THE SPY IN
MOSCOW
STATION

ALSO BY ERIC HASELTINE

Long Fuse, Big Bang: Achieving Long-Term Success Through Daily Victories

Brain Safari: 5-Minute Experiments to Explore the Space Between Your Ears

The Listening Cure: Healing Secrets of an Unconventional Doctor (with Chris Gilbert, M.D., Ph.D.)

THE SPY IN MOSCOW STATION

A Counterspy's Hunt for a
Deadly Cold War Threat

ERIC HASELTINE

THOMAS DUNNE BOOKS
St. Martin's Press 🞲 *New York*

THOMAS DUNNE BOOKS.
An imprint of St. Martin's Press.

THE SPY IN MOSCOW STATION. Copyright © 2019 by Eric Haseltine.
Foreword copyright © 2019 by Michael V. Hayden. All rights reserved. Printed in
the United States of America. For information, address St. Martin's Press, 175 Fifth
Avenue, New York, N.Y. 10010.

www.thomasdunnebooks.com
www.stmartins.com

The Library of Congress Cataloging-in-Publication Data is available on request.

ISBN 978-1-250-30116-1 (hardcover)
ISBN 978-1-250-30115-4 (ebook)

Our books may be purchased in bulk for promotional, educational, or business use.
Please contact your local bookseller or the Macmillan Corporate and Premium Sales
Department at 1-800-221-7945, extension 5442, or by email at
MacmillanSpecialMarkets@macmillan.com.

First Edition: April 2019

10 9 8 7 6 5 4 3 2 1

To my wife and soul mate, Chris
. . . and to Charles Gandy's wife and soul mate, Freda

Contents

Foreword

When I assumed command of NSA in March 1999, I quickly realized that, although the intelligence agency was a national treasure, it needed to be shaken up to meet the daunting challenges of the new millennium.

9/11 made the need to reenergize NSA even more acute, so I reached outside of the government for top industry talent to help me accelerate the agency's transformation.

Eric Haseltine, who came from Walt Disney Imagineering, of all places, was perhaps my riskiest and most audacious hire. I brought Eric into the agency to lead and to shake up NSA's Research Directorate, whose mission, in turn, was to shake up and modernize the entire enterprise.

Although parachuting a Disney executive with no intelligence experience into a leadership post at NSA raised a lot of eyebrows and generated hallway snickers about "General Hayden's Mickey Mouse hire," Eric immediately met—and surpassed—my expectations for helping to transform the agency.

Perhaps his most important accomplishment was to quickly shift NSA's research focus from "cool science projects" to technologies that made an immediate, substantial, and practical improvement to NSA's core signals intelligence and information assurance missions.

The transformation of NSA research that Eric began in mid-2002 proved very timely when the Iraq war erupted early the following year. Rather than sit at his desk in our Fort Meade headquarters, Eric traveled to Iraq and Afghanistan multiple times to get a firsthand look at the needs of NSA officers directly supporting combat operations in the two theaters of war. These trips were the first time in NSA's history a director of research had traveled to "the pointy end of the spear" in order to establish research priorities.

Each time Eric returned from one of these trips, I valued his candid take on the effectiveness of NSA's combat support activities. I especially appreciated it when Eric spoke truth to power, as when, in early 2004, he informed me that a good number of NSA's military "customers" were less than thrilled with the timeliness and effectiveness of NSA support. Based on Eric's input, I ordered immediate changes to the way NSA supported war fighters, shipping several hundred cryptologic support elements to the battlefield and integrating them with war fighters to improve NSA's responsiveness.

Getting into the spirit of combat support, Eric also directly engaged NSA research in important challenges, such as reducing casualties from roadside IEDs. For his contributions in this vital area, Eric was awarded the National Intelligence Distinguished Service Medal.

In 2005, when President George W. Bush appointed me the first principal deputy director of national intelligence, I brought Eric with me as associate director of national intelligence to lead science and technology for the entire U.S. intelligence community (IC). My hope was that Eric would do for the entire U.S. intelligence enterprise—comprised of no fewer than sixteen different intelligence agencies—what he had done at NSA: shake things up.

And shake things up he did. Eric moved swiftly to weave the disparate threads of science and technology efforts across the IC into a coherent whole, even when the threads strenuously resisted being woven. Both

I, and the IC's overall boss—John Negroponte, director of national intelligence—fielded multiple calls from agencies across the community complaining of Eric's aggressive moves to unify and rationalize science and technology pursuits across America's far-flung intelligence enterprise.

Perhaps Eric's most controversial, and important, move was to work with his deputy and successor, Steve Nixon, to create the IC's own version of DARPA, IARPA (Intelligence Advanced Research Projects Activity). IARPA filled a glaring and dangerous hole in the IC's science and technology portfolio: high-risk, high-reward endeavors that brought about revolutionary, as opposed to evolutionary, advances in mission capability.

Creating IARPA was a gutsy move, because in order to fund it, Eric and Steve had to take large sums of money away from individual agencies, most notably the CIA (where I was then director!).

We naturally butted heads a few times, but we never stopped engaging constructively or respecting each other, and when Eric left the government in 2007, we were still good friends and now enjoy serving on a corporate board together.

Reading through a draft of this book, I realize that Eric has not stopped shaking things up. His candid but accurate description of the way our intelligence agencies sometimes underestimate the Russians—badly—will not sit well in many quarters, nor will his descriptions of interagency turf fights that give the Russians an added edge against us.

The actors have changed in the forty years since the events described here, but many of the key issues and challenges have not. The Russians continue to surprise us with their audacious, innovative tradecraft, and we sometimes disappoint, even responding to Russian moves with denials and finger-pointing rather than purposeful action. Russian efforts to change the outcome of our 2016 presidential election come to mind.

So although this book describes a devastating Russian attack on our national security at the height of the Cold War, its lesson is extremely timely and important for today, and that lesson is this: we can never afford to underestimate the inventiveness and determination of highly motivated adversaries, nor can we underestimate the damage we do to ourselves when we fight each other responding to such adversaries.

To modify a phrase coined by *The New Yorker*'s Lawrence Wright, "Russia cannot destroy America. Only *we* can do that."

—General Michael V. Hayden USAF (retired),
former director of NSA and former director of CIA,
and author of *The Assault on Intelligence* and the
New York Times bestseller *Playing to the Edge*

Preface

The gleaming glass-fronted structure that serves as NSA's main headquarters building doesn't look much like a government facility on the outside. With its clean lines and tinted sides that reflect the eastern Maryland sky, OPS2, as the building is called (*OPS* standing for "operations"), would be more at home in the financial district of any large American city than on the campus of a large army base.

The inside of OPS2 is another matter. Where a commercial building would have carpeted floors, potted plants, and stylish prints adorning the walls, the raised floors of NSA headquarters are simple computer-floor tiles, which allow power and data cables to pass unmolested underneath. The walls are almost entirely devoid of decoration, save an occasional security reminder every few hundred feet or so. The overhead fluorescent lighting is bright and harsh.

In a commercial building, coworkers would be gathered in hallways, drinking coffee and engaging in informal shoptalk or gossip, but in OPS2, as in other NSA buildings, employees seldom congregate for hallway chitchat.

In fact, employees at the Fort don't talk much even *inside* their cipher lock–protected office spaces. NSA, whose job is to collect and analyze electronic information from around the globe, is a place for listening, not talking.

Coming from the gregarious entertainment business in Hollywood, and being overly talkative, I never got used to the muted, introverted culture of NSA during my three years there, and it certainly never got used to me.

Seldom was this clash of styles more evident than at my first meeting with the outside board of experts who advised my new boss, NSA director Lieutenant General Michael Hayden, on the performance of the NSA's Research Directorate, which I had taken over as chief in August 2002.

The NSA advisory board was—with a few exceptions—comprised of sober, thoughtful former senior executives at NSA, the Pentagon, or CIA along with top executives at technology companies. These were serious men on a serious mission: to make sure that I didn't screw up what they considered to be a national treasure, NSA's research-and-development group, whose mission was to invent the future of stealing and protecting electronic secrets.

The influential members of NSA's advisory board (NSAAB), which included a former DARPA director and assistant secretary of defense, had a hand in the premature and abrupt removal of my immediate predecessor, so I was eager to impress them during my first NSAAB engagement, whose purpose was to review the Research Directorate's progress over the first six months of my tenure.

At the conclusion of the grueling day-and-a-half meeting, I was exhausted and hoarse from talking almost nonstop about the directorate's new direction—and more than a little worried. While a few of the board members were engaged and offered critiques and helpful comments, most simply listened and jotted down notes, giving scant indication of their reactions to my presentation or those of my research team members.

The meeting had been civil, with a constructive atmosphere, but at its conclusion, I hadn't the slightest clue what they were going to tell General Hayden about the Research Directorate and my performance. An hour before the meeting ended, I was asked to leave so that the board could deliberate in private and prepare their conclusions for the director.

Instead of slogging through the fresh snow to my office in the research and engineering building a quarter mile away, I chose to wait in a small NSAAB conference room for the board to adjourn so that I could say goodbye to the board members as they left and to try to get a sense of how the meeting had gone. I would get the board's conclusions in writing a few days later, but was hoping to get an early read from comments and body language of different board members as they departed.

I was disappointed. Most members simply shook my hand and left immediately, while those that lingered talked among themselves. None offered encouragement or seemed eager to talk with me.

The exception was a slender, white-haired man, a couple of inches taller than I was, who had interviewed me a year earlier when I had applied for the job. In a slow, Deep Southern drawl, the man asked, "Can I grab you for a moment?"

"Sure," I answered, apprehension growing. The man, a retired NSA executive, had sat quietly, listening and making eye contact during the meeting, but had only offered an occasional comment. He had provided few clues about his thoughts during the meeting, except to briefly mention a particular area of NSA technical tradecraft that he thought deserved greater focus.

"Charles Gandy, isn't it?" I asked, dredging up his name from my encounter with him twelve months earlier.

"Yes. Gandy. We actually met at Disney about five years ago."

Oh, crap, I thought. I had forgotten that. When my boss at Disney, Bran Ferren, the president of research and development, had brought him in to consult, Gandy had hardly said a word, and my only impression of him was that he was what we techno-geeks called a *diode*, meaning that, like a semiconductor diode, information travels in only one direction. In Gandy's case, that direction had been outside–in. I didn't recall a single thing he had said at Disney, if indeed he had said anything at all. A conversation with a Disney coworker who'd sat in the meeting with Gandy came back to me. The colleague had pointed to Charles's back as he left our building and whispered, "Roach motel" (meaning, like roaches in the famous TV commercial, information checked in but didn't check out).

No wonder I had completely forgotten meeting Gandy.

Gandy and I found an empty conference room nearby and made ourselves comfortable in the stuffed chairs. Anxious, and never long on tact, I got right to the point. "What did you think about the ideas I gave the board for changing NSA's research priorities?"

"Well," he said slowly, "I was pleasantly surprised by most of it." He paused, evidently choosing his words with care. "Honestly, I didn't think you were up to the job, and I recommended against your being hired. But your presentation today showed that in this short period of time, you have really grasped what's going on and what's needed."

I swallowed hard, realizing my nervousness about the meeting had been on target. Despite his comment about there being some hope for me, I concluded that this was not a casual meeting. Perhaps in the final hour of the meeting, the board had anointed Gandy to deliver a message.

That was the way NSA worked: never confront someone in an open meeting, but send a messenger to deliver the bad news in a secluded office or empty SCIF (sensitive compartmented information facility).

"What part of my pitch didn't pleasantly surprise you?" I asked.

"It wasn't what you said but what you didn't say. That was the reason I wanted to chat with you."

I was expecting him to go on, but he just sat there, regarding me carefully through rimless glasses, wearing a neutral expression—one that I called "the NSA face." I dreaded and loathed that face, which I had seen on countless agency employees in the six months I'd been at Fort Meade. It seemed that everyone at the agency put on that same blank look when they wanted me to shut up or generally thought I was clueless.

I wondered if Gandy thought I was clueless.

Perhaps I was being tested. I thought out loud. "I left out the surveillance technique you mentioned in the meeting."

A slow smile spread on his face. "Yes, for sure. But that particular technology is just the tip of the iceberg. There's a whole universe of exploits you didn't mention in your plans—ideas that are old but as important today as they were in my time." Gathering steam, he continued, "You really need to beef up these types of things; they've fallen out of favor and could cause us major, major problems."

He proceeded for the next thirty minutes to give me a tutorial on classic NSA tradecraft that he and his team had perfected when he'd headed the legendary R9 group* in the '70s and '80s.

But R9, part of the Research Directorate, no longer existed.

Which was Gandy's point. He wanted R9, or at least the work it had been doing, to be resurrected.

As Gandy spoke, a transformation came over him, from placid diode who only took things in to an animated, energized teacher explaining a topic he loved. A distinct gleam showed up in his eyes, and his normally slow way of talking accelerated. Gandy's hands rose and fell like those of an orchestra conductor as he drew imaginary traces of radio frequency (RF) signals on the imaginary screen of a spectrum analyzer, an NSA tool of choice for their work.

The more he went into the physics of R9 old techniques, the more I found myself thinking, *Jesus, some of this stuff is older than I am!* I had no idea how sophisticated early '50s technology had been. Listening to Gandy and NSA's accomplishments from so many years ago felt like discovering that the ancient Egyptians had used gasoline engines or that the Romans had the telegraph.

Despite being in awe of the magic of the technology Gandy had just shared—not to mention the man himself—I had a problem doing as he asked.

---

* Even at the supersecret NSA, R9 had enjoyed a reputation for being especially "black," specializing in "truly spooky stuff."

I said, "General Hayden [NSA's director] just came back from the White House yesterday and told me and his other direct reports to get ready for war in Iraq. And we can't forget al-Qaeda. This technology you're talking about seems geared for big nation-states, not our current crop of hard-to-find targets."

He nodded. "Sure, but you've got plenty of money after 9/11. Why not inject new life into the things I've been talking about? Targets like Russia haven't gone away just because terrorists currently occupy our attention."

I could see Gandy wasn't going to give up easily. I didn't want to alienate him, but at the same time, I'd just finished six months of careful budgeting, and there was no extra money lying around, especially considering that the Research Directorate now had to gear up to support wars in both Iraq and Afghanistan.

Trying a different angle, I asked, "Would it really hurt that much if we put off the R9 stuff for a bit, at least until next fiscal year, when I can try to find the extra money? After all, NSA must be ahead of countries like Russia. Russia's entire economy is smaller than Texas's, and they're in a downward spiral. They have to be years, if not decades, behind us."

Gandy's white eyebrows raised abruptly, then he leaned forward in his overstuffed armchair. "Now you've really got me upset." His northern Louisiana accent, already thick, got thicker. "I can't tell you how many times I've heard that same line of reasoning. It's technology arrogance, pure and simple. Don't ever"—which he pronounced *eva*—"underestimate the Russians. I could tell you stories about them that would curl your toes."

Alarmed that I had upset an NSA legend, one who would soon be elevated to the rarified ranks of NSA's equivalent to the Hall of Fame, I blurted out the first thing that came to mind. "Uh, why don't you tell me a toe-curling story? I've got time if you do."

This seemed to calm Gandy down. He collected his thoughts, then began to tell me a story that lasted over two hours.

"Okay," Gandy said, exhaling a deep breath. "Here's one."

He cleared his throat. "In the spring of 1978, NSA director Bobby Inman called me to convey a request from CIA's chief of station in Moscow, asking for me by name and urging me to get to Moscow as soon as possible. Here's what was happening . . ."

1. Our Spies Are Dying

CIA Station, U.S. Embassy, Moscow, March 1978

Gus Hathaway sat in his cramped, windowless office on the seventh floor of the chancery building at 21 Tchaikovsky, gazing at some documents on his desktop as he toyed with a radical idea that probably wouldn't make him any friends in CIA's clandestine service, the Directorate of Operations (DO). In Moscow, March was like deep winter everywhere else, so the room's heat was turned up, contributing to the stuffiness and claustrophobic feel of the place. Hathaway knew that uninformed civilians thought of him and his brethren in the DO as spies, but that was a term he and the other intelligence officers who ran espionage operations in foreign countries never *ever* used to describe themselves. Hathaway and his DO colleagues were case officers who didn't spy at all, but rather spotted, assessed, recruited, vetted, and operated foreign "human assets" (actual spies) who stole vital secrets from "targets," such as the USSR, on behalf of CIA.

Case officers were the agency elite—whereas other CIA officers, such as technologists in the Directorate of Science and Technology (DS&T) or the academic types that comprised the Directorate of Intelligence

(DI)—were lesser beings who could only *dream* of becoming case officers one day.

Which was precisely the problem that Hathaway had with the idea he was kicking around; he had an urge to go outside of CIA for help with a vexing problem in Moscow that had just become urgent.

The culture of the elite DO was to keep their mouths firmly shut to all outsiders and to tough out gnarly problems among themselves. Sure, every now and then a case officer needed a surveillance gadget or disguise from the nerds at DS&T, or even some advice on a target from one of the ivory-tower eggheads at the DI, but to wander *outside of CIA* for help?

Not good form. Not good form at all, especially when the outside agency that Hathaway was considering asking for help was the National Security Agency (NSA). NSA had become CIA's bureaucratic archenemy over the past few years because of turf fights over which agency had authority to collect signals intelligence (electronic intercepts also known as *SIGINT*). CIA wanted to continue its long-standing practice of collecting foreign communications, while NSA argued that gathering such SIGINT should be placed under NSA authority.

Also, NSA, which had quickly grown in power and prestige under Admiral Bobby Inman, had gotten into the habit of withholding raw SIGINT from CIA—instead, feeding CIA NSA's sanitized and summarized *interpretation* of the raw intelligence—on grounds that revealing raw SIGINT would compromise NSA's covert sources and methods.[1] NSA had also been resisting CIA director Admiral Stansfield Turner's play with President Carter to take direct control of NSA on the grounds that the director of central intelligence was the titular head of the entire intelligence community.[2]

In U.S. national security circles, the bitter feud between NSA's Inman and CIA's Turner was dubbed "the war of admirals."[3]

But Hathaway was not nearly as allergic to NSA as others at CIA and was truly desperate, and it was unlikely that anyone from the DO— or CIA writ large—could solve his life-or-death problem.

Which truly *was* a life-or-death crisis. The previous year, the KGB—Russia's formidable intelligence service—had arrested two CIA assets in Moscow. One asset, a Soviet Ministry of Foreign Affairs staffer named Aleksandr Ogorodnik, had committed suicide during his interrogation at Lubyanka prison with the cyanide "L pill" his CIA case officer, Martha Peterson, had supplied him,[4] while the other asset, Colonel Anatoly Filatov of Soviet Military Intelligence (GRU), had just been sentenced to death after being caught handing over state secrets to CIA case officer Vincent Crockett.[5]

Both Peterson and Crockett had been arrested and then "PNG'd" (declared persona non grata) and booted out of Russia shortly after their respective assets had been "rolled up."

According to a source familiar with Hathaway's thinking in early 1978, Hathaway was also concerned about compromises that had led directly to execution of U.S. assets.

For certain, there was a leak—or leaks—in the ultratight security that protected the identities of case officers and their assets.

But where?

Perhaps a mole at Langley (CIA headquarters) was tipping off the KGB about identities of case officers and their Soviet assets. Such horrors did occur—if rarely—such as when senior British intelligence official and KGB asset Kim Philby betrayed numerous assets of Her Majesty's Secret Service to the Soviets.

Or maybe the KGB was intercepting and deciphering encrypted communications somewhere between Langley and Moscow Station.

Flawed espionage tradecraft by DO case officers was another troubling possibility. Had Peterson or Crockett, for instance, failed to run counter-surveillance routes (elaborate street maneuvers designed to confuse and shake off KGB tails) properly before executing brush passes or servicing dead drops (covert means of exchanging information with assets)?

Peterson and Crockett both vehemently denied making any such mistakes, but even elite DO case officers were, at the end of the day, human and therefore prone to committing errors every now and then.

Martha Peterson, for instance, was not only a novice but the very first female case officer assigned to Moscow.[6] Hathaway was an old-school gentleman from southern Virginia who did not like involving women in the dangerous, manly, meticulous work of the DO. He'd made his views known, but to no avail, as his masters at Langley, concerned about the safety of Ogorodnik, had hoped that a female case officer would escape KGB suspicion.

That ploy had obviously failed. But despite Hathaway's misgivings about female case officers there was no evidence, that Peterson—or Crockett, for that matter—had screwed up. Which raised yet another possibility: the KGB might have compromised security at the Moscow embassy itself.

Of all the possible sources of leakage, the embassy seemed like the best bet.

First and foremost, the facility was in the heart of Moscow, where the KGB could bring every tool in its vast espionage arsenal to bear. A large number of embassy staffers—including guards, switchboard operators, travel coordinators, cooks, maids, and drivers—were Soviet citizens who were guaranteed to be either KGB informants or outright KGB officers. Although CIA officers knew how to behave around such obvious threats, the same could not be said of State Department diplomats. State employees—whose job, after all, was to mingle with Russians in order to collect and exchange information to improve relations between America and Russia—were not all that security conscious and had a well-deserved reputation for being "information sieves."

Yes, diplomats, with the occasional exception of the ambassador himself, were not privy to the identities of CIA's human assets. But senior diplomats, such as the ambassador and deputy chief of mission (DCM), *did* know which of their employees actually worked for CIA. A careless word from a diplomat in the wrong place at the wrong time could tip off the KGB about a case officer's true function at the embassy and ultimately lead to the unmasking of that case officer's assets.

Ambassador Malcolm Toon, for instance, who knew Martha Peterson's real job and had made a comment while riding in the embassy's un-secured elevator the year before, clearly acknowledged that Peterson was CIA. The elevator, like most of the embassy outside of highly se-cured areas on the top three floors, which were constantly swept for sur-veillance devices, was probably bugged. State Department staffers often had dangerously cavalier attitudes about such bugging. The current number-two diplomat in Moscow, for instance, DCM Jack Matlock, fre-quently said of the presumed embassy bugs, "If they [the Soviets] want my opinion, they're welcome to it."[7]

In other words, KGB bugging of the embassy was an accepted fact of life. A decade earlier, more than one hundred microphones had been dis-covered behind radiators in the chancery.[8] And even before the United States moved into its current embassy in 1953, numerous electronic sur-veillance devices had been discovered in Spaso House, the de facto embassy and U.S. ambassador's residence as early as the 1930s.[9] U.S. ambassador Joseph Davies's wife said in 1936, for example, "We found them [microphones] in the fireplaces, we found them in the little vents, in the inner walls."[10] Then, in 1951, a truly ingenious listening device called "the Thing" had been discovered in a wooden Great Seal of the United States in Ambassador Kirk's office, a gift to the ambassador from a troop of Russian girls.

The Thing, a carefully machined acoustic cavity attached to a special antenna, consumed no electrical power whatsoever but reflected radio waves that the Soviets beamed at the embassy in such a way that voices, even at a whisper, could be clearly picked up at a nearby Russian intel-ligence listening post.[11]

That such sophisticated tradecraft was way beyond CIA's own sur-veillance technology was deeply troubling in 1951 and even more troubling in 1978, because the KGB continued to beam radio waves— in the form of microwaves—at the upper, highly sensitive floors of the embassy that housed both the ambassador's office and offices of CIA and other U.S. intelligence services.

Although the original function of radio frequency (RF) reflections off the Thing had been discovered, the current purpose of the microwave bombardment, alternately called TUMS (the unidentified Moscow signal) or MUTS (Moscow unidentified technical signal), was, as the "unidentified" term in *TUMS* and *MUTS* implied, a mystery, at least to CIA and State Department surveillance countermeasures technologists.[12]

To Hathaway, it was unacceptable that CIA and State Department technologists did not understand what the microwaves were about. Why would the KGB devote considerable resources to continuing the microwave attacks if they were not yielding productive intelligence in some way, especially after one U.S. ambassador to Russia, Walter Stoessel, had complained so bitterly to the Soviet Ministry of Foreign Affairs about the health hazards of the microwave radiation a few years before? Stoessel, a leukemia victim, suspected that his disease, and the ailments of other embassy staffers, were directly attributed to the microwaves.[13]

But despite the diplomatic problems the microwave radiation caused for the Ministry of Foreign Affairs with the United States, the KGB persisted with their mysterious bombardment.

Why? And were the microwaves somehow responsible for the devastating leaks?

As if the constant, mysterious microwave bombardment weren't troubling enough, there was the baffling case of "the chimney to nowhere" to keep Hathaway up at night.

In the summer of 1977, a secretary for the State Department's Regional Security Office (RSO), which maintained security in portions of the embassy that were the State Department's responsibility (not including CIA's or NSA's spaces on the top floors), started hearing strange scraping noises in a chimney outside her apartment on the fifth floor of the south annex of the embassy. Worried that birds might have somehow flown into and gotten trapped inside the chimney, and concerned for the animals' welfare, the secretary, GH, had asked the Marine guards at the embassy to investigate.

When the Marines aimed their flashlights down the shaft from the roof, they couldn't see very far into the gloom but heard no sign of trapped birds or any other animals.

But the soldiers did discover, while attempting to find a fireplace from which to look up the chimney shaft, that no fireplaces *anywhere* in the south annex fed into the long chimney shaft that hugged the west outer wall of the annex.

The chimney shaft, it turned out, wasn't a chimney at all but a vacant space that had been built by the Russians before the Americans took possession of the building in 1953, for some other purpose. Was that purpose to house a covert KGB observation or listening post? Were the mysterious scraping noises made by Soviet surveillance technicians installing or moving around microphones of some kind?

With the Soviets' forty-year history of eavesdropping on embassy conversations, it was a reasonable assumption that the Russians had not constructed the so-called chimney simply as an architectural ornament.

Thus, when Hathaway learned of the non-chimney chimney, he asked CIA technology operations (TOPS) officer NP to take his State Department counterpart, RSO officer FB, aside in the open courtyard behind the embassy—away from KGB microphones—to quietly suggest that the RSO break into the brick shaft to see what security threats it might house.

Although the apartments adjoining the false chimney contained no sensitive operations—apart from the private lives of embassy staffers—there was some urgency to NP's request because GH's apartment was soon to be converted into a top-secret secure space.

Unfortunately, in August of 1977, just as RSO was arranging to bring in a crew of Seabees from Frankfurt, Germany, to get into the chimney, a fire broke out on the embassy's eighth floor.

In addition to destroying much of the embassy's sensitive spaces on the upper floors, the devastating fire caused RSO to postpone their chimney investigation, as more urgent issues, such as determining the cause of the fire and rebuilding destroyed portions of the building, occupied their attention.[14]

Hathaway and others at the embassy put a high priority on discovering the cause of the blaze, because the timing of the fire, coming right after RSO had set in motion an investigation of the chimney, was suspicious. It was entirely possible that the KGB, either through one of their hundred-plus employees or informants in the embassy, or bugs in State Department spaces, had learned of RSO's plans to investigate the chimney.

Moreover, the presence of KGB agents—wearing clean, brand-new fire gear—among the ranks of legitimate Moscow firefighters who fought the blaze (some of whom even offered Hathaway oxygen) also suggested the Russians may have caused the fire, especially considering that KGB "firefighters" had broken into—and in some cases, stolen—classified information in State Department offices.[15] Although Soviet citizens weren't supposed to have access to the eighth floor where the fire erupted, both CIA's TOPS and State Department's RSO officers knew that the Soviets had several ingenious ways of remotely igniting such a conflagration. For instance, when the Soviets wanted to harass Americans in the embassy, they sometimes created overvoltages on the external power lines feeding the embassy, blowing out electronic equipment in the embassy, melting electronic equipment, and generating acrid smoke.

When, months after the fire, U.S. fire investigators ultimately discovered that a frayed electrical cord on the eighth floor had ignited the blaze,[16] the KGB-triggered overvoltage theory took on more weight, because the electrical cord in question had old-style flammable cloth insulation instead of the more fire-resistant rubber or plastic insulation that Americans used in modern construction.

(The final conclusion of the months-long fire investigation was that the fire started accidentally, but KGB defector Victor Sheymov testified before the U.S. Congress in 1998 that the KGB had, in fact, intentionally caused the fire.[17])

But on the positive side, if the fire had indeed been a smoke screen, as it were, to protect KGB secrets in the chimney, that clearly suggested the chimney might hold a clue to the recent rash of asset roll-ups and case officer PNGs.

In order to keep CIA assets alive and his case officers safe, Hathaway had to know what was in that false chimney, so, in early 1978, he pushed RSO to restart the chimney investigation as soon as fire repairs would allow.

But there was another urgent reason Hathaway needed to solve the chimney mystery, get to the bottom of the microwave threat, and to generally button up embassy security: Admiral Stansfield Turner, CIA's new director, had, as a result of the recent intelligence compromises in Moscow, shut down all human intelligence (HUMINT) operations in Russia the year before as being too risky.[18]

Many officers in the DO thought Turner was a real piece of work and a real pain in the ass. A U.S. Naval Academy classmate of the current president, Jimmy Carter, Turner was a career military officer with no intelligence experience whatsoever, who favored technical intelligence collection from overhead (spy satellite imagery, called IMINT) and NSA SIGINT over HUMINT. Turner was smitten by high-tech gadgets and mistrusted the dirty business of human espionage as inherently fraught with messy ethical and moral dilemmas.[19]

President Carter had campaigned in 1976 on a promise to restore trust in government after the Watergate scandal and revelations of CIA's occasional practice of opening American citizens' mail and assassinating (or attempting to assassinate) foreign leaders. Turner understood that part of his job was to restore ethics and morals to CIA clandestine operations.[20]

Not an easy task with espionage, which routinely involved emotionally manipulating Russian nationals to betray their country and to risk both their lives and those of their closest relatives. Just how do you persuade, cajole, bribe, or even seduce people (and CIA *has* done that, with Anatoly Filatov) *ethically?*

Easier to rely on spy satellites, communication intercepts, and other morally pure technical means than to dirty your hands with messy HUM-INT, where people can, and do, get killed.

Acting on his disdain for HUMINT, Turner had instigated the Halloween Massacre on October 31, 1977, abruptly dismissing over two hundred DO officers as unnecessary after the conclusion of the war in Vietnam.[21]

Hathaway, like other case officers, wasn't pleased with the massacre and was unhappy that HUMINT operations on his turf had been curtailed.

Hathaway was a cold warrior from way back who believed that HUMINT against the Soviet target was essential. An army veteran who had been wounded in the leg and awarded a Purple Heart while serving in France and Germany during World War II, Hathaway went right into CIA in its third year of existence after graduating from the University of Virginia in 1950. Stints as a case officer in Frankfurt, Berlin, and most recently South America had taught him that some kinds of intelligence simply couldn't be gathered through technical means.[22] Hard intelligence targets—such as Soviet officials, for instance, who'd grown up under the tyranny of Stalin and took security extremely seriously—rarely made mistakes that would allow SIGINT or IMINT to capture their deepest secrets. The really good stuff, such as what policies the ruling Soviet politburo had just approved or what new technical capabilities Soviet fighter planes were slated to get, was best obtained, in most case officers' opinions, through HUMINT.

The Moscow Station chief was also not nearly as risk averse as his ultimate boss, Admiral Turner.

The previous month, when a soon-to-be-released book by Ed Epstein provided enough details about an American asset in Moscow named Aleksey Isidorovich Kulak (codenamed *Fedora*), CIA feared for the asset's safety. After several attempts to evade surveillance, Hathaway dressed up as his secretary and was able to securely phone Kulak to warn him.[23]

Before that, during the suspicious embassy fire the previous August,

Hathaway had disobeyed direct orders from Ambassador Toon to evacuate and had planted himself outside CIA's seventh-floor offices to discourage KGB officers, who were masquerading as firefighters, from entering his sanctum sanctorum.[24]

Hathaway's bravery that night earned him the prestigious Intelligence Star medal along with the undying admiration of his colleagues in the DO.[25]

Some things, Hathaway had shown, were worth taking extreme risks to achieve.

And one of those things had definitely presented itself early the previous year—and could turn into an immense intelligence gold mine, if only Hathaway could persuade risk-averse Turner to turn HUMINT operations back on in Moscow.

The potential gold mine was a mysterious Soviet citizen who had approached Robert Fulton, Hathaway's predecessor as Moscow Station chief, while he was getting gas in January 1977. The citizen asked Fulton if he were an American, then, after the chief said yes, dropped a note on the seat of Fulton's car. The note, written in Russian, suggested a meeting to discuss "confidential matters" with "the appropriate American official." The note also included suggestions for a place where a secret follow-up meeting could take place.[26]

Although Fulton was intrigued, he did not respond to the volunteer's first overture, because the KGB was notorious for offering up "dangles" and double agents who professed to have access to juicy secrets, but whose real objective was to feed CIA false information or to learn the types of intelligence needs CIA had at the top of its list when CIA asked the dangle to collect a particular piece of intelligence.

In the convoluted logic of intelligence, using dangles and doubles to get a clear picture of what an adversary such as CIA *didn't* know but *wanted* to know was incredibly useful for two reasons.

First, if an enemy such as America desperately wanted to learn the capabilities of a particular Soviet weapon, it meant that the enemy *didn't know* what the weapon could do. So if a war with America or its allies ever broke out, Soviet military planners might be able to surprise the American military with the capabilities of that weapon, such as the weapon's operating range or lethality.

Second, if CIA *did not* ask a double agent or dangle for a particular piece of information, say, about a Soviet weapon system, this *lack* of curiosity suggested that the Americans *already knew* what they needed to know about it . . . which in turn hinted that CIA had a Soviet asset who was feeding them that information. Thus, when CIA chose *not* to ask a dangle for specific information, the KGB would sometimes launch a counterintelligence investigation to explore the reasons for CIA's lack of curiosity. Or, if the KGB already suspected that classified information was leaking out of some sensitive Soviet operation, such as their strategic rocket forces, they might create a dangle purporting to work in that operation in order to learn if CIA were curiously uncurious about what was going on in the suspect organization.

Fulton also knew that Soviet dangles and doubles helped the KGB learn more about American espionage tradecraft. If CIA should take the bait and accept a KGB-inspired "walk-in" as genuine, they would train that volunteer in covert communication, use of special equipment, counter-surveillance techniques, photography, and so forth, thereby showing the KGB how CIA assets operated, helping the KGB spot and apprehend real CIA assets.

In addition, CIA case officers in Moscow were aware that fake walk-ins could unmask which Americans at the Moscow embassy were actually CIA officers, should CIA decide to accept the dangle. Equipped with this information, the Soviets could surveil that officer in order to unravel his connections to any Soviet "traitors" he had recruited. Entrapping a CIA case officer with a dangle also allowed the Soviets to score propaganda points by arresting and expelling the officer, while publicizing that imperialist spies were constantly trying to undermine the socialist revolution.

For all these reasons, Fulton ignored three more attempts by the volunteer, who refused to identify himself for many months out of fear of exposure.[27]

However, in December 1977, the enigmatic volunteer included two typewritten pages of highly classified technical information about Soviet airborne radar systems, so the newly arrived chief of station, Gus Hathaway, asked CIA headquarters for permission to engage the anonymous Soviet.

Despite the promising nature of the technical material the Russian had provided with his last request to meet, CIA headquarters ultimately denied Hathaway permission to proceed further with the potential asset, on grounds that the stranger's overture could be a deliberate KGB "provocation." Also, Admiral Turner's order to halt all HUMINT operations in Russia was still in force.

But Hathaway got a break when the air attaché at the embassy pointed out the importance of this kind of information for the U.S. Department of Defense, which eventually made CIA headquarters consider engaging the anonymous Soviet walk-in.[28]

Here is the declassified CIA account of what happened next:

On 16 February 1978, the volunteer approached Hathaway and his wife at their car on the street after work and passed another note containing additional intelligence information. He wrote that he seemed to be caught in a vicious circle: "I'm afraid for security reasons to put down on paper much about myself, and, without this information, for security reasons you are afraid to contact me, fearing a provocation." He then suggested a secure way to pass key identifying data on himself. In his note, he provided all but two of the digits in his phone number. He instructed the recipient of the note that at a certain time at a certain bus stop he would be standing in line holding two pieces of plywood, each with a single number on it. These would be the last two digits in his phone number. At the indicated time, Hathaway's wife drove past the bus stop in question, recognized the volunteer holding the two pieces of plywood, and recorded the numbers.

Hathaway immediately sent a cable to CIA headquarters pushing for a positive response to the volunteer. This time, headquarters concurred.

On 26 February, after careful planning, John Guilsher, a case officer fluent in Russian, conducted a lengthy surveillance-detection run to determine that he was free of any Soviet surveillance and then called the volunteer's home phone from a public phone booth. The volunteer's wife answered the call, however, forcing Guilsher to break off the conversation. Guilsher repeated this exercise on 28 February, with the same lack of success.

On 1 March 1978, [the volunteer] again approached Hathaway and his wife on the street after work. This time, he passed 11 pages of handwritten materials, the bulk of which was detailed intelligence on Soviet R&D efforts in the military aircraft field. In this note, [the volunteer] finally identified himself fully, providing his name, address, exact employment, and a great deal of personal background information. He noted that he had spent "hours and hours roaming the streets in search of [U.S.] diplomatic cars," and, having found one, had returned "tens of times" without passing anything, because of unfavorable conditions. He said that he was now almost desperate for a positive response to his efforts, and, if he did not get one this time, he would give up.[29]

The walk-in had identified himself as Adolf Tolkachev, senior engineer at a Ministry of Defense R&D organization called Phazotron, where advanced Soviet airborne radars were designed. It later emerged that Tolkachev had become bitter about the Soviet system, partly due to the arrest and execution of his wife's parents under Stalin's purges in the late 1930s, and had resolved to help take down the Communist regime that he served.[30]

Despite CIA headquarters' new openness to the possibility of working with Tolkachev, whose access to highly coveted intelligence seemed phenomenal, Hathaway knew that Admiral Turner had not formally lifted his ban on HUMINT operations and might still allow the Tolkachev opportunity to slip through Hathaway's fingers.

It was essential that Turner's confidence in Moscow Station's ability to operate without leaks be restored and formal approval for the Tolkachev operation be given as soon as possible. Otherwise, in Tolkachev's own words, he would "give up."

But this urgent imperative put Hathaway in a tough spot.

Tightening up security at the embassy was the most likely way to plug the leaks that had compromised other assets over the past year, but CIA's own technical security experts at the embassy, along with those from the State Department who had formal authority over embassy security, couldn't tell Hathaway how embassy security might have been breached . . . by the mysterious microwave bombardment, for example.

Worse, those same State and CIA security officers argued that their frequent bug sweeps and inspections guaranteed that there was *no* security problem at the embassy.

An illogical assertion considering that State and CIA security officers admitted they didn't really know the purpose of the microwave bombardment or the false chimney.

Based upon Hathaway's entreaties to turn HUMINT back on in Moscow and to let him run Tolkachev, Turner planned to send Rusty Williams, "a Navy man he trusted," to Moscow to assess and report back on the security situation there. It was vital, Hathaway believed, that Williams give Moscow Station a passing grade so that Turner would let him operate Tolkachev.[31]

What Hathaway needed in the worst possible way, before Williams arrived to do his assessment, was a technical expert who *did* have a good idea how the Soviets might have breached embassy security, and Hathaway knew of such a person.

For the last decade, an NSA engineer named Charles Gandy had been making the rounds at CIA, FBI, and other intelligence agencies, trying to raise awareness about the potent and dangerous threat posed by advanced KGB surveillance tradecraft.

Some at CIA regarded Gandy as a quixotic figure, who persisted year after year in presenting a long, highly technical, highly classified slideshow describing how, for example, microwave bombardment could allow the KGB to breach otherwise tight security.

Several CIA officers told Gandy to his face that his technologies were just a modern form of snake oil, and he acquired the moniker "snake oil salesman" at CIA's DS&T.

Still others at Langley headquarters wondered if Gandy—a career NSAer, after all—was purposely feeding CIA bogus information in order to sucker them into ill-considered operations that would damage CIA's reputation and elevate NSA's own stature in the intelligence world.

But because CIA's and the State Department's relatively primitive countermeasure equipment at the time could detect no evidence of Russian snooping, most at CIA—based on the evidence of their equipment—regarded Gandy's warnings as simply Chicken Little stuff. Pure science fiction. There was no way, CIA believed, the technologically backward Russians had a prayer of conducting the kinds of ultrasophisticated attacks that Gandy warned of.

In his memoir of his tenure as CIA director, *Secrecy and Democracy*, Admiral Turner summarized the CIA's view of security experts such as Gandy this way:

> *The experts tend to see a bug under every table. Given their way, they would prescribe defensive measures that would make it impossible to carry on the business of Government.*[32]

But Hathaway had sat in on one of Gandy's talks a few years earlier and had found his fellow Southerner to be persuasive and credible. If anyone could get to the bottom of possible leaks at the embassy, Gandy could.

True, Gandy worked for NSA, and yes, Hathaway's buddies at the DO and CIA leadership on the seventh floor of CIA headquarters wouldn't like bringing in an outsider to solve an ultrasensitive HUMINT operational problem.

But the tantalizing Tolkachev opportunity, and all future HUMINT operations in Russia, hung in the balance, including the lives of future Russian assets.

In a one-on-one meeting with Ambassador Toon earlier that day, in a secure room enclosed in Plexiglas on the ninth floor, Hathaway had learned that Toon shared his belief that extraordinary measures were called for and approved bringing in an NSA man, even though the State Department mistrusted and disliked NSA more than CIA did . . . if that were possible.

Making his decision, Hathaway took out a paper and pencil and authored a cable to CIA headquarters requesting permission to engage NSA and asking them to request one Charles Gandy get on a plane to Moscow with all possible dispatch.

2. The Counterspy

NSA Friendship Annex, Linthicum, Maryland, March 1978

Gandy hung up the gray-line phone in his office—the telephone line only used for highly classified conversations—and smiled inwardly.

NSA director Admiral Bobby Inman had just instructed him to pack his bags for a trip to Russia. The admiral hadn't supplied a lot of details, only that a number of "strange things" were going on at the embassy and that CIA had asked for him by name to help identify and patch possible security holes in the Moscow embassy.

Gandy was pleased, although more than a little surprised that CIA had asked for his help. Since joining NSA in 1954 as an air force lieutenant, Gandy had worked many times with the "folks across the river," as CIA was called at NSA, and the interactions were not always harmonious.

Every now and then, such as with his frequent visits to Vietnam during the war that ended three years earlier, his relationships with CIA officers were cordial and mutually productive. CIA operatives valued Gandy's ability to locate adversary intelligence officers and assets, sometimes taking Gandy along on dangerous counterintelligence missions.

Taking Gandy along on such adventures was a show of respect, of sorts, but one that Gandy could have lived without.

But more often, relations with CIA were strained. For instance, on numerous occasions, Gandy had shared new technologies NSA had developed for collecting intelligence with officers from CIA's DS&T only to have CIA tell him that the technologies didn't work or were impractical. Frequently, though, six months later, CIA would field those exact NSA-invented technologies using their own outside contractors. Gandy supposed DS&T officers were doing this to get credit with their superiors for innovating, but it didn't stop him from continuing to share new advancements.

When NSA colleagues asked, "Charlie, why do you keep doing that? CIA keeps screwing you."

Gandy's answer was always the same: "Yes, but they've done it so many times, I'm starting to enjoy it."

Gandy didn't care much who got the credit for new inventions, as long as the new technology advanced U.S. intelligence interests. He was an old-school patriot who tried to keep the main objective—countering the Soviet threat—in mind. Gandy had also, by 1978, risen to a very high position at NSA, attaining a civilian rank that was the military equivalent of major general. In that capacity, he sat atop an organization called R9, which many viewed as the most prestigious and glamorous at NSA. Gandy had no ambitions to grab all the credit for a new technical advancement in order to move up the ladder further. He wanted to stay right where he was, regarding every day as a new "Christmas present," a new opportunity to solve a cool technical problem.

But what Gandy did object to was that the innovations he and R9 shared with CIA often ended up leaking to the Soviets—probably, Gandy believed, through a mole somewhere at CIA. Gandy harbored particularly deep suspicions about CIA's notorious chief of counterintelligence, James Jesus Angleton, who had crippled CIA's clandestine operations for over a decade by conducting one paralyzing mole hunt after another. It was simply too coincidental, Gandy thought, that intelligence sources that R9 had opened up with some new invention would dry up shortly after he shared the technical advancement with Angleton, suggesting that the Russians were using leaked knowledge of NSA technology to devise countermeasures that nullified the technology's effectiveness.

Gandy had voiced suspicions about Angleton to FBI, who themselves wondered if Angleton's zealotry at rooting out CIA moles covered up Angleton's own role as a mole. But no concrete evidence ever emerged implicating the counterintelligence chief in the leaks. Because of his debilitating mole hunts throughout the 1960s and early 1970s, however, Angleton did have a number of powerful detractors at CIA, including Director William Colby, who ultimately fired him in 1975.

Another ongoing difficulty for Gandy with CIA was that they were skeptical about his oft-stated concerns about the deep sophistication of Soviet technical tradecraft. Ever since the Vietnam War, he'd been briefing CIA about the gravity of the Soviet technical threat to U.S. intelligence, military, and diplomatic facilities, but usually CIA ignored or dismissed his concerns. "The Soviets are simply too backward to be that good" was a phrase he often heard from CIA officers at his briefings. Gandy found such reactions both frustrating and baffling. Putting aside the KGB's stellar track record of inventing new attacks on their own, such as the famous microwave-stimulated Thing discovered in the '50s, the KGB had to be aware of several of R9's own innovations due to the numerous leaks over the past few years. What made CIA think that the KGB hadn't done what CIA itself had done so often and simply reproduced R9's technologies?

Given CIA's recent skepticism about the Soviet's capabilities, it was puzzling that they had specifically asked for his help.

What could have changed CIA minds? Had the Russians breached embassy security in some way that neither CIA nor State Department security officials could detect?

For instance, over the years, FBI, NATO allies, and others had discovered a broad range of KGB implants—listening and data-capture devices—that broadcast intelligence to nearby listening posts. The Russians had also developed special implants on telephone sets that exfiltrated conversations over phone lines and special "hooks" that covertly broadcast data from text-processing technology, such as teletypewriters, teleprinters, and text encryption devices used by the military, intelligence, and diplomats. Some of these attacks monitored tiny current fluctuations on power lines feeding a denied facility, such as an embassy, that conveyed useful information about data being processed on machines such as typewriters and teleprinters.

A declassified NSA document describes the power line vulnerability this way:

> *Any time a machine is used to process classified information electrically, the various switches, contacts, relays, and other components in that machine may emit radio frequency or acoustic energy. These emissions, like tiny radio broadcasts, may radiate through free space for considerable distances—a half mile or more in some cases. They may be induced on nearby conductors like signal lines, power lines, telephone lines, or water pipes and be conducted along those paths for some distance—and here we may be talking of a mile or more.[1]*

Also, entry-level Russian textbooks on "information leakage through technical channels," asserted that each keystroke of an electric typewriter or teletypewriter causes a current draw that's slightly different from that of other keystrokes, enabling sensitive equipment attached to the power line feeding the sensitive building to pick up, differentiate, and decode typed information. When the Soviets couldn't manage to implant listening or data-capture devices inside a target's facility or attach sensors to phone or power lines, they had other ingenious options, both passive and active, for remotely capturing classified conversations and data.[2]

Passive remote attacks included what NSA codenamed *TEMPEST collection*. With TEMPEST, an adversary such as the Russians would pick up and decode unintended RF emissions from sensitive equipment at ranges of several hundred feet. In the 1950s, a British company called

Rediffusion had pioneered a technology for remotely sensing RF signals radiating from ordinary televisions sets that were turned on, in order to enforce licensing fees for operating consumer TVs in the UK. If a Rediffusion monitoring truck that was driving down a residential street detected an operating TV set in a household that wasn't paying the required fee, that house would soon be sent a notice and a bill.[3] The KGB, ever on the lookout for new spy craft, had to have learned of this technology and adapted it for remotely monitoring signals from CRT data displays and television monitors in classified facilities. Russian textbooks confirm that the Soviets did, in fact, know about this technology.

A KGB technologist named Leon Theremin (the same Theremin who invented the musical instrument bearing his name) had also created two separate active remote techniques, where focused electromagnetic energy was beamed at a target from a remote post—say, a few hundred feet away—and reflections of that energy were analyzed to decode slight but discernible voice-induced vibrations from inside a building. One technique, codenamed *BURAN* by the Russians, used infrared radiation to capture slight voice-induced vibrations from windows, while the other, termed *RF imposition* by the Russians, captured voice signals from vibrations of different kinds of electrical conductors that reflected radio frequency (RF) energy.[4] The Thing, discovered in the Moscow embassy in 1951, was Theremin's brainchild, but Gandy knew that RF flooding could also remotely capture information without a cooperative device like the Thing, relying only on electronics present in a targeted room that were routinely used by an adversary, such as telephone microphones and speakers. Gandy believed that the TUMS and MUTS signals that the KGB constantly beamed at the Moscow embassy were almost certainly examples of active RF remote attacks that grew out of Theremin's original work.

The KGB also employed a variety of "wired" remote attacks, in which they injected microwaves onto conductors that fed into a target's facility, such as phone lines, then decoded voice and data information contained in reflections of those microwaves at nearby listening posts.

In 1975, this type of microwave radiation had been detected on Ambassador Walter Stoessel's phone line at the Moscow embassy, prompting the State Department to protest the Soviet Ministry of Foreign Affairs.[5]

Gandy sometimes marveled at the inventiveness and technical sophistication of Russian intelligence. The Soviet economy was smaller than that of Texas, and yet they had somehow managed to blow past the United States in surveillance tradecraft. Part of the reason for this, he supposed, was that the Russians, who spent only one dollar on their national security for every ten dollars the American's spent, had decided that excelling in a few narrow areas could level the playing field against vastly superior American science and technology and national wealth.

The KGB, for instance, had mounted a highly successful effort to steal designs of advanced U.S. military technology, such as airborne radars and stealthy submarine propellers, so that they could field this technology for their own armed forces at only a tiny fraction of the development cost that the Americans had spent to create the technology from scratch.[6] Acquiring U.S. designs also taught the Soviets about the weaknesses of American weapons so that they could develop effective countermeasures to negate the advantage that America's technology would otherwise enjoy on the battlefield. Understanding the weaknesses of American weapons could also save a lot of money for the Soviet military, because when the Soviets knew just the right way to shoot down an attacking American bomber, they could employ one well-aimed missile instead of the multiple missiles that would have otherwise been necessary.

Spending a lot of money on high-tech spying was a great way for the Russians to dramatically reduce spending on everything else.

But Gandy knew there was more to Russia's superior technical spy craft than the heavy resources they focused on it. Studying the original Thing that the KGB had created in the 1940s, along with other Russian innovations such as optical attacks and other Russian surveillance tech, Gandy realized that the KGB focused Russia's very best minds on developing innovative bugs, implants, and remote attacks. America's brightest scientists got Ph.D.s at places like MIT and faculty positions at Harvard or Stanford, then went on to win Nobel Prizes. However, the KGB scooped up Russia's best brains, sometimes before they even went to grad school, and offered them privileges, prestige, and perks only available to KGB officers and top Communist Party officials. Gandy had a fabulous team at R9, but thinking about the intellectual achievement of Leon Theremin's Thing and other KGB marvels, Gandy wondered if the KGB's A team was, pound for pound, better than anyone else in the world.

A final crucial advantage that the KGB enjoyed, Gandy realized, was that he had been unable to convince people outside NSA—particularly at CIA and the State Department—that the Russians were as good as he knew they were. As a result, American investment in thwarting the KGB's virtuoso technology was lacking. To protect their facilities, CIA and State performed security scans against the bugs and remote attack technology that they themselves used, on the assumption that U.S. technology was the best in the world.

Expending efforts to protect against *better* than the best possible attacks in the world made no sense, State and CIA believed.

Arrogance, pure and simple, Gandy thought as he considered how devastatingly effective the KGB's remote radar and optical attacks probably were.

Active remote attacks particularly intrigued Gandy because discovering these magical techniques as an eleven-year-old had motivated him to go into intelligence work in the first place.

Shortly after the end of World War II, Gandy had gone with friends to the local theater in Homer, Louisiana, to see one of the many war movies that came out in the mid-to-late 1940s. In the movie, FBI agents monitoring Nazi spies in America remotely beamed energy from a dish antenna at a room where the spies were planning their next attack. The intrepid FBI agents were able to decode voice signals in the room from reflections off a vibrating speaker in a telephone headset and thwart the attack.

Eleven-year-old Gandy was in awe of FBI's advanced technology and vowed, at that moment, to pursue a career catching America's enemies using technology.

By that time, Gandy had already become a ham radio operator and learned from his older brother Carl and a family friend how to build and operate radio transmitters and receivers.

After watching FBI score a spectacular technical success against German spies, Gandy resolved to build on his ham radio skills to become an electrical engineer somewhere in U.S. law enforcement or intelligence, in order to keep America safe.

But the path to that dream faced formidable obstacles.

One such obstacle was Gandy's extreme distaste for going to school. Early in the first grade, when a teacher punished him for a minor infraction by lifting him up by both ears, Gandy suffered extreme pain and ear infections that lasted two weeks. On top of that, the Homer elementary schoolhouse was old, dank, and dark, not an inviting place at all for an active six-year-old.

Compounding an extreme "allergy" to school, Gandy had an undiagnosed learning disability that made it difficult for him to read. He nearly flunked second grade, and one of his high school teachers scoffed at his dreams of becoming an engineer, saying, "You will never be college material."

It wasn't until 2017 that a neuroscientist determined that Gandy suffered from an extreme case of dyslexia.

Despite this disadvantage, Gandy won two state high school competitions in physics and general science. He passed the FCC exam to earn a first-class commercial radio license at age seventeen that later enabled him to take a job as chief engineer at radio station KRUS during his junior and senior years in college. Getting this highly technical license required study of a thick manual, which his mother read to him while he lay in the family's hammock. "I absorb information best when I hear it," Gandy later said.

Midway through his senior year in high school, Gandy got accepted to Louisiana Tech, where he excelled at engineering and physics classes. English, history, and other classes that required heavy reading or writing term papers were another matter. Fortunately, he'd met his future wife, Freda Grambling (the same Gramblings who'd donated land to the university that was to be named after the family), who helped write his more difficult papers, and he graduated with a degree in electrical engineering in 1955.

Gandy then promptly joined the air force and shipped off to NSA, where he began pursuing the dream that had begun in a movie theater a decade earlier watching FBI agents surveil Nazis spies.

Twenty-three years later, it appeared he would get an opportunity to confront a dangerous enemy.

Gandy got up from his desk, poked his head out of his office, and asked his secretary, Nancy, to come inside and close the door so he could get her started on the paperwork for his trip to Moscow.

Two weeks later, the State Department informed Gandy that a major snag had developed processing a critical part of his paperwork: a travel visa to the USSR. Apparently, the Soviets knew exactly who he was and what he did for a living, perhaps from his frequent trips to Berlin, Vietnam, and other places "downrange" (intelligence jargon for a war zone or hot area) from NSA. The Ministry of Foreign Affairs had denied his visa on grounds that the only reason for his journey to the USSR was to conduct espionage.

Disappointed, Gandy assumed that would be the end of his personal involvement in any trip to Moscow. But to his surprise, State, which was not a big fan of NSA due to constant tension with NSA over the agency's constant criticisms of embassy security, took a hard line with the Soviets.

"If you won't let our man travel to the USSR," State had informed the Soviet Ministry of Foreign Affairs, "then no Soviet diplomats will be allowed to travel to the United States either." For eight days, all Soviet diplomatic travel to the United States was blocked.

Under this pressure, the Soviets relented, granting visas to Gandy and two of his top technologists for a one-month stay in Moscow.

A few days after hearing that his trip to Moscow was back on, Gandy was at CIA headquarters in Virginia, picking up his travel paperwork for Moscow, when a young man and woman Gandy had never met before approached and quietly asked him to join them in a nearby conference room.

Gandy grew more alert as he followed the pair into a cubbyhole near the spy museum on the first floor, because everything about the pair screamed DO. One clue was that they were quite attractive, neatly dressed, and well-groomed. The tall, slender woman sported shoulder-length auburn hair and makeup that had been sparingly but artfully applied. Her smile radiated a million watts. The man was shorter than the woman, but solid, with an erect, military bearing and a short haircut. Well-toned shoulder and upper-arm muscles pressed against the fabric of his cream-colored Lacoste polo shirt.

Both officers held Gandy's gaze in a way that somehow made him feel special. He'd seen the same performance in other case officers he'd met over the years. In contrast, DI analysts were likely as not to appear academic and tweedy, while DS&T officers dressed and acted a lot like Gandy did.

As he seated himself across from the pair, he suspected he was about to be manipulated into doing something advantageous to the DO.

He wasn't disappointed.

The woman began. "I'm Ellen, and this is Tony. We're from SE"— the Soviet Union Eastern Europe Division.

Gandy believed the second part of the sentence but not the first. Case officers sometimes supplied their real names, and sometimes they didn't. Gandy sensed in this case that Ellen and Tony were not really Ellen and Tony.

"We understand you're going downrange," the woman went on.

Gandy was supposed to reveal details of his trip only on a need-to-know basis. He wasn't even permitted to tell Freda his true destination until after he got back. But he decided not to be coy. "That's right," he said.

Tony's pleasant expression grew serious. "We'd like to ask a favor."

"Okay. What's on your mind?"

The CIA officers exchanged quick glances. As if by prior agreement, Ellen said, "We were wondering how you'd feel about venturing outside the embassy while you're over there to run an errand for us."

Alarm bells went off in Gandy's head. "Running an errand" sounded a lot like hard-core espionage on the KGB's home turf. He wasn't particularly worried about the physical danger—he'd been shot at and subjected to mortar attacks in Vietnam—but he didn't think Freda would care much for him wandering the streets of Moscow. Also, he didn't know how he would stand up to the KGB's notorious interrogation methods, including drugs, if caught. He had way, *way* too much ultrasecret knowledge rattling around in his head to risk falling into Soviet hands.

He asked, "You mean do the kinds of things y'all do over there?"

"More or less," Tony answered.

"I'm confused. Can't one of your own folks do this? You've got troops over there, and I'm not trained for this sort of thing."

Ellen answered, "We're in a bit of a bind at the moment and are, well, shorthanded."

Gandy edged closer to the conference table. "You do realize the other side knows who I am."

Ellen said slowly, "We might have heard something about that."

"So what am I missing? They're gonna be on me like white on rice. How do I do what you ask without getting picked up and hustled to Lubyanka?"

"We assess that risk as very low," Tony chimed in. "You're a fresh face, and we don't think they'll be looking for you to do this. They believe you NSA guys just do SIGINT."

Gandy pushed down his growing irritation. "I don't mean to be difficult, but we *do* just do SIGINT. My security folks at the Fort wouldn't agree to this in a million years. Neither would Director Inman."

Neither of the CIA officers spoke, their facial expressions unreadable. *Feels like a poker game where I'm the sucker,* Gandy thought. He said, "If all y'all are from SE, then you know about security problems over there. Plenty of recent roll-ups and PNGs, from what I've heard."

"Oh," Tony said in a neutral voice, "what have you heard?"

"Well, the Marti Peterson PNG hit the papers last year. I assumed she was one of yours. And then there was your other guy, I forget his name—Vincent something or other."

Ellen spoke up. "Those things happen from time to time; it doesn't mean you wouldn't be safe."

Gandy looked at her evenly. "I assume you know why COS Gus Hathaway asked me over there in the first place, to find and plug leaks?"

A trace of anger leaking into his voice, Tony said, "Maybe it would be most constructive to stay away from what we know and don't know and just stick to the topic at hand."

"A fair point," Gandy said. "But my being asked to help the DO find and plug a security leak is not something that happens every day—or every decade, for that matter. I've got to believe that whatever leak, or leaks, have sprung up over there could have already compromised whatever project you want my help with."

Ellen's pretty face creased into a frown. "Does that mean you won't help us?"

"I'd love to help you, and it might even be fun to play James Bond. But I'm *not* James Bond. Is this somehow related to my mission over there?"

Tony said, "Not exactly."

"Does COS know?"

"I assume so," Tony answered.

Gandy thought for a moment. *Assume so?* Weren't these guys talking to each other? What the heck was really going on? An important station like Moscow would have ample DO staff to run errands. Could it be that *all* the case officers over there had been "blown" to the KGB? If so, why hadn't CIA already replaced the officers with "fresh faces"?

Something didn't add up. Gandy thought of himself as trusting and cooperative—sometimes to a fault—but he was certain the DO wasn't giving him the whole story. It couldn't be a coincidence that the outsider-phobic DO had asked for his help *twice* in the same city in the same month. Gandy mistrusted coincidences, especially when his "cousins" from CIA were involved.

An unsettling idea began to take shape at the edge of Charles's awareness. As he dwelled on the thought, it came into sharper focus. Gandy felt a chill crawl up his spine. The previous week, FBI had arrested two KGB officers, Cherneyev and Enger, working undercover in New York, which meant that the Soviets would be eager to trade for them before they told FBI too much about their operation. Such trades happened all the time, as when the Soviets exchanged U2 pilot Gary Powers for KGB master spy Rudolf Abel back in the '60s. If Moscow didn't already have any Americans "on ice" in Lubyanka, they'd need to quickly collect a few in order to trade for their men in New York.

Perhaps these two fashion models sitting in front of him and their DO masters wanted Gandy to get caught running an errand so that he could be a convenient hostage for the swap. That way, the KGB wouldn't be tempted to arrest a CIA officer or two—or three—at Moscow Station for that purpose. The identities of case officers were supposed to be secret, but one way or another, the KGB always seemed to know exactly who they were.

Gandy was a very senior NSA executive. The way these swaps went down, he might be worth two garden-variety KGB men. And Charles's noble sacrifice would keep CIA out of any future prisoner swap.

Was that the real reason Moscow COS had asked him to come over?

Gandy looked at the two CIA officers, searching their fresh scrubbed, wholesome faces for clues.

Finding none, he chided himself for being paranoid. Not even the DO could be that devious, could they? More likely, there was a simpler explanation, maybe even the one they had supplied him. In his long career dealing with different flavors of intelligence officers, he'd learned that screwups were usually a better explanation than malice to explain why officers did the unexplainable things they did. He didn't know what screwups might have happened in Moscow to make the DO unable to perform routine errands, but something had to be seriously wrong over there if the DO really did need his help running routine operations.

Gandy later learned that "Tony" and "Ellen" had probably asked him to run the "errand" because Admiral Turner had prohibited CIA from conducting HUMINT, omitting, apparently, explicit instructions for employing U.S. intelligence officers *outside* of CIA.

But in 1978, Gandy could only guess what had gone wrong in Moscow. His intuition told him it had to be connected somehow to the COS's unusual call for NSA's help with security, but he knew better than to ask the two youngsters in front of him about it.

At length, he said, "Look. I assume you wouldn't be asking me to do this if it weren't important, but I really can't help you out. Since they know who I am, running your errand would probably scuttle both your mission and mine. Then there are the leaks to worry about."

The officers, who'd both leaned in to hear, settled back in their chairs as if they'd been expecting this answer.

Tony said, "It was worth a try." He handed Gandy a card that bore only a name and gray-line phone number. "Sorry about getting a little testy a moment ago. Call if you change your mind."

But Gandy didn't change his mind. He was headed straight into the belly of the beast and didn't want to get chewed up and spit out before he got started there.

3. In the Belly of the Beast

Gandy looked out his window as the commercial passenger jet he had taken from Frankfurt circled Sheremetyevo International Airport north of Moscow, then lined up for final approach. Through the broken clouds, he could see large thoroughfares, wet with recent rain, that encircled the Soviet capital. Like most major cities, Moscow had a loop surrounding it, but unlike many sprawling urban centers, it possessed two such loops, rippling out in concentric circles.

Or maybe rings on a target, Gandy mused.

After the plane touched town and began to taxi to the gate, Gandy breathed an involuntary sigh of relief. Despite arriving in the world's most dangerous city—at least for foreign intelligence officers such as himself—he was actually relieved to have made it to Moscow in one piece.

Gandy was traveling as a U.S. government employee but had refused the government travel office's direction to take an Aeroflot flight with a stopover in Sofia, Bulgaria, and instead had offered to pay out of his own pocket for a more expensive ticket on a U.S. carrier that stopped over in Frankfurt, Germany. In Gandy's view, a lot of things could happen on an Aeroflot flight, none of them good.

Although he had deep respect for Russian intelligence tradecraft, he did not think much of the safety record of Soviet-made commercial aircraft. On top of that, Aeroflot was owned and run by a Communist government who had made known their strong objection to his visit.

Doubtless, he would be surveilled on Aeroflot and possibly seated next to a "honey trap": a KGB female sexual operative whose goal would be to compromise him. Gandy knew he could not be seduced into giving up classified information, but the KGB had many ways of successfully employing honey traps against unwilling targets. An attractive woman seated next to him, for example, could, without warning, lean over and kiss him passionately on the lips while simultaneously placing her hand in his crotch for the benefit of surveillance cameras. Then, once he landed in Moscow, the KGB could show him the embarrassing photos and threaten to send them to his wife, Freda, or his bosses back in the States.

Or an attractive *man* could stage the same performance, creating even greater blackmail leverage.

Crude but sometimes effective.

Then there was the one-night stopover in Bulgaria, a close Soviet ally. What genius in the travel office had thought it was a good idea to park a highly valued U.S. intelligence officer—known to the KGB—in a Communist bloc country for an evening in a Sofia hotel without a personal security detail or even a weapon (which Gandy sometimes carried on other overseas assignments)?

But an Aeroflot journey wasn't the only hazard Gandy had to worry about. The Russians knew exactly when he was coming and probably which U.S. carrier and flight he had chosen, thanks to excellent Soviet SIGINT capabilities on the rooftops of diplomatic facilities in Washington and New York, where U.S. airlines transmitted passenger and flight information by microwaves—which, as mere "commercial" links, could probably be intercepted by any local foreign embassy employees in the United States.

It wasn't unheard of for the KGB to harass and rough up the opposition, although by a gentleman's agreement between U.S. and Soviet spy agencies, this sort of thing was kept to a minimum. But gentleman's agreement or no, the Soviets had strenuously objected to Charles's visit and might have caused him trouble in Frankfurt. If West German thugs mugged him at the airport, who was to say who or what had made them do it?

Modern jetways had not yet made it to Russian airports, so Gandy and the other passengers deplaned via old-fashioned mobile stairways. The late April Moscow air was chilly, and Gandy could see his breath, along with a small mounds of dirt-streaked snow in the shadows, reminding him that Moscow's latitude was just a smidgen south of Juneau, Alaska.

Carrying a government passport, Gandy was ushered by stern-faced officials into "the fast lane," where he presented his papers. The uniformed officer studied his passport and attached visa carefully, taking his time leafing through every page of the documents, then going over them again.

And again. And again.

Finally completing his elaborate perusal, the officer said nothing and made no move to stamp the documents. Instead, he fixed Gandy with an unblinking death stare. Gandy, realizing the Soviets were simply stalling so they could search his luggage in a back room, had been prepared for this, so he just stared back.

At length, the officer answered his phone, simply said, "*Da*," stamped the passport, and curtly waved Gandy through, where he picked up his luggage.

Outside of customs, Gandy was met by a driver from the embassy accompanied by Jon LeChevet from the U.S. embassy's Regional Security Office (RSO).

"Welcome to Moscow," LeChevet said, extending his hand.

In the car, a late-model American sedan, Gandy and his host kept the conversation light, avoiding any shoptalk. The driver, like most U.S. embassy employees, was either a serving KGB officer or employed by them. And the odds were excellent that the car was bugged.

Although Gandy needed no reminder to obey "Moscow rules"—the hyper-strict security protocols that Western intelligence officers followed in the Soviet capital—a forceful reminder nevertheless presented itself as the embassy sedan pulled away from the curb at the arrival terminal. Four black Russian-made sedans abruptly boxed in the embassy car, proceeding slowly into the flow of traffic.

Gandy looked over at the KGB car closest to him and spotted two officers in black fedoras—shockingly similar to those worn by the *Spy vs. Spy* characters in his son Chuck's *Mad* magazine cartoons.

The black-hatted officer looked back at Gandy, wearing a menacing expression similar to that of the immigration official.

I wonder if they teach that look at the KGB academy, Gandy thought as he settled in for the half-hour ride to the embassy.

Although Gandy was weary from the long trip, he wanted to get a feel for the country he now found himself in and the people who lived there. So instead of succumbing to a powerful urge to nap during the ride from Sheremetyevo, he took in the sights of the outskirts of Moscow as best he could given that he was still boxed in on all sides by his KGB "escort."

Putting aside his specialized knowledge of Russian technology and tradecraft, most of what Gandy knew about Russia had come from movie, television, and news depictions of a grim, dark, poor, soulless place where blocky men in fur hats and long leather coats ordered jackbooted subordinates to haul innocent civilians out of bed in the small hours of the morning for long journeys to the gulag and a life of hard labor in the Siberian wilderness.

A Stalinist hell, in other words.

But for the most part, outer Moscow looked like the surroundings of other large cities Gandy had visited. Factories, power lines, trucks and cars speeding to their destinations on surface streets. The occasional pedestrians who he spotted did not appear to be trudging ahead, heads down, occasionally looking over their shoulders for secret police, as American stereotypes of life in Russia suggested.

No, on the whole, the place and the locals who inhabited it looked surprisingly normal, with a few important exceptions.

One of those exceptions was a line of crossed-rail tank barriers in Moscow's outskirts. The tank traps were rusted and old, some with graffiti painted on them.

Clearly these defenses were left over from "the great Patriotic War" against Hitler thirty-five years earlier. Why were they still there? Did the Russians expect another attack from the West all these years later? Did they ceremonially mark the farthest point of German advance decades earlier? Or were the tank traps just another form of Communist propaganda, reminding the populace that danger was everywhere?

As Gandy took in bomb-damaged buildings also left over from the war, another explanation for the tank traps occurred to him: any country too poor to rebuild bombed-out buildings was also probably too poor to remove tank traps. It seemed that building up and maintaining their armed forces and nuclear capability took higher priority than building up their civil infrastructure.

As he entered Moscow proper, a palpable, heavy sense of his surroundings, and the men who ruled them, crept into his bones. Here was a place that would not soon—if ever—forget that enemies from the West had nearly destroyed them. And literally nothing—including rebuilt housing for its people or factories for its industry—was worth sacrificing for military strength against Western adversaries like America, its main enemy.

Nothing.

After unpacking in his room at the north annex of the U.S. embassy at 19 Chaikovskova, a short walk from Red Square, and getting a good night's sleep, Gandy went down to breakfast in the embassy snack bar. Loading food on his tray, he scanned the tables, looking for tourists who had stopped by the embassy to check in and to get a reasonable meal, as good food was scarce in Russia, even for Western tourists with hard currency.

From many previous trips abroad, Gandy had learned how to spot tourists in American embassies: they were usually bright-eyed and excited about being where they were, talking fast and smiling a lot—and they wore cameras around their necks. Career diplomats, especially in Iron Curtain countries, were not so cheery. And they rarely carried cameras in the snack bar.

Gandy needed to avoid diplomats in the cafeteria at all costs. He was supposed to be in Moscow working as a routine government employee and didn't want to draw the usual questions about which section of the department he worked in or what his job was.

But if he ate alone, some diplomat or other, exhibiting the normal social graces of people who are selected for their relationship-building skills, would seek him out, if for no other reason than to keep him company.

So Gandy looked for nearly full tables of tourists. Finding a family of three seated at a table for four, Gandy asked if he could join the group and sat down. A pleasant-looking couple from New Jersey in their mid-forties was in the middle of breakfast with their daughter, already dressed in a brightly colored down coat for the chilly weather, and welcomed him.

It turned out, after quick intros, that the family were not, strictly speaking, tourists, because only embassy staff and their guests, along with the occasional student, were allowed into the Moscow embassy snack bar. These people were guests of the embassy, but they were almost as good as tourists for Charles's purposes.

As was usually the case when Gandy sought out nongovernment types, the family asked Gandy no questions except for his name, and they proceeded to talk about their visit, what they had bought, how horrible the food was in Moscow, how hot the hotel rooms were, and how grim the locals looked. The embassy snack bar seemed to offer the only digestible food in the city, if not the country.

Gandy loved every second of the boring one-way conversation, because no return conversation from him was expected—or apparently desired. He nodded and smiled at all the right times as he worked through his plate of scrambled eggs and sipped his coffee.

God, he loved tourists, even if they weren't really tourists!

Breakfast completed, Gandy wished the New Jersey family a fun outing and found his way up to Jon LeChevet's office for his first appointment.

Jon offered him a seat, and they chatted for twenty minutes, filling each other in on their backgrounds.

Gandy learned that LeChevet was from Oneonta, New York, and had a mother who, in a post–atom bomb world, had encouraged him to study physics in high school and to become a physicist because "the country needs more physicists."

So Jon earned a Ph.D. in solid state physics from Northeastern University, only to discover when he graduated in 1971 that the world did not need more physicists. Academic and private-industry jobs for physicists were scarce, so Jon took a postdoctoral position at Georgetown University, where he applied his expertise to develop ultrasensitive weapons detectors for airports. He developed a detector capable of sensing the location, type, and shape of weapons, but the FAA passed on his device because it was an eight-foot-long tunnel that made passengers feel claustrophobic.

His postdoctoral work at an end, Jon decided to try his luck in private industry and took a job working for a company that made superconductors, where, among other projects, he worked on applying superconductor technology to detecting submarines.

But after a couple of years, Jon decided to do something more meaningful with his life and accepted a job at State Department security, protecting diplomatic facilities overseas. After working in the research-and-development section for a couple of years, Jon shifted over to the operational side of diplomatic security and trained in a government interagency TSCM (technical security countermeasures; basically, finding bugs) program and shipped off to Moscow, accompanied by his family.

After Gandy sketched out his own background, the two got down to business. "I wanted to fill you in on what I've learned here before we go downstairs to see the COS and the boss"—CIA chief of station Gus Hathaway and Ambassador Malcolm Toon, respectively, whom they were slated to meet an hour later.

"I'd appreciate that," Gandy answered. He'd already thoroughly prepared for the trip at Fort Meade by poring over security data collected at the embassy, but he was always open to learning more.

"I've been here since last June," LeChevet began, "mostly repairing all the damage from the fire last year that destroyed the eighth floor, damaged parts of the ninth and most of the tenth, gutted the attic, and collapsed the roof. When I can, I do the usual security work: making sure event detectors—room-entry alarms, metal detectors, and so on—work properly, monitoring the microwave signals beamed at the upper floors, and checking for bugs and hidden microphones in the State Department's sections of the embassy. As you probably know, CIA officers do security in CIA areas."

Gandy nodded.

"Bugs and microphones in the residences and nonsecure offices are, despite a never-ending battle to find and remove them, a constant presence," Jon continued. "And with over a hundred Soviets running around the building, including maids, cooks, drivers, secretaries, administrative staff, and even security personnel, it's impossible to stop the Russians from planting the devices."

Gandy thought, *The walls don't have ears; the walls* are *ears.*

Gandy had heard from a State Department man named Javits, who had been posted in Moscow, that his eight-year-old son, who lived with him in the residence section of the embassy, had his bike stolen. Infuriated, and accustomed to Russian harassment, the boy screamed at the wall in his bedroom, "Wall, give me my bike back!"

The next day, the bike magically appeared outside his room.

"Can you tell me about the microwaves?" Gandy asked.

LeChevet slid a thin, stapled document across the table. "I do these measurements every day."

Gandy studied the documents, which typically looked like this cable sent from Ambassador Toon to the secretary of state, Cyrus Vance, containing LeChevet's measurements.[1]

SECRET

PAGE 01 MOSCOW 16931 212255Z ACTION SY-05 INFO OCT-01 IS0-00
/006 W R 211452Z NOV 77
FM AMEMBASSY MOSCOW
TO SECSTATE WASHDC
4764 S E C R E T MOSCOW 16931 SY CHANNEL FOR A/SY/OPS/T E. O.
11652: XGDS-3

SUBJECT: SPECIAL MEASUREMENT 076532 220226Z

MUTS SIGNAL ACTIVITY RECORDED THROUGHOUT THE PERIOD BE-
GINNING AT 18:00 HOURS ON 18 NOV AND ENDING AT 18:00 HOURS
ON 21 NOV FOLLOWS:

DATE	MUTS ONE	MUTS TWO
18 NOV	19:15-19:25 (B)	
18 NOV	21:30-22:25 (C)	
19 NOV		10:25-10:35 (B)
19 NOV		12:00-12:10 (B)
19 NOV		13:35-13:50 (B)
19 NOV		15:15-15:25 (B)
19 NOV		16:50-17:00 (B)
19 NOV		18:20-18:35 (B)
20 NOV		09:40-09:50 (B)
20 NOV		11:15-11:25 (B)
20 NOV		12:50-13:00 (B)
19-21 NOV	1	SEE PARA 3
21 NOV		09:20-12:00 (B)

21 NOV   12:25-12:35 (B)
SECRET

SECRET PAGE 02

21 NOV MOSCOW 16931 212255Z 13:00-18:00 (B) 2. POWER DENSITY
FIGURES CALCULATED USING POWER LEVEL MEASUREMENTS (IN
PARENS) MADE DURING CERTAIN OF THE PARA ONE REVIEW AU-
THORITY: ACTIVITY PERIODS WERE AS FOLLOWS:

DATE	TIME	SIGNAL POWER
21 NOV	11:10	TWO (B).20 (13)
21 NOV	16:05	TWO (B).48 (32)

3. MECHANICAL FAILURE (JAMMED PAPER FEED) CAUSED LOSS OF
INFORMATION FROM 19:30 ON 19 NOV TO 09:20 ON 21 NOV FOR MUTS
TWO ONLY. RUSTRAK SHOWED ONLY NORMAL B ACTIVITY DURING
THIS PERIOD.

4. HIGH POWER B AND C MODES OBSERVED FOR MUTS ONE ON 20
NOV FROM 00:10 TO 00:15. NO STEADY STATE REACHED.

5. BRITISH TECHS OBSERVED MUTS TWO (B) SIGNAL THIS DAY FROM
DETAILS TO FOLLOW.

TOON

SECRET

The rows of numbers denoted the date of measurement, time, frequency band (*A* for 0.5–1.5 GHz, *B* for 1.5–3.0 GHz, *C* for 3.0–
9.0 GHz), and power levels. MUTS 1 and MUTS 2 referred to signals
originating from different locations outside the embassy.

The MUTS 1 and 2 were descendants of TUMS—the technical unidentified Moscow signals—that had bombarded different chancery buildings since the late '40s. Although the original signals were related to the Thing implant at Spaso House (the ambassador's residence, not the chancery), the purpose of the continued radiation of the chancery was something of a mystery to many State and CIA technical officers, because they knew of no further instances of Thing-like implants.

But the signals were no mystery to Gandy. He was certain that, despite rising in frequency from VHF into the microwave bands, their function had never changed from the original emissions: extracting information from the embassy. He had been trying, without success, to raise alarms at State and CIA about the very signals described in the document before him for almost ten years.

Gandy studied the data carefully because he had not seen such detailed records back at Fort Meade. As he scanned down one page after another, the numbers spoke to him, telling him what the Russians were probably up to.

"Can I keep these?" he asked.

"I don't see why not," LeChevet answered. "What do you think?"

Gandy considered how much to tell the State Department man. He was not into interagency turf fights, and he normally liked to cooperate outside of NSA as much as possible. But he couldn't talk about NSA's own ultrasensitive sources and methods that guided his interpretation of the MUTS signals described on the documents in front of him.

At length, Gandy said, "Well, one thing's for sure—they hunt for resonances, then seem to find them." He pointed to the long row of numbers on one page.

"You mean like the Great Seal?"

"Yes. Except with the seal, they knew exactly which frequencies to use because it was their own implant. My impression here is that some of these constant-frequency CW signals never change and may be stimulating another resonant microphone like the Thing, but the others shift regularly, then lock on to one frequency as if they are hunting for one of our unintended radiators, then find one to exploit."

"Go on," LeChevet said.

Choosing his words carefully, Gandy explained that microwaves, by analogy, were like sunlight that reflected off any shiny or metallic object. Whenever that object moved, changing its angle to incident sunlight, an observer would see the sunlight wink on and off, similar to a signaling mirror used by the army for long-distance communication before the telegraph was invented. Microwaves worked this way, too, sort of, but unlike sunlight, which would reflect well off any sized shiny surface, microwaves mostly return a strong signal from conductors (typically metal) that had a physical dimension that was resonant (had the same dimension as half the length of a microwave) with the microwave frequency.

Thus, when the length of a metal conductor illuminated with microwaves of a single frequency changed, even slightly, the energy returned to a microwave receiver would also change, similar to the way the amount of sunlight reflected from a mirror changed with the mirror's angle.

The Thing worked because voice vibrations slightly changed the electrical length of a small microwave antenna, allowing a remote radar to sense and decode those voice signals from small changes in received microwave energy.

But the systematic shifts in frequency of the MUTS signals suggested that the Soviet microwaves were hunting for conductors of *unknown* length that might carry classified information. According to entry-level Russian language texts on leakage of information through technical channels, conductors such as electrical traces in digital circuits that oscillate (periodically change effective length) whenever transistor logic connected to that conductive trace shifts from zero to one can leak information to remote RF imposition (MUTS/TUMS) devices. The same Russian language textbooks say that any oscillatory electronic or mechanical movements, such as back-and-forth movements of swinging typewriter arms, will inform a remote radar which letter had been typed every time a new key was struck.[2]

A declassified NSA document, "Tempest: A Signal Problem," also said that information typed on text-processing equipment, such as code machines and typewriters, could leak out of a secure facility through microphones that picked up the sound of the text equipment operating, because—on many machines—the typing or printing of different letters made different sounds that could be decoded. If an acoustic resonator, such as an implanted microwave Thing-like microphone or fortuitous vibrating membrane, such as an audio speaker, were close enough to a text-processing machine, then MUTS or TUMS could "hear" the typing through acoustic vibrations of that resonator.[3]

Not knowing beforehand what the resonant length of such telltale reflectors might be, the KGB could be systematically increasing and decreasing the frequency of microwave energy until they detected strong, resonant return signals that varied slightly with voice or data information. Once such reflectors were found, the microwaves would then lock on to that frequency and "read" the classified information it contained.

"Look here." Gandy pointed to the time stamps on the document LeChevet had given him. "The frequencies shift every ten minutes, then dwell for two hours and forty minutes on just one frequency. This means that they were hunting for an information source at different frequencies, then, finding one that was productive, stopped at that frequency."

"Stopped to do what?" LeChevet asked.

"To listen and to decode a voice or data implant, or both. The signal would not dwell like that if it weren't producing useful intelligence. I'm afraid this is very bad news. The other side is stealing from you, for sure. We need to listen to those same frequencies to see if we can learn what those guys"—Gandy pointed across the street—"are collecting."

LeChevet looked like he was digesting all this, but Gandy couldn't be sure. He'd learned, from explaining such things before, that even bright Ph.D. scientists like Jon found the subject to be arcane and incomprehensible. Microwaves were like microbes—you couldn't see them and had a hard time grasping that something invisible could be so dangerous. The strange, nonintuitive nature of microwave interactions with conductors was one reason that Gandy constantly encountered skepticism when raising the possibility of microwave attacks, even though the Thing was widely known.

The meeting over, Gandy and Jon ventured down to the seventh floor for the first meeting with Hathaway.

Although it might have been his imagination, on his way to Hathaway's office in Moscow Station—the term for CIA's operation in the embassy—Gandy thought he could smell damp, charred wood, a reminder of the fire that had swept through the embassy the previous August.

Hathaway was tall and slender and moved with athletic grace. A Southerner like Gandy, Hathaway did not immediately get down to business, but offered Gandy and Jon a cup of bad embassy coffee, then inquired about Gandy's trip, his quarters, his ride from Sheremetyevo, and other small talk. The two had met in the States during one of Charles's briefings on the Russia threat at CIA headquarters, and Hathaway praised Gandy for his excellent presentation and offer of technical assistance. Hathaway's voice was soft, and he spoke in an unhurried cadence that Gandy had grown up hearing in the Deep South.

Gandy was pleased he had made an impression but reminded himself he was talking to a skilled CIA case officer whose job, after all, was to recruit people using flattery and any number of other tools of persuasion. In the intelligence community, getting stroked, cajoled, pressured, or bullied by a DO case officer who wanted something from you was referred to as "being DO'd." When dealing with someone like Hathaway, however sincere he might appear—and Hathaway seemed *very* sincere—it was always a good idea to keep in mind that one might be being DO'd.

Finishing his coffee, Hathaway said, "Let's go to the box." Hathaway led them up two floors to a secure area on the ninth floor.

The box was a small cube inside the ninth-floor SCIF, whose walls were made entirely of clear Plexiglas with special supports that prevented sound waves from propagating into the building's structure (vibrations the KGB could decode by attaching special sound transducers to pipes, air ducts, or any other structure capable of transmitting vibrations).

Outside the box was a powerful air blower, which turned on when Hathaway flicked the lights on in the tiny room, further masking their conversation.

Shortly after Jon, Gandy, and Hathaway were seated, Ambassador Malcolm Toon appeared outside the box and gestured that he wanted to come in.

The ambassador was a distinguished gentleman with light gray hair, a tailored suit, and a no-nonsense manner. He had learned to speak Russian while serving five years in Moscow as a junior diplomat in the 1950s, including during the Stalin era, and was considered to be a hard-line cold warrior. The Soviets, unhappy with what they considered to be Toon's harsh, anti-Russian views, had effectively vetoed his appointment to Moscow with Henry Kissinger and Richard Nixon in the early '70s. Toon's wife, Elizabeth, who had spent five grim years in Moscow before, had added her veto to the Russians', telling Malcolm that he could accept the appointment there "over my dead body."[4]

But Toon, who wanted to exert influence over U.S.-Soviet relations, ultimately prevailed over both Nixon's secretary of state, Kissinger, and his wife to relent, and the Toons took up residence in Spaso House in late 1976. President Carter wasn't enthusiastic about keeping Toon when he took office a few months later but was eventually persuaded to stick with him in order not to look soft on communism.[5]

After Toon seated himself, Hathaway said, "We've got serious problems." He went on to describe the recent roll-ups and expulsions, implying that a security leak, or leaks, in the embassy was the source. Hathaway did not, however, explain the urgency surrounding the pending Tolkachev recruitment, the pending inspection by Turner's man Rusty Williams, or his campaign to rebuild Admiral Turner's trust so that he could resume HUMINT operations. Interagency cooperation was called for here—but only up to a certain point. Gandy did not learn of CIA's internal problems in Moscow until forty years later.

Hathaway concluded, "What do y'all think? Any ideas where the other side might be getting their information?"

Gandy looked over at LeChevet and wondered if the State Department officer caught the nuance. *Y'all* in this context, as any Southerner knew, was employed in the singular, meaning just Gandy. If Hathaway had also wanted LeChevet's opinion, he would have said *all y'all*.

Apparently, Hathaway already knew LeChevet's views.

Gandy was aware that both career diplomats such as Toon—known as *black dragons*—and CIA officers did not hold State's RSO officers in high esteem, discounting their expertise and bringing in intelligence technologists, such as Gandy, for the most challenging problems. From his conversation with LeChevet, the State Department man seemed perfectly competent to Gandy, but what could you do? Gandy knew that prejudices died hard.

Gandy turned to Jon. "You've been here a while. What's your sense?"

"Where to begin?" LeChevet answered. "The possibilities are endless. Mics, implants workers [Soviets employed in the embassy], maybe that mysterious chimney. We've got a couple of engineers helping Seabees [navy construction engineers] here right now about to break in to the chimney and check it out."

Gandy nodded. For the benefit of Toon and Hathaway, he asked, "What about MUTS and TUMS?"

LeChevet leaned forward. "That's been my main focus since getting here. I've recorded them and carefully analyzed their modulation schemes—which are all over the map, by the way. Frequency hopping, direct spreading, you name it. But I still haven't figured out exactly what they're doing, other than the fact they seem to be aimed at the top floors."

Gandy asked, "Where do they come from?"

"Two different sites. One is an apartment across Chaikovskova"—the street the embassy was located on. "And the other?" LeChevet pointed in the direction of the old Russian Orthodox building nearby. "We call that Our Lady of Telemetry or Our Lady of Observation."

Gandy smiled at that. "Well, I have an idea or two about the microwaves." Looking at Hathaway, he said, "I think they could be very significant to your problems here."

"How so?" Hathaway asked.

"Do you know about the Great Seal implant?"

Hathaway and Toon nodded in unison.

"Well, you might have some more like it, but they'd be quite a bit smaller, and harder to find, because the MUTS signals are higher frequency than the 400 MHz signals that energized the Thing in the Great Seal."

Gandy had learned not to explain to nontechnical people the relationship between resonator size and microwave frequency, because their eyes usually glazed over. As he'd expected, neither Toon nor Hathaway asked for an explanation. But Toon did ask, "Exactly how small are we talking about?"

Gandy did some mental calculations. "The highest frequency is 9 GHz, which is resonant at a little less than half an inch, give or take a fraction of an inch, allowing for capacitive effects."

Gandy then held out his hand as if he had such a device in his palm and leaned in to the ambassador. Then he blew on his hand, propelling the imaginary microwave bug into the ambassador's neatly groomed hair. "Could be pretty small," he added.

Toon recoiled, swatting the top of his head, trying to brush away whatever Gandy may have blown out of his palm.

"Sorry," Gandy said. "I didn't mean to startle you. I was just trying to make a point."

The exact details of the rest of the conversation among Gandy, Jon, Hathaway, and ambassador in the box are not available for public consumption, even forty years later, but careful analysis of Gandy's unclassified descriptions, declassified NSA, CIA, and State Department documents, and particularly, study of Russian-language texts on information leakage and Russian training materials regarding microwave attacks provide a reasonable idea of what was said that day, given that Gandy was aware in 1978 of Russian capabilities and microwave tradecraft, information that was highly classified then but openly available in Russia today.

Based upon this informed guesswork, here is a summary—derived solely from the information-leakage textbooks and other public sources—of what Gandy might have told Toon and Hathaway about how microwaves could be a problem.*

Consider the radar detectors that police used in 1978 to catch speeders. These handheld microwave emitters radiate a pure "tone" that bounces off the metal of traveling cars and travels back to the handheld device. Microwave energy returned from a moving car will shift up in tone and frequency in exactly the same way that the whistle of an approaching train seems to increase in pitch as it approaches, even though the whistle is actually emitting sound at a constant tone.

This phenomenon, called Doppler shift, occurs because the motion of an object emitting a sound compresses sound waves, making them shorter, increasing their frequency and pitch. Conversely, a receding object will elongate sound waves emitted from it, lowering their frequency and pitch. When police detect a very large Doppler shift in a moving vehicle traveling toward or away from them, it means that the car is traveling faster than the speed limit; a small shift in tone signifies that a driver is obeying speed limits.

The Russians used Doppler principle and other radio frequency principles such as nonlinear mixing ("parasitic and parametric" phenomena, according to Russian-language texts) to detect minute motions—including

---

* Nothing written here indicates that the U.S. government, where I worked as an intelligence officer, acknowledges either the validity or U.S. employment of techniques described in public documents such as Russian-language textbooks.

those triggered by acoustic energy from voices—of small metallic objects inside buildings upon which they wished to spy.

Robert M. Clark, writing in the 2011 unclassified book *The Technical Collection of Intelligence*, states:

> *Since at least the 1960's, radio frequency [microwave] flooding of installation has been used for intelligence data collection. The flooding signals are used to collect data remotely, much as a radar senses its target. The flooding was directed at devices [with moving metallic parts] such as typewriters. Signals directed at the typewriters were modulated by the keystrokes [e.g., by Doppler shift as keys moved toward and away from the radar] and the modulated signals received by other antennas, thereby compromising the information typed.[6]*

Thus, after raising the possibility of Thing-like implants for voice recovery, Gandy probably informed Ambassador Hathaway and Jon that the KGB could be using microwaves to read messages as they were typed on typewriters or other text input devices, *without any implant or bugs whatsoever!*

Yes, information about assets' true identities was never supposed to be typed or openly discussed outside of the SCIF or the box, which were shielded against microwave radiation. But was the door of the microwave-impervious SCIF always closed? Was it ever left open by accident or by negligence or simple convenience? If so, microwave signals beamed into the building could easily travel through open doors and compromise typewriters and other equipment, as described later.

Having worked at many embassies worldwide, Gandy knew that embassy SCIFs were often left open, despite claims by local intelligence officers that such lapses never happened.

A recent translation of an account of a former KGB officer who claimed to have surveilled the U.S. embassy in Moscow described other things that the Soviets picked up using what they call RF imposition or high-frequency pumping (what Clark earlier referred to as radio frequency flooding).

I saw with my own eyes and heard with my ears the information [conversations] not only from the phone disconnected from the automatic telephone exchange, but also the doorbells, electromagnetic starters, electric meters . . . in short everything that has inside at least a hint of an oscillatory circuit. [Back-and-forth movements of typewriter arms are mechanical oscillators.] This was achieved with the help of high frequency pumping. The secret pumping device at the time was called "area 69."[7]

A modern Russian textbook used in introductory information security courses at the college level describes in more detail how RF imposition with microwaves can recover voice information from any device containing a nonlinear element such as a transistor: in other words, any modern piece of electronics, including telephones, televisions, stereo systems, scanners, printers, and computers.

Extraction of information by high frequency imposition is achieved as a result of remote action [microwaves beamed at a target facility] by a high frequency [microwave] electromagnetic field or electrical signals on elements capable of modulating their information parameters [voice or data] by primary electrical or acoustic signals with voice information. . . . More often, a non-linear element is used as a modulation element [source of voice or digital data] including in the telephone system. In this case high frequency imposition is provided by bringing a high frequency harmonic signal to the telephone apparatus. . . . The principle of operation here is similar to the operation of a radio mixer.[8]

In simpler terms, the phenomena described in the Russian textbooks means that when a microwave signal hits a nonlinear device such as any transistor or diode, it will cause that device to radiate multiple frequencies different from the microwave signal itself in a process called mixing. These new radio frequencies, in turn, increase and decrease in volume as a transistor or diode changes electrical conductivity with voice signals, or change current with data signals, so that a sensitive microwave receiver located nearby can pick up unintended radiation of voice or data signals.

Yes, weird and magical as it seems—according to Russian textbooks— whenever you talk around any piece of electronics, your voice slightly vibrates that device, allowing a sensitive microwave to pick up and decode your voice. A similar principle allows microwave sensors to read data being processed in digital electronics.

In sum, Gandy, based upon his research, likely would have suggested to Hathaway and LeChevet that the KGB learned the identities of CIA assets and CIA case officers by planting undetectable descendants of the Thing in classified regions of the embassy or extracting the information via microwave flooding.

And the ingenious, nearly impossible-to-understand physics underlying such virtuoso technical feats made such Russian attacks all the more dangerous: Who could believe that such bizarre things were possible, especially from the backward third-world Soviets?

After the meeting, Gandy walked over to the north annex of the embassy, where he knocked on the door of the quarters of an absent embassy staffer who had, conveniently, left for a month. The door opened a crack, showing a sliver of the face of one of the two coworkers Gandy had brought with him from Fort Meade. The man opened the door, admitting Gandy, then swiftly closed it. Navigating around a black drape hung over stacked cardboard boxes that blocked any view inside the room from the door and covered all their electronics, Gandy followed his man inside and surveyed the room.

Stacks of sophisticated electronics, some with antennas attached, had been set up on tables and boxes, cables running everywhere. NSA had shipped this equipment ahead of Gandy via diplomatic pouch, which was theoretically safe from KGB prying. His man had worked through the night. Now it was Gandy's shift. A third man was sleeping nearby, who would take over for Gandy in ten hours or so, so that NSA could keep their mission going 24-7.

With lives at stake, time was short.

"Everything working okay?" Gandy asked.

Charles's partner, a tall, blond engineer of few words, only nodded. Because the room, inside a heated embassy, was draped in shielded black material and there was no air-conditioning, the temperature exceeded ninety degrees Fahrenheit. The blond man wore only his skivvies to keep cool, but Gandy, who had worked under exactly these conditions before with his team, hardly noticed. Downrange, sacrifices had to be made.

Gandy took off his own shirt to stay cool and said, "Okay, let's get started." The two men set to work, sweating profusely as they concentrated.

As with the second half of the meeting in the Plexiglas box earlier that morning, only fragmentary information is publicly available about what Gandy did the rest of the day in that room, and the following weeks must remain a subject of informed speculation based upon declassified documents and Russian textbooks on TSCM procedures.

But if Gandy and his team did what state-of-the-art bug hunters did in 1978—which is very likely—here is a rough idea of what went on in their temporary quarters.

Given that LeChevet had conducted routine bugs hunts and found nothing in the secure areas of the embassy, Gandy, in a hurry to find possible compromises, is likely to have used methods and technologies that were *beyond* those available to State Department security at the time, in order to avoid wasting time repeating what LeChevet had done many times recently.

One such advanced approach would have employed expensive, state-of-the-art low-noise radio scanners and spectrum analyzers capable of detecting and demodulating (turning encoded radio transmissions into format such as speech and text that humans could understand) RF signals, along with sophisticated antennas capable of plucking faint signals from the air.

The State Department, who didn't put the same priority on technical countermeasures that NSA did, lacked the latest and greatest equipment available to the intelligence agency.

Gandy and his colleagues, if they had followed standard TSCM practice, would have meticulously scanned the RF spectrum around the clock (ergo the 24-7 shift arrangement), searching for any signals that did not belong to the normal background of transmissions from TV and radio stations, police and fire dispatches, microwave telecommunication data links, and, in 1978, car telephones.

The goal of such needle-in-a-haystack searches is to find exfiltrated signals from bugs, microphones, or data-gathering implants, especially those transmitted in ultrashort, hard-to-find bursts favored for covert communications.

The hunt for ephemeral bursts was especially important because, in the intelligence world, any attempt by an adversary to hide information—with encryption or use of burst transmissions—ipso facto merited close attention. In a never-ending cat-and-mouse game between spies and counterspies, the trick with exfiltrating stealthy transmission was to *hide* the fact that you were hiding, in order not to draw attention to the fact that you were hiding.

TSCM textbooks provide another tantalizing clue about what Gandy and colleagues might have been doing to track down the lethal information leaks. Electronic circuits in rooms where conversations are occurring can vibrate slightly with acoustic energy generated by speech, exactly as the diaphragm of a microphone vibrates. Just as microphones convert such vibrations into a voltage that is then amplified and transmitted (e.g., via a telephone receiver, a public address system), minute vibrations of electronic circuit boards cause subtle changes in the electrical properties of transistors and other components. When such changes occur in a circuit that oscillates (such as a digital clock that oscillates between one and zero in most electronics), voice signals that vibrate an electronic circuit having an oscillator will slightly modulate (change the amplitude, or pitch) of that oscillation. Since, according to principles of physics, any oscillation in an electronic circuit will transmit some RF to the outside world, a sensitive receiver can pick up and decode unintended voice transmissions from many types of electronic equipment.[9]

The KGB (as evidenced by many Russian-language TSCM textbooks) was well aware of the dangers of unintended RF transmissions of voice signals and therefore, like other intelligence organizations, routinely shielded electronics in sensitive areas capable of radiating such signals or placed them in electrically shielded rooms (SCIFs), or both.

Here is a translated excerpt from a modern Russian TSCM primer:

Acoustic energy arising during a conversation can cause acoustic (mechanical) oscillations of electronic equipment elements, which leads to the appearance of electromagnetic radiation [unintended RF transmissions] or to its change under certain circumstances. The most sensitive elements of radio electronic equipment for acoustic influences are the inductors and capacitors of variable capacity, piezo and optical converters.[10]

Thus, if the KGB was recovering voice signals from the embassy and playing them on loudspeakers (or possibly even headsets) in their listening posts, Gandy might have been able to hear what the KGB was hearing, despite Russian efforts to electrically shield the rooms from which they were surveilling the embassy. Shields didn't always work as intended. Gandy might also have been able to pick up voices of KGB operatives themselves, commenting on their "take" (the intelligence collected from the embassy) or problems they were having zeroing in on suitable signals.

In the spy trade, listening to listeners is called robbing the highway robber.

Again, no information has emerged that indicates that Gandy actually did "rob the robbers" in Moscow in this way. But if he were aware of these techniques in 1978 and motivated to learn what the KGB was learning about human assets and their controllers, he had the skills to do so.

For the next several weeks, Gandy lived a *Groundhog Day* existence, repeating the same activities for twelve to eighteen hours each day, including the weekends. Rising early, he would go down to breakfast, find a fresh batch of nongovernment visitors or guests to sit with, listen attentively to the same stories and complaints, nod and smile in all the right places—but say little—then bus his cafeteria tray and make his way up to the work quarters to relieve the night shift.

But it wouldn't have been right for him to return from an exotic city like Moscow without some souvenirs for his wife, Freda, and their children, Chuck and Beth, so Gandy requested an embassy driver and car and ventured out into the city for some shopping at a Beriozka store, where embassy staff had told him that foreigners could spend their hard currency. Given that the KGB knew who he was, there was some danger in leaving the protective, if overly acquisitive, walls of the embassy.

Gandy and his team had indeed experienced a sophisticated form of harassment while working in the temporary quarters. One night, there was a deafening *pop* inside their room, accompanied by a blinding flash and smell of ozone, just before the power went out. The KGB, who controlled electrical power fed to the embassy, had created an overvoltage on the power circuits feeding the admiral's quarters in order to blow out their electronics.

The power surge destroyed a stereo and TV in the room but caused only minor damage to Gandy's gear, because he had anticipated and protected his equipment from just such an attack.

Later checks of the embassy revealed that the power surge had only hit the circuit feeding the admiral's room, proving that the KGB had somehow figured out exactly where he was working.

And Gandy had a fair idea of how the KGB knew about his work location.

When showing up at the beginning of his shift each day, Gandy had to step around a neat, ten-by-ten matrix of cigarette butts left at the stairway landing on the floor where he worked. Although he never saw the smoker who left signs of a stakeout, Gandy believed the smoker was a KGB surveillance officer who managed to get into the embassy each day (not much of a challenge, given that much of the embassy's outside security was provided by the KGB), then parked himself at the top of the stairs and watched who entered and left Gandy's work space.

A few times, Gandy had even caught fleeting glimpses of the KGB sentinels who sat at the top of the stairs, waiting for him to emerge.

With listening devices everywhere and over a hundred pairs of eyes of Soviet employees working in the embassy, it could not have been hard for the KGB to learn where Gandy and his team were working and to plan a stakeout.

The well-organized cigarette butts were another message, Charles supposed. "We own you, even inside your 'secure' embassy."

"Smoking kills," Gandy mused. "I wonder if *smokers* also kill."

But if the KGB were going to harm him either inside the "safe" confines of the embassy or when he ventured outside, as he planned to do now, they probably would have done it two weeks earlier right after he entered the country, so Gandy felt reasonably safe leaving the embassy with a driver and security escort.

Getting into the same sedan that had ferried him from the airport, Gandy noted that the early May air carried the scent of diesel exhaust mixed with the ubiquitous odor of cooked cabbage, onions, and cheap cigarettes. When his limo cleared the embassy compound, black-hatted drivers in KGB chase cars once again boxed his car in.

The KGB drivers and their passengers fixed him with the by-now-familiar KGB death stare. Gandy smiled back at his grim escorts, mustering his maximum northern Louisiana charm. *Bless their little hearts,* he thought.

The wide boulevards of downtown Moscow were well maintained, and the façades of many buildings ornate and sometimes colorful with pastel exteriors and white trim. Not third world at all, Gandy thought. Scarf-headed women in long skirts were everywhere, wielding long-handled brooms to sweep the streets. LeChevet had told Gandy that these *veniki* ("broom ladies") were usually KGB paid informants who kept an eye on the streets for the authorities.

Gandy was mesmerized by the rhythmic back-and-forth motion of the *veniki*'s brooms, which kept the main boulevards spotless.

But Moscow's side streets were dingy and piled high with trash.

The nicely groomed boulevards reminded Gandy of a story he'd once read about Czarina Catherine the Great's minister and sometime lover, Grigory Potemkin. Shortly after Russia's 1789 annexation of the Crimean Peninsula, when Catherine asked to see Russia's new possession, the inventive Potemkin had created moveable picturesque villages to be placed along the czarina's route from Saint Petersburg to the Crimea so that the ruler would only see new, well-maintained buildings and well-fed peasants along her journey and think her country had prospered under Potemkin's administration.[11]

The term *Potemkin village* had been born on that trip, and apparently, its lessons had not been lost on modern Russians.

Arriving at the Beriozka store, Gandy selected an iron bust of Lenin (he thought it would sit well on his desk back at NSA), along with wood boxes delicately painted with single-hair brushes, and the Matryoshka dolls-within-dolls-within-dolls toys.

While checking out at the cashier, a commotion erupted at the store's entrance, catching Charles's attention. Two six-foot-five-plus guards, probably KGB, had closed ranks at the store's entrance, blocking a scarf-headed babushka in her seventies accompanied by a small girl from entering. "*Nyet,*" one behemoth simply said in a deep baritone, informing the woman that the store only permitted foreigners. Face growing pale, the woman clutched her little girl's hand and scampered away.

That's odd, Gandy thought. The Russian woman must have known that Beriozka stores catered exclusively to foreigners. Why would she call the KGB's attention to herself?

Ten minutes later, while returning to the embassy, he got his answer. When his car stopped at a red light, once again surrounded by the four KGB escorts, Gandy caught a blur of motion to his left, then heard a loud screech of brakes and the dull thud of one car slamming into another. An elderly woman with a young girl, closely resembling the pair who'd been barred from the Beriozka store, had tried to cross the street in front of Gandy's group of five cars, when the KGB car on his left had abruptly accelerated, then collided with the rear of the car in front of it, blocking the woman's path. The woman and little girl turned and sprinted down a side street.

Observing the agility and speed of the old woman, Gandy realized she wasn't old at all. And now that he thought about it, he realized she didn't just *resemble* the woman from the Beriozka store, she *was* the babushka from the Beriozka store.

I get it, he thought. *The KGB put on a show, complete with a woman in disguise, to deliver a message: we own this town, and, if the message of cigarette butts wasn't clear enough, we own you, too.*

4. The Chimney

The next day, as they had done about once a week since Gandy arrived, Jon LeChevet and his wife, Dawn, invited Gandy to breakfast at their residence, where they chatted about Charles's Beriozka adventure.

Breakfast over, Jon said, "Got something for you—follow me."

The two walked over to the South Annex and climbed to the seventh floor, which housed apartments for State Department employees. LeChevet stopped in front of the door of a west-facing apartment and knocked.

The door opened almost immediately, and a mustached man wearing white coveralls smeared with reddish-brown dust poked his head out and motioned them in before closing and locking the door.

"John Bainbridge," the man introduced himself, offering his hand. Bainbridge wore long brown hair that Gandy thought had gone out of style a decade earlier, and he was excited, a distinct gleam in his eye.

"John is from our Frankfurt operation," LeChevet said. "We asked him here to check out the chimney."

But Gandy hardly heard Jon, his attention riveted on a crude, two-by-two-and-a-half-foot opening that had been carved out of the brick in the west wall of the apartment. Beneath the opening were fractured bricks, dust, and debris, along with a sledgehammer, a massive chisel, and an electric demolition hammer, which Bainbridge had apparently used to smash through the apartment wall.

The opening in the wall, which extended almost four feet through a mass of mortared bricks, had a patch of old gray carpet laid on its lower lip, with cables and ropes running from the apartment into a black void.

Pointing into the void, LeChevet said, "That's the chimney I told you about, except it's not actually a chimney."

Gandy poked his head through the opening and looked up and then down the shaft but could see little.

"Got a flashlight?" Gandy asked.

LeChevet and Bainbridge exchanged knowing glances, then Bainbridge handed Gandy a light from his utility belt, saying, "Be careful not to fall in."

Lying on his stomach on the crude ledge Bainbridge had carved out of the brick wall, Gandy wormed his way into the opening and played the flashlight along the inner walls of the shaft. About one floor above him, he spotted a glint of aluminum and focused the flashlight's powerful beam on it.

A three-element, Yagi-style beam antenna was mounted in the shaft, aimed up and to the right. An aluminum box about the size of a carton of cigarettes was attached to the antenna, connecting to it through a short coaxial cable. Another cable emerged from the box and dropped to the bottom of the shaft. The mechanical assembly holding the antenna had simple pulleys, with cords hanging down, all the way to the shaft's bottom.

Gandy backed out of the shaft and dusted off the redbrick dust from his shirt and pants. "The pulleys and cords are interesting," he offered, handing the flashlight back to Bainbridge. "Like they are used to pull the antenna up and down and to tilt it. The mysterious 'bird' scraping noises that your secretary heard the previous year before the fire may have been the other side"—the KGB—"manipulating the antenna with those cords and pulleys."

"You mean to aim the antenna?" LeChevet asked.

"Probably. If it's a beam antenna, as it appears, it will have a main lobe of greatest sensitivity along its long axis. The pulleys could allow the other guys to aim the beam at different targets on different floors. Right now, it seems to be aimed at the upper floors of the southeast corner of the main building." Gandy pointed in the direction he thought the antenna was aimed. "What's over there?"

Again, LeChevet and Bainbridge exchanged a look. LeChevet said, "Among other things, the chief of mission's office."

The three men were silent for a moment, pondering the implications. The KGB had obviously hidden the antenna in the false chimney to get close to a target of interest, probably to pick up weak signals from a bug or data implant. If the antenna truly were pointed at the ambassador's office, it was possible that conversations in his office were being routinely monitored and recorded. Or a covert KGB implant in an information appliance, such as a fax machine or typewriter, might be sending data that was typed or faxed in the office straight to KGB headquarters.

Given the ultrahigh classification and sensitivity of ambassadorial conversations, this possibility was too horrible to even think about—especially because LeChevet's frequent TSCM scans of the embassy, including the ambassador's office, had not found any implant or bugs. Was it possible the Soviets had developed an entirely new generation of undetectable bugs? If so, was any part of the embassy safe, including the box?

Gandy felt an involuntary shudder as he thought about the American assets who had been arrested, tortured, and executed over the last year. "When can I hook into the antenna to hear what it's hearing?"

"Well, you see, that's the thing," LeChevet offered. "It could be booby-trapped, so whoever touches it could have body parts blown off. It's happened twice before with TSCM operators who tried to check out Sov implants: once in England and once in the U.S. And then there's the normal diplomatic BS. The Soviets may claim it's on their territory." The

U.S. embassy was officially American soil, but exactly where the embassy ended and Russia began was sometimes a topic of hot debate with the Soviet Foreign Ministry.

"Okay," Gandy said. "Please let me know when I can get my hands on it." Thanking the two men, Gandy retreated to his office in the temporary quarters to think about the new discovery and to chart his next steps.

Later the same day, a series of cables passed between the State Department in Washington, D.C., and the Moscow embassy. The back-and-forth communication continued for several days as State Department officials grappled with how to react to the discovery of the chimney antenna.

The following account of what happened after the initial communication between Moscow and Washington, D.C., is pieced together partly from declassified archives from the Carter Library (Jimmy Carter was president in 1978) that provide a historical, blow-by-blow official account of what happened—along with reactions of senior White House officials to the discovery—in chronological order. Some of the archival records are copies of cables between the Moscow embassy and D.C., while others are memoranda from State Department officials describing conversations with the Soviets regarding the chimney antenna find and real-time observations of national security staff members in the White House commenting on the chimney antenna discovery.[1]

The account is also based upon interviews with Jon LeChevet, Charles Gandy, and an officer stationed at the embassy during the chimney discovery (whom we'll call Carl), along with oral accounts drawn from *The History of the Diplomatic Security Service of the U.S. Department of State.*[2]

In the cable traffic from Moscow, note that the signatory of the cables from Moscow was Jack Matlock, deputy chief of mission, because Ambassador Malcolm Toon had flown to D.C. for talks between Soviet foreign minister Andrei Gromyko and Secretary of State Cyrus Vance. Also, Jon LeChevet wrote the technical descriptions of the chimney antenna discovery, which were forwarded under Matlock's signature.

Missing from the official communication is the original message from the Moscow embassy to the State Department in D.C., which was transmitted through the SY (state security) channel and remains classified.

In contrast, all the following cables were transmitted through the diplomatic/political channel, which is why they are available in the Carter Library.

MOSCOW, MAY 25, 1978, 1407Z

11713. SUBJECT: PROBABLE PENETRATION. REF: MOSCOW 11684.

1. ANTENNA APPEARS TO BE A MODIFIED 3 ELEMENT YAGI (SIMILAR TO SOVIET TV ANTENNAE) DIRECTED IN A NORTH EASTERLY DIRECTION. POLARIZATION IS VERTICAL.

2. ANTENNA IS LOCATED APPROXIMATELY AT THE TOP OF THE SEVENTH FLOOR INSIDE THE CHIMNEY.

3. ANTENNA FEEDS A WHITE BOX ABOUT 4″ × 2″ × 10″ THAT IS PROBABLY A PREAMP SINCE "12V" [12 volts] IS CLEARLY VISIBLE. [This white box contained electronics that filtered and amplified received signals, presumably either from bugs in the embassy or from intercepted U.S. RF communications.]

4. SECOND WHITE BOX ABOUT 3″ × 1½″ × 6″ IS TAPED TO ABOVE BOX AND MAY BE A COMBINING NETWORK [mixing multiple RF signals together].

5. OTHER WRITING VISIBLE IS "1361XOJ" AND "N003."

6. ANTENNA HAS BEEN LEFT IN PLACE AND CABLES ARE INTACT.

IT HAS BEEN SECURED BY LINES AND STEEL BARS TO PRECLUDE
ATTEMPT AT RECOVERY BY OPPOSITION [KGB].

7. CHIMNEY SHAFT MAY INCLUDE MULTIPLE CABLES AT LOWER
LEVELS THAT APPEAR TO ENTER BOTH THE EMBASSY AND SOVIET
BUILDING. CABLES CONTINUE DOWN SHAFT AND ENTER SOVIET
BUILDING AT BASEMENT LEVEL.

8. WE WILL SOON ENTER SHAFT TO INSPECT LOWER SUSPECTED
CABLING.

MATLOCK

In order to enter the chimney shaft and descend to its bottom, Le-Chevet had the Seabees make a boatswain's chair, which allowed a man to be lowered on thick ropes from specially constructed braces at the top of the chimney shaft, down through the shaft. Only John Bainbridge, who had a slight build, could use this flimsy contraption because, according to LeChevet, "neither mine nor Carl's corpulent bodies would have fit."

On John Bainbridge's first excursion into the shaft on the boatswain's chair, he looked closely at the cords holding up the antenna and discovered that they were actually thick fishing-line nylon monofilaments.

Dropping farther into the shaft, Bainbridge reached the bottom, where he discovered a rotor control mechanism attached to the nylon monofilaments, which allowed a KGB technician to raise and lower the antenna and to change its orientation. The monofilaments ran through heating coils that, if activated, would melt the nylon control lines for the antenna, causing the antenna to fall to the base of the shaft, where it could be retrieved in an emergency.

At the base of the chimney, Bainbridge also found a headset and microphone, presumably for a KGB operative manning the chimney listening post to communicate with other KGB technicians as he manipulated the controls on the antenna. Whatever the KGB was listening to, the technicians listening to the antenna inside the Soviet apartment building next to the U.S. embassy must have wanted the man manipulating the antenna with nylon leads inside the chimney to hear their feedback: "A little left," "A little right," "Higher," "Lower," and so on.

Playing his flashlight along the brick walls of the shaft, Bainbridge discovered an oval-shaped tunnel leading toward Russian sovereign territory: an apartment complex adjoining the embassy. There appeared to be a trapdoor access from the floor of the changing room where the Soviet maids and janitors (the char force) changed clothes at the beginning and end of each work shift.

Rather than proceed farther, aware that the tunnel might be booby-trapped with explosives, Bainbridge stopped his exploration and pulled himself back up the shaft.

Jon LeChevet was waiting for him in the apartment, where Bainbridge and the Seabees had created the original access hole into the shaft. Carl, the security officer, was also present.

"What did you see?" LeChevet asked.

Dusting off his white coveralls, Bainbridge described his discoveries. He concluded, "I'm not sure the Russians know we've broken into the shaft. The control lines haven't been severed yet."

LeChevet rubbed his chin. "That's hard to believe. They had to have heard us hammering away in here."

Carl added, "It's not like them to leave the space without monitoring microphones. Why have an antenna retrieval system without intrusion sensors to activate the heating coils? They did have at least one mic in there, right?"

"Yes," Bainbridge said. "It looked like a standard Uher [handheld] mic, but I think it was for communicating between the LP [listening post] and antenna tech in the chimney."

The three men considered this for a moment.

LeChevet broke the silence. "Maybe the heating coils malfunctioned."

"Maybe," Carl said. "But whether they malfunctioned or not, it's only a matter of time before those guys discover our discovery and come for their antenna. We need to go back into the shaft now."

LeChevet and Bainbridge looked at Carl but did not say anything. Dropping to the bottom of the shaft inside American territory was one thing, but venturing into a tunnel that almost certainly led to sovereign Soviet territory was another. The State Department employees, even security personnel, were essentially diplomats. The derring-do shit was clearly in Carl's lane.

"Okay, I'll do it. But I'll have to find another way into that tunnel. I can't fit into that," Carl said, pointing through the hole in the wall at the boatswain's chair hanging limply inside the shaft. "I'll wait until the end of the day shift, then try to get into the tunnel from the trapdoor you saw in the changing room."

MOSCOW, MAY 25, 1978, 1502Z

11720. SUBJECT: TECHNICAL PENETRATION OF U.S. EMBASSY MOS-COW. REF: (A) MOSCOW 11684, (B) MOSCOW 11713.

1. WE HAVE ENTERED THE CHIMNEY AND FOUND A TUNNEL AT THE BOTTOM. TUNNEL HEADS 30 FEET NORTH AND THEN TURNS WEST. HATCH ENTRANCE APPEARS TO ENTER SOVIET CHANGING ROOM IN EMBASSY.

2. LISTENING POST LOCATED AT BOTTOM OF SHAFT WITH HEADSET AND MICROPHONE. LINE BOX WITH 8 DUAL PIN JACKS ALSO FOUND. HEADSET PLUGGED IN AND APPEARS DEAD.

3. WE WILL ENTER TUNNEL AT THIS TIME.

4. STILL POSSIBLE THAT OPPOSITION [KGB] HAS NOT BEEN ALERTED.

MATLOCK

When Carl felt confident he would not be discovered, he dressed in coveralls, slipped into the char force changing room, quickly found the trapdoor, and lowered himself into the tunnel connecting to the chimney shaft. He snapped on his powerful light and looked around. A short distance into the tunnel, stretched across the sandy floor, his flashlight revealed a parallel set of taut piano wires.

Playing his light against the tunnel walls where the wires attached, he noticed a parcel with electrical cords running to a box where the piano wires terminated.

The package was almost certainly high explosive—probably plastique—attached to trip wires. Carl backed away a few steps and turned off his light. Better not to alert the Russians, who might decide to detonate the plastique remotely. An explosion in the confined space would collapse the tunnel and probably blow the antenna right through the top of the chimney.

Carl considered what to do next. The KGB must have a way of deactivating the trip wires when their technicians entered the tunnel to move the antenna around. Should he try to engage the deactivation mechanism and go farther? Upon reflection, he decided the move would be too risky. In the darkness of the tunnel, he squinted to see if light was leaking into the tunnel from another opening, through which opposition might materialize.

Peering into the darkness ahead, he saw light seeping through the cracks of an access door to the basement of the Russian apartment building. Recalling the layout of the south annex where the chimney he had just come through attached and the geometry of the adjacent Soviet apartment complex, Carl concluded that that light was coming from a room in the apartment complex, offering a second KGB access route into the tunnel.

Turning on his flashlight once again, Carl advanced as far forward as he thought safe, taking note of the rough distance traveled, until he was certain he had left American territory and was trespassing on Russian soil.

Returning to the trapdoor, he gently pushed it up, saw that he was alone in the changing room, and exited the tunnel, closing the trapdoor after him.

He told LeChevet and Bainbridge what he had found, then said, "We can't go through that tunnel farther or even try to wall it off. Who knows what will happen if they blow the explosives. We might be able to disable the explosives, but the explosives themselves could have anti-tamper circuits that would trigger an explosion."

The other two agreed. LeChevet said, "But sooner or later, probably sooner, they're going to realize we've broken into the shaft and burn the control lines to get their antenna back."

Carl said, "Maybe they already know we're in the shaft, but the heating coils have malfunctioned, as you suggested earlier. If so, they're going to come for the antenna some other way. We need to get it out of there ASAP."

"Hmmm," LeChevet said. "Not that simple. My bosses, the diplomats here, haven't decided whether we should pull the antenna out. That could complicate the diplomatic situation. The Soviets might argue we violated their sovereignty and stole their property."

"Okay," Carl said. "Let's write up what we found for the chargé d'affaires"—Matlock—"and have him help us with the next steps."

MOSCOW, MAY 25, 1978, 1933Z

11770. SUBJECT: TECHNICAL PENETRATION OF US EMBASSY MOSCOW. REF: (A) MOSCOW 11684, (B) MOSCOW 11713 (C) MOSCOW 11720.[2]

1. WE HAVE ENTERED AND EXPLORED TUNNEL. IT HEADS ABOUT 25 FEET DUE NORTH THEN MAKES A GRADUAL LEFT TURN AND FURTHER PROGRESS IS BLOCKED ABOUT 40 FEET FURTHER ON BY A SHEET METAL BARRIER. BARRIER APPEARS TO DEFINITELY BE OFF THE EMBASSY COMPOUND [meaning in sovereign Soviet territory].

2. THERE ARE FOUR CABLES EXITING THE CHIMNEY THAT HEAD DOWN THE TUNNEL. ONE SERVICES THE ANTENNA, TWO GO INTO THE BACK OF THE LINE BOX MENTIONED IN REFTEL [reference telecommunication] C, AND ONE CONNECTS TO A UHER MICROPHONE

WITH A SWITCH ENCASED IN A PLASTIC BAG. ALL FOUR CABLES TERMINATE IN A JUMBLE OF CABLE LOCATED ABOUT TWO FEET IN FRONT OF THE SHEET METAL.

3. ABOUT TEN FEET BEYOND THE BEND THREE HEAVY BLACK CABLES ENTER WHAT APPEARS TO BE THE BASEMENT OF THE SOVIET APARTMENT BUILDING. THESE CABLES CONTINUE DOWN THE TUNNEL AND ENTER THE JUMBLE IN FRONT OF THE SHEET METAL.

4. TWO HEAVY BLACK CABLES EXIT THE JUMBLE AND GO THROUGH THE ROOF OF THE TUNNEL.

5. TUNNEL CEILING TURNS FROM BRICK TO SHEET STEEL BEYOND POINT WHERE THREE CABLES ENTER BUILDING BASEMENT [from the Soviet apartment building, presumably where the KGB listening post for the antenna was located].

6. SMALL OPENING (TWO FOOT SQUARE) IS LOCATED TO THE SOUTH JUST IN FRONT OF SHEET METAL BARRIER. THIS OPENING IS BLOCKED OFF BY LOOSE BRICK.

7. THERE APPEARS TO BE FIVE TRIP WIRES CONNECTED TO THE LOOSE BRICK FILL. THESE WIRES ARE SOLDERED TO HEAVIER GAUGE WIRES THAT EITHER ENTER THE WIRE JUMBLE OR A PLASTIC WRAPPED OBJECT ABOUT THE SIZE OF A TRANSISTOR RADIO. [Trip wires would trigger alarms, alerting the KGB that U.S. staff had entered the tunnel. Trip wires could also trigger explosive booby traps to kill or injure American investigators. The KGB had booby-trapped their surveillance devices in the past.]

8. TWO TUNNEL ACCESSES ARE IN THE SOVIET CHANGING ROOM AS REPORTED IN REFTEL C.

9. WE ARE NOW TRYING TO TRACE ALL CABLES WITHOUT DISTURB-
ING TRIP WIRES.

10. SINCE OPPOSITION WILL DEFINITELY BE ALERTED AT 8:00 A.M.
WHEN SOVIET WORKERS WILL BE DENIED ACCESS TO CHANGING
ROOM, WE REQUEST IMMEDIATE DEPARTMENTAL GUIDANCE.

11. ONCE OPPOSITION IS ALERTED, WE SUSPECT THEY WILL ENTER
TUNNEL FROM THE FAR END AND SEAL OFF ACCESS OR REMOVE
AS MUCH CABLING AS POSSIBLE.

12. PHOTOGRAPHIC DOCUMENTATION CONTINUES.

MATLOCK

After Jack Matlock had sent the above cable, he met with LeChevet, Hathaway, and Carl in the secure bubble on the ninth floor to discuss next steps as Carl had suggested. Carl addressed Matlock.

"Sir, if we want to recover as much equipment as possible to analyze what they have been doing to us in the chimney, we need to try to recover cables and any gear attached to the cables, but I estimate a lot of the stuff is actually in Sov territory."

Hathaway asked, "What will it take to retrieve it?"

Carl said, "Two options. I can go back in and try to grab as much as possible by hand, hoping to avoid the trip wires, or we can toss hooks out there from our side and try to snag it, then drag it back, never leaving our turf. That's tougher, of course, but the only way if we want to avoid violating Sov turf."

Matlock said, "We can't make this decision here. It's too far above our pay grade."

Hathaway asked, "Cable State?"

Matlock nodded. "We cable D.C. and wait for an answer."

MOSCOW, MAY 25, 1978, 2304Z

11786. SUBJECT: TECHNICAL PENETRATION OF U.S. EMBASSY MOSCOW. REF: (A) MOSCOW 11684 (B) MOSCOW 11713 (C) MOSCOW 11770.[2]

1. WE BELIEVE WE ARE FACED WITH A DECISION IN THE NEXT FEW HOURS OF WHETHER OR NOT WE SHOULD ATTEMPT TO REMOVE CABLES DESCRIBED IN PARA 3.

OF MOSCOW 11770. WE ARE CERTAIN THAT THIS CABLE AND THE MATERIALS DESCRIBED IN PARAS 4, 5, 6 AND 7 ARE LOCATED IN SO-VIET REPEAT SOVIET TERRITORY.

2. WHILE WE DO NOT REPEAT NOT KNOW WHETHER OR NOT THE SOVIETS ARE AWARE OF OUR DISCOVERY, THEY WILL CERTAINLY LEARN OF IT BY TOMORROW MORNING (ABOUT 6 HOURS HENCE) WHEN WE DENY SOVIET WORKERS THE USE OF THEIR CHANGING ROOMS. BY THEN IT WILL PROBABLY BE UNSAFE FOR US TO GO BE-YOND THE EMBASSY'S TERRITORIAL LIMITS. IF THE DEPARTMENT BELIEVES THE MATERIALS IN SOVIET TERRITORY WOULD BE USE-FUL IN DETERMINING THE EXTENT AND TYPE OF SYSTEM, WE BE-LIEVE WE CAN STILL SAFELY ATTACH HOOKS AND ROPES TO THE CABLES AND EQUIPMENT IN SOVIET TERRITORY AND DRAG PARTS OF IT BACK INTO U.S. TERRITORY FROM A POSITION OF SAFETY. WE MUST HOWEVER, HAVE THE DEPARTMENT'S INSTRUCTIONS IN THE NEXT FEW HOURS IF THIS IS TO BE DONE.

3. ANY DECISION TO REMOVE EQUIPMENT FROM TUNNEL UNDER SOVIET TERRITORY SHOULD OF COURSE HAVE HIGH-LEVEL POLITI-CAL APPROVAL, INCLUDING THAT OF AMBASSADOR TOON.

MATLOCK

The answer to Moscow's urgent request from the State Department in D.C. did not take long.

WASHINGTON, MAY 26, 1978, 0019Z

134109. SUBJECT: TECHNICAL PENETRATION. REFS: MOSCOW 11770, MOSCOW 11786.[2]

1. DO NOT REPEAT NOT ATTEMPT TO PENETRATE ANY BARRIERS. WE BELIEVE RISKS OF SUCH ATTEMPTS OUTWEIGH POTENTIAL GAINS.

2. IN ORDER TO HOLD DETAILED DISCUSSIONS WITH OTHER AGENCIES WE WOULD LIKE TO LEAVE ALL DISCOVERED EQUIPMENT IN PLACE FOR ADDITIONAL 24 HOURS IF POST CAN DEVISE MEANS OF PROTECTING ALL DEVICES WHICH WOULD NOT FURTHER ALERT SOVIETS. THIS WOULD PRECLUDE BARRING SOVIETS FROM CHANGE ROOM.

3. IF SUCH MEANS CANNOT BE DEVISED ALL DISCOVERED EQUIPMENT ON OUR TERRITORY SHOULD BE REMOVED AND SECURED WITH AS MUCH OF THE CABLING ON OUR TERRITORY AS POSSIBLE. BEFORE CUTTING CABLES PERFORM TESTS TO DETECT DC VOLTAGES, AUDIO OR RF ON CABLES AS TIME PERMITS BEFORE SOVIETS ARE ADDITIONALLY ALERTED. THIS HAS BEEN CLEARED AT POLICY LEVEL IN DEPARTMENT [meaning Vance or Warren Christopher, the deputy secretary of state] BUT NOT WITH AMBASSADOR TOON, WHO IS UNAVAILABLE.

4. ADVISE US OF ALL ACTIONS TAKEN BY THE CLOSE OF BUSINESS IN MOSCOW ON FRIDAY.[3]

5. PLEASE INCLUDE COMMENTS ON APPARENT USAGE OF TUNNEL

OR EQUIPMENT, I.E. ANY INDICATIONS OF FREQUENT AND RECENT USE OR DISUSE. ALSO INDICATE IF POSSIBLE USE COULD BE DE-TERMINED FOR THREE CABLES ENTERING TUNNEL BEYOND BEND, I.E. MULTIPLE PAIR CABLES SUITABLE FOR MICROPHONE SYSTEM, POWER CABLES, COAX CABLES, ETC.

6. BASED ON YOUR ACTIONS WE WILL FURTHER ADVISE BY THE COB [close of business] IN WASHINGTON ON FRIDAY.

7. ASSUME YOU WILL TAKE WHATEVER MEASURES ARE POSSIBLE TO PRECLUDE INADVERTENT PUBLICITY.

8. WOULD APPRECIATE EMBASSY RECOMMENDATION ON PROTEST.

CHRISTOPHER

The following day, LeChevet, armed with some test equipment and tools, entered the tunnel through the trapdoor in the changing room. He spent most of the day—firmly on U.S. territory—cutting, probing, and measuring the cables that traveled to the chimney. He wrote up his findings and passed them to Matlock for transmission to D.C. late that afternoon.

MOSCOW, MAY 26, 1978, 1428Z
11855. SUBJECT: TECHNICAL PENETRATION OF UNITED STATES EM-BASSY MOSCOW. REF: (A) MOSCOW 11792, (B) MOSCOW 11720, (C) MOSCOW 11770 (D) STATE 134109.[2]

1. PENETRATION APPEARS TO BE LIMITED TO AN ANTENNA LO-CATED IN THE SOUTH WING CHIMNEY THAT CAN BE LOWERED OR RAISED BY A PULLEY SYSTEM AT THE BOTTOM OF THE CHIMNEY SHAFT. LISTENING POST REPORTED IN PARA 2 OF REFTEL B AP-PEARS NOW TO BE A TWO WAY COMMUNICATIONS LINK BETWEEN

THE ANTENNA OPERATOR AND MONITORING SITE. DETAILED IN-SPECTION OF LINE BOX AND CONNECTIONS WILL BE NEEDED TO VERIFY THIS HYPOTHESIS. ONLY THE FOUR CABLES REPORTED IN REFTEL C, PARA 2, ARE IN AMERICAN TERRITORY.

2. PER PARA THREE OF REFTEL D, VOLTAGE AND AUDIO CHECKS WERE PERFORMED ON THE FOUR CABLES WHICH SERVICE THE CHIMNEY.

A. THE UHER MICROPHONE WAS FOUND TO BE PASSING AUDIO. THE CABLE WAS CUT AT THIS TIME. DC AND AC VOLTAGES WERE FOUND ON THE MIKE CABLE.

B. THE ANTENNA CABLE WAS SPLICED WITHOUT BREAKING THE CONDUCTOR PATHS TO THE ANTENNA AND A DC VOLTMETER WAS APPLIED. AT 0705 HOURS, PLUS 12 VDC AND 25 VAC POWER WAS AP-PLIED FROM THE OPPOSITION END OF THE CABLE. AT 0715, THE VOLTAGE FELL TO ZERO, AT 0733 12 VDC RETURNED, 0743 OFF AGAIN, AND AT 0855 ON AGAIN UNTIL WE CUT THE CABLE AT 1304 HOURS. SEVERAL FREQUENCY SCANS WERE CONDUCTED FROM 20–1000 MEGACYCLES [frequency scans were looking for signals from bugs or implants picked up by the chimney antenna] WHILE VOLTAGE WAS APPLIED [so that the Soviet amplifiers and circuits that received, filtered, and processed received signals from bugs would operate while frequency scans were conducted; in essence, LeChevet was substituting himself for the KGB, trying to hear what they were hearing] AND BEFORE THE CABLE WAS SEVERED.

C. CABLES THREE AND FOUR WERE ALSO CHECKED FOR VOLTAGE AND IMPEDANCE DATA. THE SMALLER OF THE TWO CABLES REG-ISTERED 1000 OHMS OF IMPEDANCE FOR THE SECTION LEADING BACK TO THE CHIMNEY AND AN OPEN CIRCUIT FOR THE OPPOSI-TIONS CABLE END. THE LARGER CABLE ALSO READ AN OPEN

CIRCUIT FOR THE OPPOSITIONS [meaning the KGB's] SEGMENT OF CABLE AND ONE OHM FOR THE CHIMNEY SECTION.

3. SIGNIFICANT EVENTS IN CHRONOLOGICAL ORDER WHICH OCCURRED FRIDAY:

0600–0700—Cable voltage and impedance measurements conducted.

0640—First char force [cleaning crew of Soviet citizens] personnel was refused permission to enter south wing char force change room.

0710–0855—B plus [high voltage] applied repeatedly by opposition [KGB] to the antenna cable.

0855–1205—B plus remained steady.

1015–1205—Frequency spectrum scans of antenna cable conducted.

1240—Pounding sounds emanating from opposition end of tunnel [the KGB was trying to intimidate U.S. investigators].

1245—Light coming from opposite end [controlled by the KGB] of tunnel first observed.

1255—Visual sighting occurred approximately halfway down tunnel between resident Seabee and opposition.

1305—Antenna cable cut to preserve antenna electronics.

1320—Watch posted by opposition at point where three large cables enter the tunnel. Observation post was basement area of adjoining apartment building controlled by opposition.

1326—Four cables retrieved at demarcation between opposition and embassy grounds.

4. AT 1400 HOURS WORK COMMENCED TO GAIN ACCESS TO THE SECOND TUNNEL ENTRANCE HIDDEN UNDER THE CHAR ROOM SUB-FLOORING. THIS ENTRANCE WILL BE ENLARGED TO PERMIT THE MATERIALS REQUIRED FOR A BARRIER WALL TO BE ERECTED AT THE EMBASSY GROUNDS BOUNDARY IN THE TUNNEL PROPER.

5. ONCE CHIMNEY AND CHAR ROOM TUNNEL ARE SECURE FROM FURTHER COMPROMISE WORK WILL COMMENCE ON ANALYZING THE ANTENNA ARRAY ASSEMBLY. DEPARTMENTAL GUIDANCE IS REQUESTED SOONEST REGARDING ANTENNA DISASSEMBLY AND/ OR RETRIEVAL.

MATLOCK

Twenty minutes later, Matlock followed up this cable with a request.

MOSCOW, MAY 26, 1978, 1445Z
11859. SUBJECT: TECHNICAL PENETRATION. REF: STATE 134109.[2]

1. SUBJECT TO AMBASSADOR TOON'S CONCURRENCE [Toon was in D.C., so Matlock couldn't contact him easily], EMBASSY RECOMMENDS STRONGLY THAT VIGOROUS PROTEST BE LODGED WITH SOVIETS REGARDING MAJOR PHYSICAL PENETRATION OF EMBASSY PREMISES, IN TOTAL VIOLATION OF ALL PRINCIPLES OF EXTRATERRITORIALITY AND INTERNATIONAL AGREEMENTS GUARANTEEING IT. PERTINENT FACTS WHICH MIGHT BE MENTIONED INCLUDE:

A. CONSTRUCTION AND MAINTENANCE OF SURREPTITIOUS ACCESS TO EMBASSY PROPERTY.

B. EVIDENCE OF SYSTEMATIC AND REPEATED VIOLATION OF EMBASSY PREMISES BY SOVIET PERSONNEL.

C. INSTALLATION AND OPERATION OF ELECTRONIC DEVICES ON EMBASSY PROPERTY.

2. CONSIDERATION MIGHT BE GIVEN TO DELIVERING PROTEST TO GROMYKO DURING WEEKEND MEETINGS, PARTICULARLY IF HE WEIGHS IN HEAVILY ON CHERNYAYEV AND ENGER ARREST.[3] [These

were two undercover KGB officers working at the Soviet mission to the UN in New York. Gandy was well aware of their arrest and concerned that he might be arrested to swap for Cherneyev and Enger.]

3. THIS WOULD SEEM APPROPRIATE OPPORTUNITY TO REITERATE AT HIGH LEVEL OUR STANDING DEMAND THAT MICROWAVE SIGNALS DIRECTED AT EMBASSY BE SHUT OFF FORTHWITH. (ALTHOUGH FINAL JUDGMENT MUST AWAIT FULL TECHNICAL ASSESSMENT, IT IS QUITE POSSIBLE THAT THE DEVICES WE DISCOVERED ARE ASSOCIATED WITH MICROWAVES [MUTS])

MATLOCK

MOSCOW, MAY 26, 1978, 2352Z
11787. **FOR DEPUTY UNDERSECRETARY READ FROM CHARGE** [Chargé d'Affaires Matlock]. **SUBJECT: MAJOR TECHNICAL PENETRATION OF EMBASSY MOSCOW.**

1. ASSUME SY [State Department security] HAS BRIEFED YOU ON DETAILS OF MAJOR PENETRATION OF EMBASSY PREMISES DISCOVERED TODAY. WE FACE URGENT AND CRITICAL DECISION WHETHER TO ATTEMPT TO REMOVE CABLING AND OTHER EQUIPMENT FROM PORTION OF TUNNEL WHICH IS OUTSIDE THE BOUNDS OF EMBASSY TERRITORY. WE CONSIDER IT PROBABLE, BUT NOT ABSOLUTELY CERTAIN, THAT THE SOVIETS ARE AWARE OF OUR DISCOVERY. NEVERTHELESS, OUR PEOPLE ARE CONFIDENT THAT THEY CAN RETRIEVE MUCH OF THE CABLING WITHOUT MAJOR PHYSICAL DANGER (THERE IS WITHOUT QUESTION SOME DANGER INVOLVED) IF THEY DO SO TONIGHT.

2. TECHNICIANS CONSIDER IT IMPORTANT TO RETRIEVE FOLLOWING FROM SOVIET END OF TUNNEL TO DETERMINE PURPOSE AND CHARACTERISTICS OF SURVEILLANCE SYSTEM:

- A. SECTION OF EACH OF 3 CABLES WHICH RUN FROM METAL PLATE UP TUNNEL, AND INTO SOVIET APARTMENT HOUSE. THESE ARE BELIEVED TO BE RF CABLES BUT MAY CONCEIVABLY BE POWER CABLES.
- B. DEVICE (PROBABLY COUPLER) IN PLASTIC BAG WHERE TRIP WIRES AND SOME CABLING TERMINATE.
- C. SECTION OF EACH OF TWO CABLES EXITING TUNNEL ROOF SEVERAL FEET IN FRONT OF METAL BARRIER.

3. I AM INFORMED THAT THE CABLE CAN BE CUT WITHOUT DANGER TO PERSON CUTTING. RETRIEVAL OF PLASTIC BAG WOULD BE AC-COMPLISHED BY ATTACHING ROPE AND PULLING FROM OUR END WHEN ALL PERSONNEL ARE OUTSIDE TUNNEL, IN CASE THE TRIP WIRE SHOULD ACTIVATE EXPLOSIVE OR GAS.

4. ASIDE FROM PHYSICAL RISK, WHICH IS PROBABLY ACCEPTABLE IF RECOVERY OF ITEMS IS CONSIDERED CRUCIAL, THERE IS OF COURSE THE POLITICAL RISK INVOLVED IN REMOVING OBJECTS FROM SOVIET TERRITORY. INASMUCH AS ALL OF THIS EQUIPMENT APPEARS TO BE A PART OF A SYSTEM WHICH HAS FLAGRANTLY VIOLATED EMBASSY TERRITORY, A DECISION TO REMOVE WOULD PROBABLY BE DEFENSIBLE, IF THE SOVIETS SHOULD COMPLAIN. HOWEVER, THIS IS A QUESTION OF SUFFICIENT GRAVITY THAT I BE-LIEVE IT SHOULD BE DECIDED AT A HIGH POLITICAL LEVEL. IF IT WERE MY DECISION, I WOULD GIVE IT A TRY.

5. IF WE ARE TO PROCEED, WE MUST HAVE INSTRUCTIONS NO LATER THAN 6:00 A.M. MOSCOW TIME (11:00 P.M. EST).[2]

MATLOCK

After Carl, LeChevet, and Bainbridge had made multiple forays into the chimney and tunnel, the chances that the Soviets knew of the chimney discovery were quickly rising, so, to protect the chimney from interference, LeChevet requested an armed Marine guard station himself with a flash camera at the base of the tunnel to wait for the Russians to inspect the shaft. The three also agreed to cut an observation panel into the wall opposite the antenna to monitor it, and possibly grab it, if the Russians tried to recover it first.

Jon got to work directing the Seabees to create an observation port, as well as a shelf below the antenna to prevent it from falling to the chimney floor, then paid the commander of the embassy Marine guards a visit.

The next day, a Marine stationed himself at the base of the shaft in total darkness and waited. After a few hours, he heard the creak of hinges—probably from the basement door that Carl had seen the day before. Looking into the gloom, the guard saw no light at all from that direction. But after sixty seconds, he did hear labored breathing approaching. When the guard judged that the man—or men—who were advancing toward him were within a few feet of him, he pointed his camera in their direction and activated the flash.

For the briefest instant, he caught a ghostly impression of a very surprised KGB technician, who promptly turned and scurried back the way he had come.

Mission accomplished, the guard climbed up through the trapdoor in the changing room and emerged from the tunnel with his camera.

When the film in his camera was developed later that day, it clearly showed the face of a very surprised KGB man in coveralls.

If the Russians hadn't already known about the Americans getting into the chimney, they certainly did now.

MOSCOW, MAY 27, 1978, 1516Z

11950. **SUBJECT: TECHNICAL PENETRATION OF US EMBASSY MOS-COW. REF: STATE 135571.**[2]

1. PHYSICAL BARRIER WAS ERECTED [by LeChevet's team to protect the chimney] EARLY THIS MORNING. BARRIER IS BRICK, REINFORCED

CONCRETE, AND SHEET STEEL AND LOCATED APPROXIMATELY TWO FEET WITHIN EMBASSY PROPERTY. BARRIER ERECTED AT NORTH EDGE OF SECOND HATCH ENTRANCE IN SOVIET CHANGE ROOM. THIS IS ABOUT 18 FEET DOWN TUNNEL FROM CHIMNEY ENTRANCE.

2. WE ATTEMPTED TO ERECT BARRIER AT EMBASSY PROPERTY LINE, BUT EFFORTS WERE THWARTED BY SOVIET HARASSMENT (POUNDING ON WALL, ERECTION OF TRIP LINE IN TUNNEL, PRODDING INTO TUNNEL WITH STEEL BARS FROM SOVIET BASEMENT, AND VERBAL ABUSE). [The Soviets were now overtly reacting, possibly due to the flash photography incident.]

3. [One line not declassified.] A 24 HOUR MARINE POST REMAINS AT SOVIET CHANGE ROOM.

4. PER PARA 1 OF REFTEL WE HAVE BARRED ALL SOVIETS AND CHARS FROM THE CHANCERY. IT WOULD BE IMPRACTICAL TO BAR CHARS FROM ALL AREAS OF BUILDING (APARTMENTS, BASEMENT, FIRST FLOOR) AND WOULD PROBABLY ALERT PRESS.

5. RESIDENT TSOS [technical security officers] WILL SURVEY BUILDING FOR OTHER CHIMNEYS AND SHAFTS THAT MIGHT POSSIBLY BE USED FOR SIMILAR INSTALLATIONS.

6. EQUIPMENT IS ON SITE TO CONDUCT LIMITED NON-DESTRUCTIVE TESTS OF ANTENNA. WE HAVE LEVELED GENERATORS, CALIBRATED DIPOLES, RECEIVERS, SPECTRUM ANALYZERS, AND PREAMP POWER SUPPLY. FIRST PRIORITY WILL BE TO DETERMINE BANDWIDTH OF SYSTEM [the bandwidth, or range of frequencies that the antenna and attached circuits spanned, would give clues to which types of bugs were used and how they transmitted information to KGB listening posts].

7. TEST PROCEDURES SUGGESTED IN PARA 4 OF REFTEL WILL BE CARRIED OUT TO EXTENT POSSIBLE.

8. EXTENSIVE PHOTOGRAPHIC DOCUMENTATION IS BEING MAINTAINED.

9. PER PARA 7 OF REFTEL, ACCESS AT SEVEN LEVEL AND SOVIET CHANGE ROOM WILL BE PRESERVED.

10. MUTS MONITORING CONTINUES AS BEFORE. NO CHANGES IN TIME OF ACTIVITY OR GENERAL SPECTRAL SHAPE HAS BEEN OBSERVED.

11. PER PARA 10 OF REFTEL:

(A) GENERAL APPEARANCE OF ANTENNA INDICATES RECENT (PAST YEAR OR SO) INSTALLATION. GENERAL APPEARANCE OF MACHINERY AND ELECTRONICS AT BOTTOM OF SHAFT INDICATES MUCH OLDER INSTALLATION. GRILL INSTALLED AT TOP OF CHIMNEY ALSO APPEARS TO BE OF RECENT VINTAGE. PLEASE NOTE THAT CLOSE VISUAL INSPECTION OF ANTENNA OR GRILL WOULD REQUIRE DISTURBING ANTENNA. [These descriptions are emphasized to imply that the antenna was actively listening to a bug or implant, or to U.S. wireless communications within the bandwidth of the system.]

(B) ANTENNA CAN BE HOISTED SEVERAL FEET ABOVE SOUTH WING ROOF LEVEL. CONFIRMATION OF THIS FACT WILL REQUIRE ACTUAL MOVEMENT OF ANTENNA.

(C) AS VERY ROUGH ESTIMATE:

(1) FRONT ELEMENT IS 4 FOOT LONG.

(2) MIDDLE ELEMENT IS 5 FOOT LONG.

(3) END ELEMENT IS 6 FOOT LONG.

(4) ELEMENT SPACING IS 18 INCHES AND 24 INCHES READING FRONT TO BACK.

12. WHEN CAN WE EXPECT ARRIVAL OF ANALYSIS GROUP? UNLESS SPECIFICALLY DIRECTED OTHERWISE WE WILL UNDERTAKE NO TASK THAT HAS THE SLIGHTEST CHANCE OF CHANGING ANTENNA POSITION OR ORIENTATION OR DAMAGING ELECTRONICS. ALL TECHNICIANS CONCUR THAT WE HAVE SEIZED A DEVICE IN CURRENT OPERATIONAL CONFIGURATION AND RECOMMEND AGAINST ANY MEASURES THAT WOULD ALTER THIS CONFIGURATION.

MATLOCK

Four hours later, Matlock got an answer about his earlier suggestion that a protest be lodged.

WASHINGTON, MAY 27, 1978, 1951Z
135977. SUBJECT: TECHNICAL PENETRATION PROTEST. REF: MOSCOW 11859.[2]

1. THE SECRETARY [of State, Cyrus Vance] MAY 26 ORALLY PROTESTED PENETRATION TO GROMYKO, WHO SAID HE HAD NO INFORMATION BUT WOULD LOOK INTO THE MATTER. WE PLAN TO HOLD OFF ON A FORMAL PROTEST UNTIL YOU HAVE DEVELOPED INFORMATION ON THE SCALE OF THE PENETRATION.

2. AMBASSADOR TOON CONCURS. [Ambassador Toon was in D.C. for talks then.]

VANCE

In the midst of this string of Moscow-D.C. cables, State Department officials met with officials from the Ministry of Foreign Affairs in D.C. to discuss the "technical penetration" (that is, the chimney antenna).[3] Several passages have been deleted for brevity.

MEMORANDUM FOR THE RECORD
Washington, May 29, 1978, 7 p.m.

SUBJECT
Intelligence Cases; Jailed Soviets and Embassy Penetration; U.S.-Soviet Relations

PARTICIPANTS
U.S.
Dr. Marshall D. Shulman [special advisor to the secretary of state for Soviet affairs]
Sherrod McCall, Acting Director, EUR/SOV [European Soviet Group at State]
U.S.S.R.
Minister-Counselor Alexander A. Bessmertnykh [senior Soviet diplomat]

Secretary . . . then raised the matter of listening devices in the U.S. Embassy in Moscow. Firyubin[3] in Moscow had given the Soviet part of the story and view of the matter, which was quite different from the U.S. assertion of the case.

[Deleted] Gromyko had promised some information on U.S. acts of the same calibre against the Soviets here in Washington, New York and San Francisco, and Bessmertnykh was instructed to give some brief information on that subject. Reading from a Russian language nonpaper, which he did not hand over, Bessmertnykh said:

Begin Quote. In the last several years there were found in Soviet installations in the U.S. more than 50 various special electronic devices which were used for listening to conversations held in buildings and over telephones.

—1977: a special cable was discovered, and a special device, which was connected to the internal telephone system at the country residence of the Ambassador at Pioneer Point.

—1975: in the building occupied by the Soviet Trade Mission in the U.S., on Connecticut Avenue, several radio transmitters were discovered, designed for listening to conversations in working offices, including the office of the Trade Representative himself. Earlier, several special pre-amplified microphones were found in the former trade office building at 1511 16th Street, N.W. (these were found when the Soviets were moving out of that building).

—1973 and 1974: in the building of the Soviet Consulate General at San Francisco, there were found several radio transmitters, pre-amplified microphones and two cables used for listening to conversations in the offices and living quarters.

We informed U.S. authorities and the U.S. side requested no publicity. This is the same way we have proceeded in cases of agents, acting at the specific request of the U.S. side in giving no publicity. *End Quote.*

[Two paragraphs deleted]

[Deleted] We were frankly astonished by the report we had of Firyubin's remarks to Charge Matlock,[5] and Shulman thought Bessmertnykh would be, too. Firyubin had said the Embassy's actions violated health and fire codes affecting a neighboring Soviet building. This was not true. The chimney was wholly within the U.S. Embassy property and did not touch the Soviet building.

Shulman showed a copy of a Soviet drawing of the Embassy floor plan and located the chimney for Bessmertnykh to see. Looking up from the drawing, Bessmertnykh grinned and said he understood that, indeed, some protective system had been located in the chimney by the Soviet side. Nothing directed at the Ambassador's office— something—a protective device on the Soviet side. Gromyko had some more information on this; it was not at all a device to listen into the U.S. building, but maybe to follow what was going out from there.

Shulman said we had to reject what Firyubin said as being ridiculous. We are taking the matter seriously and considering what to do. The tunnel, which runs for 20 and more feet on our property, was clearly a serious intrusion. We have not wanted to act hastily, and we wanted to have the facts before expressing ourselves. But we would have to express ourselves, and forcefully. We would do so at the proper time.

Here in the time line of events, the cable traffic between Moscow and Washington resumes with instruction from Cyrus Vance to Matlock on how to proceed with the Soviets.

WASHINGTON, MAY 31, 1978, 0010Z

136975. SUBJECT: TECHNICAL PENETRATION: PROTEST. REF: MOSCOW 12011.[2]

1. THE CHARGE [Matlock] SHOULD SEEK AN IMMEDIATE APPOINTMENT AT AN APPROPRIATE LEVEL IN MFA [Soviet Ministry of Foreign Affairs] AND DELIVER THE FOLLOWING NOTE. CHARGE IS AUTHORIZED IF NECESSARY TO CORRECT THE FACTS IF THEY DO NOT ACCURATELY STATE THE CASE LOCALLY.

2. BEGIN TEXT. THE EMBASSY OF THE UNITED STATES OF AMERICA INFORMS THE MINISTRY OF FOREIGN AFFAIRS OF THE UNION OF SOVIET SOCIALIST REPUBLICS THAT THE EMBASSY HAS UNCOVERED A SECRET LISTENING POST AND ELECTRONIC SPYING DEVICES WITHIN ITS CHANCERY BUILDING AND AN UNDERGROUND TUNNEL EXTENDING A CONSIDERABLE DISTANCE THROUGH THE EMBASSY'S PROPERTY CONNECTING THIS INSTALLATION WITH A NEIGHBORING SOVIET APARTMENT BUILDING. FOLLOWING DISCOVERY OF THIS INSTALLATION, THE ELECTRONIC CABLES OPERATING THE POST WERE

FOUND TO BE ENERGIZED. MOREOVER, SOVIET PERSONNEL HAVE BEEN OBSERVED TO ENTER AND OCCUPY THE TUNNEL FROM THE END CONNECTING TO THE SOVIET APARTMENT BUILDING. THUS THERE CAN BE ABSOLUTELY NO DOUBT THAT THIS LISTENING POST HAS BEEN ACTIVELY OPERATED BY THE SOVIET SIDE.

THE EMBASSY IS INSTRUCTED TO PROTEST THIS CRUDE INTRUSION INTO ITS CHANCERY. IT IS TOTALLY UNACCEPTABLE AND RUNS COUNTER TO EFFORTS TO IMPROVE RELATIONS BETWEEN OUR TWO COUNTRIES.

THE EMBASSY DEMANDS IN THE STRONGEST POSSIBLE TERMS THAT THE MINISTRY TAKE IMMEDIATE MEASURES TO PUT AN END TO SUCH INTRUSIONS INTO THE EMBASSY'S DIPLOMATIC PREMISES. RESPONSIBILITY FOR THE CONSEQUENCES OF THIS ACTION REST FULLY WITH THE SOVIET SIDE.

THE UNITED STATES RESERVES THE RIGHT TO RETURN TO THIS MATTER AND TO TAKE ACTIONS IT DEEMS NECESSARY WHEN IT HAS COMPLETED ITS INVESTIGATION. END TEXT.

3. THE CHARGE MAY STATE ORALLY THAT THIS EVENT HAS AROUSED A STRONG NEGATIVE REACTION IN WASHINGTON WHERE SOVIET ESPIONAGE ACTIVITIES AGAINST THE UNITED STATES HAVE ALREADY BECOME A CAUSE OF INCREASING CONCERN. CHARGE SHOULD, IN DELIVERING THE NOTE, ALSO PRESENT PHOTOGRAPHS OF THE EAVESDROPPING EQUIPMENT AND RELATED INSTALLATION.

4. CHARGE SHOULD STATE ORALLY THAT THE MINISTRY'S NOTE OF MAY 28[3] IS SO PATENTLY FALSE AND SO ABSURD AS TO BE INSULTING, AND THAT HE IS INSTRUCTED NOT TO REPLY BUT TO ORALLY REJECT IT OUT OF HAND. CHARGE MAY MAKE POINTS AND SHOW

DOCUMENTS AS SUGGESTED IN REFTEL, BUT SHOULD AVOID LET-
TING POINT OF DEMARCHE APPEAR TO BE REPLY TO SOVIET NOTE.
POINT SHOULD BE OUR PROTEST OF THEIR INTRUSION INTO AND
SPYING ON OUR PROPERTY.

5. AMBASSADOR TOON CONCURS.

VANCE

At this point in the back-and-forth, State in D.C. recorded an account
of a meeting between Secretary of State Cyrus Vance and his counterpart, Soviet Foreign Minister Andrei Gromyko, discussing the chimney
antenna.[4] Passages have been deleted for brevity.

MEMORANDUM FOR THE RECORD
New York, May 31, 1978, 2:40–5:20 p.m.

SUBJECT
Vance-Gromyko Private Meeting

PARTICIPANTS
U.S.
Secretary of State Cyrus R. Vance
Mr. Wm. D. Krimer, Interpreter
USSR
Foreign Minister A.A. Gromyko
Mr. V.M. Sukhodrev, Interpreter

Penetration [via chimney antenna]
. . . Gromyko wanted to inform the Secretary that his people had
discovered more than 50 listening devices installed in various Soviet premises in Washington, San Francisco and New York. He would
give the Secretary three packages of photographs, together with a

list referenced to the photographs, containing a brief description of each. The information sheet was in Russian, but he was sure the Secretary would get it translated. Of course, his people had many more photographs of the same kind in their possession, and they might have made them public long ago if they had wanted to. However, proceeding from a broader approach to Soviet-American relations, they had refrained from doing so, especially since the U.S. side, too, had intimated that it would not like to see matters of this kind made public.

In addition, Gromyko wanted to draw the Secretary's attention to the fact that Soviet nationals working in the U.N. General Secretariat had been the targets of numerous approaches by agents of the U.S. side. By Soviet count, at least 200 U.S. citizens in the Secretariat had links to the special services of the United States. He repeated that the Soviet side had many such photographs at its disposal, some of which were quite interesting and "spicy." They would make quite an exhibit, for which a large hall would be required. As for the two individuals they had discussed, much would depend on the turn of events that this case would take. He noted the Secretary's statement to the effect that after the trial he would be in a position to see what could be done. The Soviet side would therefore wait and see, and then decide what response might be appropriate.

The Secretary told Gromyko . . . there was serious concern over the recent case involving our Chancery in Moscow, a case the Secretary had brought to Gromyko's attention.[3] Our investigation of the circumstances there was continuing, and a matter of particular concern to us was the Soviet tunnel which crossed our property for 20 feet or more. This represented a gross intrusion upon the property of our Chancery, and we were continuing to look into that matter. As he had already indicated, he would be in touch with Gromyko about the two individuals after their trial.

Gromyko said he would wait and see. As for the incident mentioned by the Secretary, he had already informed him that according to the information Gromyko had received, things appeared in quite a different light. Indeed, what the Secretary had described appeared to distort the facts of the matter. He would ask the Secretary to have someone on the U.S. side take an objective look at these things. After all, neither side was interested in distorting that kind of information. The purposes of the things to which the Secretary had referred were totally different—he would describe them as having a protective nature, among other things aimed at fire prevention. No spying of any kind had been involved there. It would have been primitive indeed in this day and age of electronic equipment to try to dig a tunnel for intelligence purposes. Modern technology simply made such things unnecessary. This was not the immediate post-war period of 1945/47 when the Soviets had discovered a western tunnel on the territory of East Berlin, which had been dug for intelligence purposes. Gromyko concluded this subject on the note of saying he would be in touch with the Secretary and would see what happened.

Next in the time line of events was an urgent message from Matlock to his boss Toon, who was in the United States for high-level talks with Gromyko and Vance.

MOSCOW, JUNE 21, 1978, 1423Z
14313. CINCEUR [commander in chief U.S. European Command] FOR ECJ3 TO BE PASSED URGENTLY TO AMB TOON ONLY. URGENT EYES ONLY FOR AMBASSADOR TOON SCHEDULED TO BE AT EURCOM FLIGHT OPERATIONS. SUBJECT: TECHNICAL PENETRATION—OPPOSITION ACTIVITIES. [Toon was at European Command headquarters.]

1. AT APPROXIMATELY 1000 THIS MORNING, JACK-HAMMER TYPE NOISES WERE HEARD WHICH EMANATED FROM BEHIND THE WALLS

AT THE BASE OF THE CHIMNEY SHAFT IN THE SOVIET CHANGE ROOM. IT WAS SUSPECTED THAT THE OPPOSITION [KGB] WAS ATTEMPTING TO BREAK INTO THE SHAFT FROM THE BASEMENT OF THE BUILDING WHICH ADJOINS THE EMBASSY'S SOUTH WING. CONSEQUENTLY, A PARTIAL DEMOLITION OF THE NORTH WALL OF THE SHAFT FROM WITHIN THE CHANGE ROOM WAS CONDUCTED IN AN EFFORT TO DE-TERMINE WHAT THE OPPOSITION WAS ATTEMPTING TO DO. NO TECH-NICAL PENETRATION WAS DISCOVERED AS A RESULT OF THIS DEMO.

2. BELOW THE FLOOR OF THE CHANGE ROOM ALONG THE WEST WALL WHICH ADJOINS THE SOVIET BUILDING, THERE IS LOCATED AN APPROXIMATE 12″ × 12″ LIGHT CONCRETE VENTILATION SHAFT WHICH RUNS IN A NORTH-SOUTH DIRECTION. WE BROKE INTO THIS SHAFT AND DISCOVERED A PENETRATION FROM THE BASEMENT OF THE APARTMENT BUILDING WHICH MEASURES APPROXIMATELY 18″ SQUARE. THIS PENETRATION IS NOT THE LOCATION FROM WHERE THE ORIGINAL JACK-HAMMER NOISES CAME FROM. ONCE THE OP-POSITION LEARNED THAT WE WERE AWARE OF THEIR ACTIVITIES ALL JACK-HAMMERING CEASED. [Two and a half lines not declas-sified.] WE ARE MAINTAINING SURVEILLANCE IN THE CHANGE ROOM.

3. AT 1445 THE CHARGE [Matlock] AND COUNSELOR FOR ADMINIS-TRATION WERE CALLED INTO UPDK (THE DIPLOMATIC SERVICE AGENCY). THE RESULTS OF THIS MEETING AND POST'S RECOM-MENDATIONS ARE BEING TRANSMITTED BY SEPTEL.[2]

MATLOCK

Following this message, State in D.C. got back to Moscow with a status update, along with instructions from Vance to Matlock about what to tell the Soviet MFA.

WASHINGTON, JUNE 21, 1978, 2344Z

158602. SUBJECT: TECHNICAL PENETRATION PROTEST. REF: MOS-COW 14311, 14313.[2]

1. SECRETARY [Cyrus Vance] RAISED LATEST CHIMNEY DEVELOP-MENTS WITH DOBRYNIN [SOVIET ambassador to the United States] JUNE 21 (SEPTEL) [separate telecommunication].[3] EMBASSY SHOULD SEEK IMMEDIATE APPOINTMENT AT APPROPRIATE HIGH LEVEL IN MFA [Ministry of Foreign Affairs] AND STATE THAT EM-BASSY IS UNDER INSTRUCTIONS TO PROTEST WHAT CAN ONLY BE VIEWED HERE AS A SERIOUS PROVOCATION AGAINST THE EM-BASSY. IN ADDITION TO REITERATING THE FACTS ABOUT THE LO-CATION OF THE CHIMNEY, EMBASSY SHOULD POINT OUT THE ABSURDITY OF ANY ATTEMPT TO ASSERT THAT THE CHIMNEY AND TUNNEL HAVE HAD IN RECENT TIMES A FUNCTION, HEATING, VEN-TILATION, OR WHATEVER, OTHER THAN AS A PENETRATION OF OUR EMBASSY.

2. EMBASSY SHOULD SAY THAT THE U.S. IS TOTALLY UNABLE TO COMPREHEND WHAT THE SOVIET SIDE HAS IN MIND AND HOPES TO ACCOMPLISH. BUT IF THIS PROVOCATION CONTINUES IT CAN ONLY ADD FURTHER STRAIN TO RELATIONS. THE U.S. HAS NO DE-SIRE TO SEE THIS HAPPEN. BUT IF THE PROVOCATION CONTIN-UES, AND THOSE RESPONSIBLE FOR IT ON THE SOVIET SIDE ARE NOT RESTRAINED, THEN RESPONSIBILITY FOR THE CONSE-QUENCES SHALL REST FULLY WITH THE SOVIET SIDE.

VANCE

Matlock did as instructed and reported back the result.

MOSCOW, JUNE 22, 1978, 1544Z

14472. SUBJECT: TECHNICAL PENETRATION PROTEST. REF: STATE 158602.[2]

1. CHARGE [Matlock] DELIVERED PROTEST, AS OUTLINED IN REF-TEL, TO FIRST DEPUTY FOREIGN MINISTER KORNIYENKO AFTER-NOON OF JUNE 22. IN ADDITION TO MAKING POINTS SUGGESTED IN REFTEL, CHARGE REFERRED TO HIS JUNE 21 MEETING WITH AM-BASSADOR KUZNETSOV[3] ON SAME SUBJECT, AND ALSO SHOWED KORNIYENKO OFFICIAL COPY OF SOVIET GROUND PLAN OF EM-BASSY BUILDING WHICH CLEARLY INCLUDED CHIMNEY AS PART OF EMBASSY PROPERTY.

2. KORNIYENKO RESPONDED ALONG FAMILIAR LINES, "MOST DE-CISIVELY" REJECTING ASSERTION THAT USSR WAS INVOLVED IN ANY SORT OF PROVOCATION AGAINST EMBASSY, AND ARGUING THAT CHIMNEY HAD NO CONNECTION TO EMBASSY AND INDEED WAS AN "ESSENTIAL PART" OF THE HEATING SYSTEM OF THE NEIGHBORING BUILDING. THE OCCUPANTS OF THAT BUILDING DE-MAND RESTORATION OF DAMAGE CAUSED BY EMBASSY, AND IF EM-BASSY DOES NOT COMPLY THEY HAVE THE RIGHT TO REPAIR THE DAMAGE THEMSELVES. PERHAPS THE HEATING SYSTEM HAD NOT BEEN USED FOR A WHILE, BUT THE CHIMNEY HAD TO BE USEABLE IN CASE THE FURNACE WERE FIRED UP.

3. CHARGE SAID HE COULD ONLY REITERATE THE EMBASSY'S PRO-TEST, STRESS THAT THE FACTS WERE CLEAR AND OUR POSITION WAS FIRM, AND EXPRESS HIS HOPE THAT THE SOVIET GOVERN-MENT WOULD TAKE NOTE OF U.S. POSITION AND AVOID FURTHER EXACERBATION OF SITUATION.

4. AS REPORTED SEPTEL, THERE HAS BEEN NO DISCERNIBLE SO-VIET ACTIVITY AROUND CHIMNEY TODAY.

MATLOCK

During internal State Department discussions, LeChevet grew increasingly concerned that the KGB might remove the chimney antenna and associated electronics before he and RP could get their hands on them.

So as soon as a formal protest to Gromyko had been filed, and the Soviet counterprotest had been rejected, LeChevet got the green light from Ambassador Toon (who had recently returned from Moscow) to reenter the shaft and recover the antenna. But with the Russians now on high alert, LeChevet and his team had to proceed carefully, despite the urgency.

So the first thing LeChevet's team did was observe the antenna through the access panel they had installed a few days earlier. The antenna had not been touched.

After some discussion, LeChevet, Bainbridge, and Carl agreed that the heating coils must have failed, or when LeChevet cut the cables he had disconnected the heating coils. In any case, the Russians would be working furiously on an alternate way to recover their prize, or at least to prevent the Americans from getting their hands on it. Perhaps the Soviets might try to access the antenna from the apartment building west of the annex, where the chimney abutted the Soviet-controlled apartment on the fourth floor.

That afternoon, while exploring the chimney, Bainbridge noticed something new on the far inner wall of the chimney that could be a sign of the KGB's plan B to recover the antenna: down at the level of the fourth floor, where the west face of the chimney shaft merged with the east wall of the Soviet apartment building, three parallel water stains, each about two inches wide, streaked down the sides of the brick.

LeChevet and Bainbridge could talk through the observation panel, so when Bainbridge informed him of the new features, LeChevet shouted, "Check out the bricks above the water stains, just below the antenna!"

Running his hands along the brick wall, Bainbridge felt a change in the texture of the surface and pressed hard on the bricks immediately above the three water stains. The bricks felt spongy, rather than hard.

Aiming a light at the bricks while he probed further, Bainbridge said, "I'll be damned."

"What is it?" LeChevet asked with a touch of irritation, straining to hear three floors below. "Tell me."

"Sorry," Bainbridge answered, "it's just that these aren't bricks at all but some kind of rubbery material molded to *look* like bricks."

"Can you pry the fake bricks loose?" LeChevet asked.

"Trying now." Bainbridge worked his fingers into the seams between the real and fake bricks and pried the rubbery material away. Behind the fake bricks, there was a black anodized aluminum panel.

LeChevet, who was illuminating the area with his own light, instructed, "Can you remove that panel, too?"

Bainbridge placed his hand flat on the panel and pushed on it, feeling some give, as if it were attached to a spring. Pushing harder, the panel receded an inch or two, then slammed back into place.

Someone who was clearly on the other side of that panel didn't want the Americans to explore further.

Underscoring this point, the panel pulled back into the wall and three pointed steel spikes advanced through three holes that had just been drilled in the brick, almost certainly with circular, water-lubricated drill bits that had left the water stains. The long spikes proceeded at a leisurely pace to a spot just under the observation portal on the opposite wall. Then, the spikes withdrew into the wall from which they had come, but almost immediately snapped quickly back across the shaft, below the antenna.

The message was not subtle: if Bainbridge—or any American—attempted to descend into the shaft again, they would be impaled.

Bainbridge screamed, pulling on the boatswain's chair hoist, "Get me up! Now!"

LeChevet thought, *It looks like the opposition is about to retrieve their prize by pushing the row of bars across the shaft to catch the antenna when it falls, manually cutting the monofilaments to make the antenna fall into their clutches.*

He called down to Bainbridge. "Okay, but first we'll bring you up to the antenna, where you can hold on to it. Then I want you to cut the signal and power cables and nylon control lines, retrieve the antenna and that aluminum box, and get the hell out of there."

Bainbridge did as he was instructed.

The Americans never again ventured into the shaft.

5. Clues to the Mystery

During his regular morning meeting with LeChevet the day after the antenna had been retrieved from the chimney shaft, Gandy looked at the antenna. He asked, "Exactly where was this when you pulled it out?"

"Near the top floor."

"And can you confirm where was it pointed?"

LeChevet pointed toward the upper southeast corner of the main chancery building. "Looks like the ambassador's office, as we feared."

Gandy thought for a moment. "Would you mind getting on the roof and mapping out precisely how high up it was and where it was pointed?"

"Sure," LeChevet answered, "but why?"

Gandy placed his hand on the antenna. "Small details matter—a lot."

"Okay. I'll measure the distance from the antenna to the ceiling here, then use that distance as a reference from outside the building to figure out exactly where it was. I'll be back in a bit."

A half hour later, LeChevet returned. "Well, the antenna was almost exactly level with the roof of the main chancery building next door, tilted up at the same angle as the sloping roof of the chancery."

"What is the roof made of?" Gandy asked.

"Copper, I think. Definitely some kind of metal."

"That's what I would have predicted," Gandy said.

"Why does a metal roof matter?" asked RP, who had joined the meeting.

"I believe the metal roof channels RF energy from some kind of implant in the chancery, probably the ambassador's office, directly to the antenna, greatly increasing its sensitivity. That increase in sensitivity, along with the proximity of the antenna, would allow the implant to broadcast at extremely low power to avoid detection." Gandy looked up from the antenna and caught LeChevet's gaze. "That could be why your TSCM scans never caught it."

"Maybe," LeChevet said. "Or maybe it's no longer in use."

Gandy didn't think that was likely, given the great lengths the KGB went to in order to retrieve the antenna. He asked, "When can I take the antenna for analysis?"

"Well, I can't just hand it to you to take back to your work area, because you shouldn't be seen by Russian embassy staff carrying it over to the north annex."

"True enough," Gandy said. "What do you propose?"

LeChevet considered that. "What if I boxed it up and brought it to you at midnight?"

"Tonight?"

"Yes, tonight," LeChevet said.

Fourteen hours later, at exactly midnight, Gandy heard a knock on the door of the quarters where he was working.

Expecting LeChevet, he opened the door wide and got what he would later call "the shock of my life."

Standing before him, instead of LeChevet, was one of the most beautiful women he had ever seen. She wore a frilled, very low-cut Russian peasant blouse with patterned trim and a big smile. Gandy's gaze involuntary wandered to the blouse, which did a poor job of covering the woman's ample, braless breasts. Part of his brain registered the woman's intense blue eyes and blond hair cascading down to pale, bare shoulders.

Her face wore a playful, confident expression that somehow seemed to say, "Yes, you can get in trouble for sleeping with me, but it would be *so* worth it." Her glossy lipstick was impossibly red, and Gandy caught a heady whiff of perfume.

"I went on automatic," Gandy later said, "not really thinking at all because I wasn't accustomed to the HUMINT side of things. Here was obviously a KGB honey trap. For a full minute, I didn't know what to do and just heard myself talking to the woman. I could feel my heart thumping away in my chest."

But Gandy did have the presence of mind to close the door all but a crack. Peering through the opening, and glad he had blocked a view of the room's interior with stacked boxes, he asked, "What can I do for you?"

The woman leaned forward, giving Gandy a more generous view of her breasts. In lightly accented English, she said, "I used to live in this apartment and left some valuables here. Can I come in to get them?"

"There's nothing in here like that," he answered.

Wrapping the fingers of one hand around the edge of the door as if to open it, the Russian said, "Perhaps I could come in for a drink?" With her other hand, the woman held up a bottle of Stolichnaya vodka up where Gandy could see it. "You could help me practice my English."

Gandy decided then to end the encounter and stepped out of his room, closing the door behind him. Immediately to his left, he saw a large man in an ill-fitting suit, pressing his back against the wall.

The woman's smile disappeared, and red blotches appeared on her face, which then drained of all color. "It was the fastest I had ever seen anyone pale in my life," Gandy said.

Abruptly, without a word, the woman and her escort turned and fled down the nearby stairs.

Shaken by the encounter, Gandy did not immediately answer the next knock on the door a few minutes later. "Who is it?" he asked through the door.

"Jon," LeChevet responded. "I've brought what you asked for."

Gandy opened the door, ushered LeChevet in, and quickly closed it. As the two stepped around the stack of boxes in front of the door, Gandy asked, "Did you tell anyone you were coming?"

"No, why?" LeChevet asked, putting the box with the antenna down on a table behind the stacks of boxes.

Gandy briefly described the encounter he'd just had with the blond woman and her escort.

"I don't see how that's possible," LeChevet observed. "How would they get past embassy security and the outside guards?"

"The guards are Russian," Gandy responded, "and probably saluted when she went by."

"That's not supposed to happen."

"Well, yeah," Gandy said, "but the Russians knowing you were bringing me the antenna exactly at midnight was also not supposed to happen either. I can't believe the woman's timing was just a coincidence."

LeChevet sighed. "Troubling."

"Yeah," Gandy agreed. "Troubling."

Even though it was past midnight, Gandy didn't go to bed; he was eager to check out the antenna and the aluminum box connected to it. With normal beam antennas, he could infer a great deal about what frequencies the antenna was "listening" to by measuring the length of the crossbeams, which in turn, would narrow down the possibilities for what bugs or implants the antenna had been picking up. An antenna crossbeam is cut to respond best to the frequency band it works in because antennas are most sensitive to frequencies whose wavelength are exactly twice the antenna length. FM radio and the old TV broadcast system operated in the very-high frequency (VHF) band covering wavelengths from 1 meter to 10 meters while the ultrahigh frequency (UHF) band encompassed wavelengths between 0.1 meters and 1 meter.

But the antenna in front of Gandy was not a normal Yagi, because all three of its elements were "active," meaning that each of them fed signals via a coaxial cable to the aluminum box. Most Yagi antennas have only one active element that connects to a receiver or transmitter, while the other cross members are unconnected to any electronics, acting solely as passive reflectors and directors of RF energy (sort of like echo chambers for acoustic energy). The antenna wasn't really a Yagi at all, where all elements worked together, but three separate antennas operating independently.

In order to learn the antenna's operating frequencies—a critical step to identifying and capturing the signals the device was designed to listen to—Gandy would have to activate the electronics, stimulate the antenna with a signal generator, and observe its response on a spectrum analyzer.

Turning his attention to the aluminum box, Gandy attached new connectors to the coaxial cable and power lines into the box that had been cut when the antenna was removed. Then he connected the antenna elements to his receivers and spectrum analyzers and hooked up a power supply to the box.

Because he didn't know what voltage the box required—even though LeChevet had told him it was probably 12 volts, he gradually walked the voltage up until the box came to life, telling him he had found the proper operating voltage. It turned out LeChevet had been right: the device operated nicely at 12 volts DC.

First, Gandy used a variable-frequency signal generator attached to a small antenna of its own to stimulate the antenna at different frequencies. He soon discovered that circuits in the aluminum box maximized sensitivity of each of the three active elements at 30 MHz, 60 MHz, and 90 MHz.

Now it was time to listen to what the antenna was hearing. Donning headphones, he picked up the antenna and pointed it in different directions, rotating it so that the cross members were alternately parallel and perpendicular to the floor. Because the antenna was most sensitive to signals arriving along its long axis, systematically moving the antenna around like this could help direction find (DF) a signal. Rotating the antenna parallel and perpendicular to the floor aligned the device to either vertical or horizontal polarizations of energy (the plane of oscillation of the radio frequencies in question). The antenna had been mounted in the chimney with the elements vertical, suggesting that they were oriented to receive vertically polarized signals, but Gandy wanted to be as thorough as possible.

Gandy spent the most time pointing the antenna at the southeast corner of the embassy, in a vertical orientation, replicating as much as possible the aim of the antenna from its original chimney position, reasoning that, when the antenna was discovered, it had been listening to a bug or implant in the ambassador's office or somewhere close by.

The first thing that struck Gandy as highly unusual about the sounds coming through his earphones was not what he heard trying various angles and polarization orientations—even pointing at the antenna's presumed target in the Southeast embassy—but what he *didn't* hear. As he tuned his ultrasensitive receivers and spectrum analyzers across the VHF band, he *did not* hear two Moscow TV stations that were broadcasting megawatt signals from a few miles away.

Incredible! This silence of these hyperpowered TV stations was the equivalent to sitting in a hotel room next to railroad tracks and never hearing trains go by.

The spectrum analyzer told the whole story of what the antenna *wasn't* hearing. Where enormous spikes and sidebands of the TV signals should have been were only flat traces, signifying that no energy was being relayed out of the aluminum box at broadcast wavelengths.

What in tarnation was *in* that aluminum box? Gandy assumed it was some kind of preamplifier that boosted received signals prior to sending them down the coaxial cable to a KGB listening post, but the strange box seemed to be doing the opposite of that, thoroughly *eliminating* powerful signals.

By watching the traces on his spectrum analyzer while listening on his headphones, Gandy could tell, through elevated noise (random background clutter generated by a wide range of electrical machines and appliances) at 30, 60, and 90 MHz, that the antennas and circuits in the aluminum box were tuned to, and most sensitive to, signals 10, 5, and 3.33 meters, respectively, but not TV stations. Gandy also observed that the amplifier circuits in the box had unusually high noise floors, meaning that they were not designed, as he'd expected, to pick up faint, stealthy signals but to capture signals over an extremely large dynamic range of everything from relatively weak to incredibly strong signals.

The strange behavior of the antenna and box suggested to Gandy that the device had special "notch" filters that eliminated strong TV signals, while at the same time amplifying signals in the gaps between adjacent TV stations where intermodulation products would normally appear.

Intermodulation products are to radio frequencies what acoustical beats are to acoustic frequencies. If you strike two piano keys at the same time, simultaneously generating two distinct frequencies of acoustic energy, those two frequencies will "beat" against each other as the two acoustic waves constructively interfere (reinforce) each other at frequency intervals equal to the sum and difference between the two frequencies, generating overtones.

In the same way, two pitches of radio frequency will beat against each other in a radio receiver, generating overtones called *intermodulation products* at sum and difference frequencies.

Local TV stations did not broadcast at the peak frequency sensitivities of the chimney system at 30, 60, and 90 MHz, so Gandy suspected that the antennas were not designed to pick up TV stations, but rather signals hidden inside intermodulation overtones of TV stations that were broadcasting 30, 60, and 90 MHz apart from each other.

Gandy's heart raced as he realized what he had discovered: an incredibly clever, stealthy way to hide signals from bugs or implants where no one using normal amplifiers and antennas would ever find them.

Normal TSCM antenna/amplifier systems, such as what LeChevet employed for bug scans, did not "notch out" certain frequencies but were designed to pick up all frequencies equally well. Also, normal TSCM gear, even if it were designed to minimize intermodulation effects, would still generate extremely strong intermodulation products while receiving energy from nearby megawatt TV transmitters, because the sheer power of these transmissions would overwhelm anti-intermodulation circuits in the TSCM equipment. Overwhelmed in this way, TSCM spectrum analyzers would display a strong spike at 30, 60, and 90 MHz that completely masked any weaker signals that might hide there.

Switching to normal amplifiers connected to his spectrum analyzer, Gandy confirmed that—without the KGB special aluminum box—he did indeed see strong intermodulation signals coming through the Soviet's chimney antenna.

Gandy was impressed by the KGB's ingenuity. The aluminum box in front of him, by blocking out the powerful TV signals themselves, would completely eliminate intermodulation signals so that it could hear what normal TSCM gear could never hear: signals from bugs and implants.

"I'll be dipped and rolled in cracker crumbs," he said under his breath, invoking a phrase oft heard in the Deep South. He had never seen anything like this sophisticated surveillance scheme.

For a full ten minutes, Gandy stared at the antenna and aluminum box that came with it, working through the elegant genius of the KGB's design. The hide-in-plain-sight approach to masking signals from bugs with intermodulation artifacts was one he had never seen before, but it totally fit the way the Russians did things. The KGB made a point of knowing, somehow, exactly what types of equipment U.S. security personnel used to find bugs and implants, then designed around that equipment to avoid detection. The original Thing, for instance, consumed no power and had no active elements—such as amplifiers—that could be detected by U.S. TSCM equipment of the time.

Another aspect of the chimney antenna system that seemed clever to Gandy was the simple pulley system by which KGB technicians, crawling to the bottom of the shaft through the tunnel from the nearby changing room, could grab the nylon monofilaments and move the antenna up and down, while simultaneously pointing it in an optimal direction.

If Soviet technicians listened to the bug or implant while manipulating the antenna, they could use the pulleys to optimize reception.

By raising and lowering the antenna, the KGB officers could also aim the antenna at different targets on different floors.

Sobering. The strong implication was that the Russians had planted multiple bugs or implants on multiple floors of the embassy—and LeChevet's TSCM scans had found none of them.

Gandy's regard for his Soviet adversaries, already very high, climbed a couple of notches. He appreciated true technical competence wherever he encountered it and found himself imagining the Russian mind that had conceived of the exfiltration system that lay before him on the table. He imagined the fun he could have chatting up the KGB technologist who had designed this system, comparing notes and "heterodyning" (bouncing ideas off each other).

Gandy took a deep breath, let it out, and got back to work, realizing that such a chat should never—and would never—happen.

Listening through his earphones for an hour to signals that might come through the antenna and box, while watching his spectrum analyzer, Gandy could not hear or see any meaningful signals in any of the antenna's three frequency bands.

He was disappointed but not surprised at the lack of signals. Bugs and implants often transmitted in ultrashort bursts to reduce the time over which TSCM scans could detect them. Also, given that it was 1:30 a.m., no one in the target zone where the antenna had been pointed in the chimney was at work, so he didn't expect voices or data from typewriters or faxes to be transmitting.

Well, that was what tape recorders were for. He could leave the system on and record what it heard 24-7.

Before setting up his recorders, Gandy debated whether or not to open up the aluminum box and to probe it with an oscilloscope to study the way it processed signals. LeChevet told him that he had x-rayed the device and found no explosives, but Gandy, recalling that the Russians

were experts at designing around sensors like x-rays, knew there were ways of masking such booby traps to x-rays.

He couldn't risk having the circuit self-destruct, because it was the only one he was ever likely to get.

And it would also be nice not to have his hands and face blown off. How would he explain that to Freda?

Waking early the following morning after a fitful sleep, tired but satisfied with his previous night's work, Gandy asked for and got a meeting with Hathaway in the box.

Hathaway met Gandy at the entrance to CIA's SCIF, wearing tennis whites and what looked like brand-new tennis shoes. Gandy noticed that three tennis rackets and two cans of balls lay on the floor by Hathaway's desk. Gandy had spotted Hathaway dressed this way before, with his wife, Karin, who also was an avid tennis player. It was now June in Moscow and time to get back on the courts for serious players.

Hathaway led Gandy back to the box. As Gandy settled into his seat, Hathaway turned on the light, activating the external blower, then took his own seat across from Gandy. "What's on your mind?"

Gandy started by describing his midnight encounter with the woman in the peasant's blouse. That blouse, and the treasures it contained, had been burned into his memory—probably forever—although he did not tell the CIA man that. Gandy concluded, "You've got some serious problems with embassy security."

Hathaway shook his head. "That can't have happened. Impossible."

Gandy suppressed his disappointment about not being believed. What did Hathaway think, that Gandy was lying about the encounter? Gandy said in an even voice, "Well, if you want confirmation, I can bring in the two NSA guys who were listening to the whole thing right behind a stack of boxes."

Hathaway started to say something, then evidently thought better of it and remained silent for a few moments, lost in thought. It seemed to

Gandy that Hathaway still didn't believe him but didn't want to argue. At length, Hathaway asked, "What did you conclude about the chimney antenna?"

"I haven't had time to study it thoroughly, but the bottom line is that you almost certainly have at least one, and probably more, implants here that are not detectable by either State or your TSCM gear. My guess is that the devices are in or near the ambassador's office and on several floors below it."

Hathaway regarded Gandy for a moment, thinking. Then he said, "First, I want to thank you for coming out here. You've been very helpful. But please understand, I'm going to have to convince headquarters about your conclusions, and I'm expecting it to be a hard sell."

"I expect so."

"So I'm going to play devil's advocate here and ask you the hard questions I know will come up. I hope you won't take my comments the wrong way."

Gandy smiled. "Well, I imagine in your business you hear lots of things of dubious validity. And I've gotten used to skepticism from your side of the river. So shoot."

"Okay," Hathaway began, "why do you say that the antenna is aimed at Toon's office? That antenna might be left over from an old operation. How can you know it's still active?"

"I can't, until I hear what it's hearing and find the source or sources. But it seems to me the other side has used this recently. Didn't one of State's secretaries hear a scraping noise in the chimney a few months ago? Those noises were probably the antenna bumping against the chimney's brick walls when it was raised or lowered."

Hathaway, eyebrows raised, fixed him with a skeptical look.

"Not hard evidence, I agree," Gandy went on, "but the aluminum of the antenna and box are tarnished, but not that much. I doubt they've been there more than two or three years."

Hathaway still didn't look convinced.

"And one more thing," Gandy observed. "Why leave the antenna where we might find it if they weren't actively using it? It would have been smarter to remove it and all the other gear in the chimney so that, if we ever went in there, we wouldn't suspect the chimney's true purpose. They would almost certainly want to use the chimney again sometime."

Hathaway's expression was neutral, and as Gandy watched him jot down some notes, he couldn't tell if Hathaway was just playing devil's advocate or harbored deep doubts himself. Gandy knew that good intelligence officers—and Hathaway was a good one by all indications—did not jump to conclusions or marry themselves to the first plausible idea. So skepticism was healthy, up to a point.

Hathaway said, "I don't know. You're implying that the Russians, who can't even keep food on the shelves of their state-run stores, are so far ahead of us that they can make bugs that state-of-the-art equipment can't detect."

"I'm not implying it, Hathaway; I'm *saying* it outright. They've done it before, with the Thing. And what do you suppose the radar flooding [microwave attacks on the embassy] is all about? They wouldn't sustain such a large operation if it weren't producing results. But the technical folks here really haven't a clue what the Russians are up to."

Hathaway waved his hand, dismissing the argument. "When we complained about the microwaves a couple of years ago, the Russians said the transmissions beamed at us were just jamming whatever listening gear we might have. My own guys think that may be the explanation."

Realizing Hathaway was probably just testing him, Gandy said, "That's not what the microwaves were doing back in '51, with the Great Seal bug. Why would it be any different now?"

"Okay," Hathaway said. "Suppose I believed you—and I'm not saying I do yet—what should we do about it?"

"For one thing, we should take out every piece of electronic gear in the embassy and x-ray it carefully—but not here, where the KGB knows our every move. We should ship it all back to the States where we can go over it at our leisure with a fine-tooth comb."

"You've got to be kidding."

"Dead serious," Gandy said. "It's the only way we can know for sure. You don't have the special equipment or expertise here to do the job properly."

"You do realize," Hathaway said, failing to mask a growing impatience, "that's wildly impractical. The disruption to our workflow would be catastrophic. And you're talking about, literally, tons of equipment: faxes, teletypes, scanners, electric typewriters, crypto gear. State has no money to replace all that. Work here would grind to a halt."

"I don't know about that," Gandy answered. "In the grand scheme of things, it's not a lot of money, and we could fly in clean replacements before we shipped stuff out."

"Not a lot of money to NSA, maybe, but the State Department is dirt poor. They would fight this tooth and nail. Hell, they already think intel officers are paranoid and see spies under every bed."

Gandy smiled at that. "This is Moscow, Hathaway. There *are* spies under every bed."

Hathaway smiled back. "Good point, but those ubiquitous microphones are in the residences and common areas, not in our secure areas up here."

"I'm not so sure about that. My midnight visitor proved the locals can go pretty much anywhere they want. There are a whole lot more of them in this building than there are of us."

Hathaway, apparently not wanting to argue the point further, glanced at his watch. "Look, I can't miss my court time with Karin. We're in a tournament, so I have to go. But I need more than you've given me—a lot more—if we're going to convince Langley, not to mention State, to do as you suggest with all the gear here."

"What exactly do you need?"

Hathaway rose from his chair. Reaching for the light switch, but before turning the light and blower noise off, he said, "Bring me solid proof about what the chimney antenna is doing. Bring me a smoking gun."

Back in his quarters, Gandy played back the conversation with Hathaway in his mind.

A smoking gun.

To Gandy, the presence of the antenna in the chimney *was* a smoking gun. The constant microwave bombardment was another. Who in their right mind would take seriously the Russians' claim that they were broadcasting microwaves in order to jam (block with high noise) the embassy's own electronic gear? All you had to do was look at the very low power levels of the microwave signals (just a few milliwatts) and the broad range of microwave frequencies that the KGB were using, along with the rapidity with the frequencies hopped around, to know instantly that the microwaves had nothing to do with jamming. Gandy had spent a lot of time in Berlin listening to East German and Russian high-power jamming signals and knew exactly what Communist jamming transmissions sounded like.

The Russian microwave attacks in Moscow were nothing like what he had heard in Berlin—or anywhere else, for that matter.

What would it take to convince Hathaway and his skeptical masters at Langley: Finding the implant (or implants) the chimney antenna was picking up? Uncovering newer, stealthier versions of the Thing that responded to microwave activation?

Probably not, Gandy decided. CIA could argue that whatever bugs or implants might be found were left over from an earlier time, just like the chimney antenna. Random microphones were always popping up around the embassy, some of very old design, that had probably gone dead years earlier.

No, finding an implant, by itself, would not prove that particular implant was the source of the recent HUMINT roll-ups.

Hathaway was setting the bar of proof extremely high. Considering the various reasons Hathaway might do that—other than a need to convert skeptics at Langley—an uncomfortable thought crept in: What if CIA didn't really *want* NSA to find the source of the devastating leaks? NSA would look like heroes if they found a leak, while CIA, in contrast, would look like incompetent bumblers. Perhaps Hathaway had summoned Gandy to Moscow just to go through the motions of looking for the leaks. "I left no stone unturned," he could argue to CIA headquarters. "I even brought in NSA's best. If *they* couldn't find bugs, then there probably aren't any, so we need to look elsewhere."

Perhaps saving face and making CIA look good was more important to Hathaway than saving the lives of his Russian assets.

Harsh, but Gandy had seen this type of bureaucratic cover-your-ass behavior before in CIA case officers (and elsewhere in the intelligence world, if truth be told).

However, sizing up Hathaway, Gandy decided bureaucratic asscovering was not the Moscow COS's game. He genuinely seemed to want to find the leaks and stop them, and he seemed a lot less into protecting CIA's turf than other agency men he'd met.

Another reason that Hathaway was acting like such a hard sell could be that he actually *did* buy everything Gandy was saying but didn't want NSA to follow up with the bug hunt, reserving that task for CIA's own technical support officers at the embassy. Unlike Gandy, CIA officers were directly under Hathaway's control and could be relied upon to keep their mouths shut about what they found (or didn't find).

Gandy had experienced this tactic at Langley many times, giving rise to him saying, "They screwed me so many times, I've grown to like it." Most folks at CIA hated, hated, hated relying on outsiders for anything. On the surface, Hathaway didn't seem to fit the CIA mold, but one never knew.

Leaning back in his chair and staring at the water-stained ceiling of his room, Gandy pondered his options.

Coming to a decision after a few minutes, he thought, *To deliver a smoking gun, I somehow have to demonstrate not only that the KGB could be stealing secrets from the embassy but that they actually are stealing secrets.*

And he knew just how to do that.

Gandy sprang from his chair and set out for the equipment room, where he had left the chimney antenna.

Over the next two weeks, Gandy and his team played and replayed recordings of equipment that he had hooked up to the chimney antenna. He took most of the recordings with the antenna aimed at the southeast corner of the embassy's main building, where the ambassador's office sat, reproducing as best he could the original geometry from the chimney.

It occurred to Gandy that the Soviets had carefully chosen the chimney as the best place to hide the antenna for that very reason. Indeed, they may have *built* the false chimney in the first place back in the '50s knowing that it would be the perfect location from which to spy on the ambassador's corner office.

One afternoon, shortly before he was scheduled to return to the States, Gandy heard a series of clicks on the tapes from the previous few days. To Charles's trained ear, they sounded like burst transmissions from a covert communication device. Putting on the earphones hooked up live to the antenna, Gandy heard the same clicks again occurring in real time.

Although he was encouraged by the clicks and strongly suspected they represented exfil transmissions from active implants in the embassy, the clicks were far from the smoking gun that Hathaway had demanded. Such clicks could result from light switches turning on and off or appliances throwing off electrical transients. Arc welders had been known to generate such clicks, too. Even flushing toilets generated such RF noises. Who knew where the clicks were coming from?

The only thing Gandy knew for certain, after reviewing tapes for the past two weeks, was that the clicks only showed up during embassy working hours. That implied that they originated in activity that uniquely occurred during the workday.

But if the clicks represented what Gandy thought they did, he had a pretty good idea what kind of implant he was dealing with and what type of information might be leaking out.

Gandy had gathered other information during the previous two weeks (still too sensitive to describe here) that was entirely consistent with his theory.

Because of a lack of publicly available records on Charles's activities in Moscow, we can only speculate about the sources of this information. Perhaps he had somehow managed to rob the highway robbers.

What is more certain is the substance of what transpired during Gandy's final out-brief with Hathaway and Jon LeChevet a few days later.

After the three men settled into the box for their final meeting and turned on the light and blower, Gandy summarized his findings from all sources, ending with the clicks he had heard the previous few days through the chimney antenna.

"What do the clicks tell you?" LeChevet asked.

"Well," Gandy began, "they're not voice signals. Too narrow bandwidth."

Hathaway leaned forward, resting his elbows on the small conference table. "What does that leave?"

"Text, almost certainly," Gandy said. "A teleprinter, typewriter, crypto machine or OCR [optical character reader]. And the other information I just told you about corroborates that. I'm quite certain we're dealing with some kind of text exfil. It could very well be the source of the leaks you brought me here to find."

Hearing this, LeChevet looked uncomfortable.

"What is it?" Hathaway asked.

LeChevet cleared his throat. "Well, it's probably nothing, but after the fire, one of our IBM Selectric typewriters—you know, the ones with the ball heads that are all over the embassy—was damaged. We're on a very tight budget here, so I asked the husband of one of the folks living here at the embassy, a guy who used to repair those IBM typewriters for a living, to see what he could do to fix it."

"Go on," Hathaway urged.

"Anyhow, the guy came to me and showed me parts of this typewriter that he'd never seen before on any Selectric: springs on switches, stuff like that. He didn't understand what those extraneous things were doing and thought I ought to know about it, even though the features could simply be a new modification on late models."

"Did you x-ray the machine?" Gandy asked.

"Yes, I did, and found nothing. I've wired D.C. for instructions about what to do next—you know, should I send the typewriter back for closer study or just keep it. I haven't heard anything back yet. In the meantime, based on the negative x-ray findings, I'm using that typewriter now myself. It's all fixed."

"You think it's safe?" Hathaway asked.

"Well," LeChevet answered, "unless the Russians have magically figured out how to make electronics that won't show up on x-rays, I'd say, yes, it's safe. Anyhow, I don't type any really sensitive stuff on it. The RSO secretary, Dotty, does all our classified typing on her machine."

Listening to this exchange, Gandy agreed that, as clever as the Russians were, they hadn't yet figured out how to violate the laws of physics, which dictated that metal conductors, which were present in all electronics, would show up on x-rays.

But the fact that LeChevet's machine probably hadn't been compromised didn't mean that *other* embassy text machines, such as other IBM Selectrics, teleprinters, or crypto gear, hadn't been messed with. For example, the electric typewriter that Dotty used might be one source of the mysterious clicks that Gandy had recorded.

"So where do we stand?" Hathaway asked Gandy.

"I believe from all the data my team has collected that you now have your smoking gun. We should organize an equipment swap and bring all text-processing devices back to Fort Meade for careful study as soon as possible." He looked over at LeChevet and smiled, half kidding. "Including your typewriter."

Hathaway stood, bringing the meeting to an end. "Okay, I'll think this over and discuss it with some folks at headquarters. You'll be hearing from me."

They shook hands all around and parted on good terms.

But Gandy wondered—for very good reasons, as it turned out—how long the fragile new relationship with Hathaway and the CIA would last.

6. Obstacles

Arriving back at Fort Meade for work on a Tuesday, Gandy tried to shake off the eight-hour jet lag from the long journey back from Moscow as he rode the elevator up to Admiral Bobby Inman's office to brief the NSA director on his findings.

You had to be sharp when briefing the admiral, who was legendary for having an honest-to-god, no-bullshit photographic memory. Gandy recalled a story that had become folklore at the agency about a time when one Captain Inman was sitting at the back of the room while his boss, a civilian head of R&D, testified in front of a congressional budget committee. When Inman's boss was asked, half in jest, about an obscure budget line item from fifteen slides earlier, the admiral demurred, saying, "I'll have to get back to you on that." But Inman spoke up, supplying the dollar figure of the budget item. The room laughed as if Inman were joking, but when a staffer resurrected the true budget number, it turned out that Inman, working only from memory, had gotten the amount correct—to the exact dollar.

The admiral never made mistakes when performing such memory feats, adding to his fast-growing legend.

Bobby Ray, as he was known to friends and close colleagues, was crisp, precise, and hardworking, often arriving at work before dawn and staying well into the night. He was famous for exhausting subordinates.[1]

To the Washington bureaucracy, the energetic Inman was considered a force of nature, and under his leadership, NSA's budget and importance in the intelligence firmament had soared.

Born in the east Texas town of Rhonesboro and the son of a gas station owner, Bobby Ray graduated from the University of Texas at nineteen, joined the navy as a reserve officer, and began to rise through the ranks of naval intelligence at meteoric speed, becoming the head of naval intelligence at the age of forty-three. Three years later, he was promoted to vice admiral and appointed director of NSA.[2]

Gandy liked Inman and had developed an easy working relationship with him. It didn't hurt that the admiral frequently praised Gandy to others, dubbing him a "wizard" and a "magician."

Inman had also shipped a lot of money to R9, encouraging Gandy to "keep the magic coming."

Entering the director's office, Gandy was met by Inman, who, in June, was already wearing his navy summer whites, and Bob Drake, the deputy director who'd just moved into the number-two job a few weeks earlier. The admiral's golden shoulder boards, bearing the three stars of his vice admiral rank, glinted in the July sunlight.

Gandy was relieved that the NSA deputy director was now Drake, not his immediate predecessor, Benson Buffham, with whom Gandy had crossed swords a number of times, most recently over security lapses that Gandy had uncovered at NSA's European headquarters during Buffham's tenure there as NSA European chief. Gandy had buried the hatchet with Buffham a few years earlier but was still happy to be dealing with his replacement.

Another reason that Gandy appreciated Drake's presence was that the executive had previously served as head of NSA's A Group, which focused on the Soviet Union. Drake would understand—and hopefully support—the daunting nature of the task ahead of Gandy working the Moscow embassy problem. A former B-24 Liberator pilot in the Pacific theater of World War II, Drake was known for his thoughtful, low-key management style. Drake, true to his reputation for listening more than speaking, shook hands and simply nodded at Gandy, who nodded back.

The admiral offered Gandy a chair facing the window at his large conference table, then sat next to his new deputy, directly across from Gandy.

Through the expansive window in the director's office of the OPS1 headquarters building, Gandy noticed that morning traffic on nearby Route 32, just a couple of hundred yards to the west, had ground to a halt. Route 32, a major thoroughfare, was close enough that Gandy could make out the figures of individual drivers.

How strange, Gandy thought, not for the first time, that random drivers could look right into the office of DIRNSA (director of NSA). Until the 1975 congressional hearings on Nixon's domestic use of the intelligence services, NSA was so secret that it didn't officially exist, although locals knew all about it—how could you miss such a mammoth organization right next to the Baltimore-Washington Parkway? Locals affectionately called NSA No Such Agency, and NSA employees themselves often said NSA stood for Never Say Anything.

Gandy wondered if adversaries such as the KGB took advantage—or even caused—traffic jams like the current one on Route 32 in order to create opportunities to surveil the nearby agency from a van or semitruck. Perhaps he ought to do just that someday, Gandy mused, and present whatever he was able to collect from the experiment to Director Inman in order to improve security.

After many weeks in Moscow, going up against the A team, Gandy was acutely aware of what a skilled adversary like the KGB might do to NSA given such close access to the agency's headquarters.

Interrupting Charles's reverie, Inman dispensed with pleasantries and got right to the point. "Welcome back. What did you find?"

Gandy produced documents he had prepared describing his findings in Moscow, laying them on the conference table. "They've got serious problems over there."

For the next thirty minutes, he presented his measurements and other findings and described the lapses that allowed KGB officers into the depths of the embassy, including secure areas.

Inman said, "Impressive. What are your next steps?"

"Until I hear back from Hathaway there's not much I can do. As you know, NSA has no real authority over there: security is handled by State and CIA."

Inman considered that for a moment. "Yes, and the admiral [CIA Director Stansfield Turner] and I are not on good terms right now. About the only thing we agree on lately is that we don't agree on anything."

No one in the room laughed. The turf struggle with CIA over which agency controlled SIGINT, along with budget issues, had been steadily growing worse and had recently moved into the category of open warfare.

Gandy said, "I sit on an interagency security panel that meets regularly across the river. How would you feel about me presenting this information at our next meeting there? It might light a fire under State and CIA."

"Fine with me," Inman said, rising from his chair to indicate the meeting was ending. "You might also want to brief Bill Perry downtown."

"I will do that. Wish me luck," Gandy said on his way out the door.

"You'll need it," Inman came back, only the slightest trace of a smile on his lips.

To prepare for the next interagency security group meeting, Gandy put together a 35 mm slideshow describing the chimney antenna and his recordings from it, along with other smoking-gun evidence of KGB penetrations of the Moscow embassy. Then, after a month of preparation, he took his show on the road.

At the first meeting of the interagency group, which included CIA's head of counterintelligence, Hugh Tovar, Gandy clicked through his 35 mm carousel of slides in a darkened room deep in the bowels of CIA.

He took forty-five minutes to work through the technical presentation, receiving very few questions.

The FBI representative to the group seemed impressed by the presentation and asked several good questions, but the State and CIA representatives sat through the slideshow stone-faced.

"Any questions?" Gandy asked the group as he flipped on the room lights.

The CIA representatives looked at each other, and eventually the most senior officer among them, Hugh Tovar, spoke up. "We are pretty up to speed here on KGB tradecraft, and I can't say I share your concerns about the chancery. Guys on the other side just aren't nearly as smart as you give them credit for."

From his previous failed attempts with the group to raise red flags about Soviet technical intelligence prowess, Gandy had expected this. "Fair enough," he answered. "Would any of you like to see a demonstration I've prepared to prove the art of the possible? The demo reproduces some of what I recorded over there."

This elicited a reluctant nod from the CIA officers present.

As he jotted his classified line phone number on a notepad, Gandy said, "Okay. Please call my office, and they'll arrange for you to come to NSA, where I can show you the demo. Then we can discuss what happened during my trip in Moscow with all of us on the same page."

As the meeting adjourned, most of the men present from other agencies copied Charles's phone number as they filed out.

Two weeks later, at Fort Meade, after Gandy presented a demonstration of the technology he believed the Soviets were employing against the embassy, he invited those who had seen the demo into a nearby SCIF for a discussion.

Gandy addressed the group. "I hope it's now clear that what I said the other side is doing to us in Moscow is entirely possible."

"Theoretically possible, yes," Tovar came back, "but probable . . . no. The fact that you can do it doesn't mean the Russians can do it. They're simply too backward."

Gandy controlled his mounting frustration and tried to keep his voice even. "What about the collection from over there that I presented at our last meeting demonstrating exfil? How else do you explain that?"

Another CIA officer, who had said nothing in the security group meeting two weeks earlier, spoke up. "There are several plausible explanations for what you showed us and multiple reasonable interpretations of each explanation. You are not a Soviet all-source analyst or Russian linguist, are you?"

"No," Gandy answered, sensing where this was going. "Of course not."

"I thought so," the CIA man said. "You've done what many armchair analysts do and have become wedded to your first idea without carefully weighing alternatives. Why don't you leave the job of translating and analyzing collection to the expert Soviet analysts here, who know the target intimately, and just stick to your job of making and breaking codes?"

Here at last, the elephant in the room had reared its head. CIA's job, along with collecting HUMINT, was to analyze collection from all the other agencies in their all-source analyst group, the DI. That was why, in CIA's view, it was the *Central* Intelligence Agency, as in the center of the universe: the Rome of the Roman Empire. CIA deeply resented other agencies "trespassing" on their analytic turf and jumping to "naïve" conclusions about what targets like the Russians were doing and—as a result of their amateurish conclusions—stirring up trouble around D.C.

CIA was also growing increasingly angry with NSA for withholding raw SIGINT collection so that NSA could issue its own, exclusive analytic reports to important "customers," such as the president.

In an internal CIA memo written a couple of years earlier, a CIA staffer summarized a long list of beefs the CIA had with what they perceived to be NSA's bad behavior.

Three paragraphs from that declassified internal memo sum up CIA's feelings toward NSA.[3]

TOP SECRET

20 August 1976

MEMORANDUM FOR: Assistant Comptroller [CIA], Requirements and Evaluation

1. SUBJECT: The CIA/NSA relationship

2. REDACTED

3. REDACTED

4. NSA's new feeling of importance became evident in many other ways, such as footnotes to various political and military NIE's [national intelligence estimates], in public and, not so public forums in which NSA reps let it be known in numerous ways that there was little or no need for "middlemen" such as CIA, DIA etc., to chew, digest and regurgitate perfectly good SIGINT data and provide it to the real intelligence consumers such as the President, the Secretary of State and the NSC [National Security Council] chair.

5. As a part of its ceaseless effort to assert itself more vigorously in the intelligence process, NSA began a policy of "gradualism" with regard to the format and content of its output. More and more it put less and less data in its publications, always with the explanation or excuse that it wanted to improve its or the Community's security and provide "better service" to its customers. Almost all of these changes made the SIGINT product less meaningful and more difficult for our analysts to interpret. Most such changes were instituted unilaterally by NSA and announced after the fact; if at all. In almost all instances, however, consumers objected, but almost always to no avail. NSA began more and more to hide behind the "technical information" dodge which meant that users of SIGINT

data had no need for and weren't really to be trusted with information on intercept positions, collection capabilities, traffic volume, crypt systems, etc. Such practices have usually been at the heart of most CIA analyst complaints.

6. During this period (which extends to the present), CIA representatives at various levels from all agency directorates objected to the NSA way of doing business. More and more as NSA became stronger and more aggressive it became an uphill battle for Agency reps in defense of the DCI's and Agency's position and responsibilities in the intelligence business. The increasingly aggressive, determined and sometimes overbearing policy on NSA's part, and the lack of a steady, coherent, reasoned and positive Agency policy supported by top Agency [CIA] management have resulted almost by default in the emergence of NSA in a Community role in which the tail too often wags the dog.

[Redacted Signature]
Requirements & Evaluation Staff
Office of the Comptroller

TOP SECRET

The attitudes about NSA expressed in this CIA memo, by 1978, were widely shared in the intelligence community and the Defense Department, who were, in theory, NSA's customers. As a result, NSA's customers often said that NSA's true motto about its "customers" for SIGINT was "We're not happy until *you're not* happy."

Aware of the negative attitudes about NSA of many in the national security community, Gandy noticed that the State representative was nodding vigorously during the CIA's officer's smackdown of NSA. "Yeah, you tell 'em," the nods seemed to say. The relationship between CIA and State was not much better than the CIA-NSA relationship, but State and

CIA did agree on one point: uppity NSA should stay in its own backyard.

Gandy exchanged a look with his assistant, who had helped him with the demo. *I told you so,* the other man's shrug said.

Realizing that enmity toward his agency was very broad and deep, Gandy addressed the room. "Okay, thanks for your time. You know where to reach me if you have any follow-up questions."

A few weeks later, acting on Director Inman's suggestion, Gandy drove directly from his home in College Park, Maryland, to the Pentagon to brief Under Secretary of Defense Bill Perry on his Moscow trip. Based on the cool reception he'd received at CIA and the hostility he'd encountered after the demo at NSA, he knew he was going to need all the help he could get to fix the problems he had uncovered in Moscow and plug the leak (or leaks) that had produced the recent HUMINT roll-ups and asset death sentences. Perry was a beltway heavyweight who was fast making a reputation as an innovator who got things done. (Bill Clinton would later appoint Perry secretary of defense).

Gandy was looking forward to the meeting for more than professional reasons. He and Freda had become good friends of Bill and his wife, Lee, when Bill ran Electromagnetic Systems Laboratories (ESL). One reason Perry occupied a special place in Gandy's heart was that, during a spelunking adventure Gandy had organized for Bill, Beth Gandy—Charles Gandy's daughter—had met her future husband.[4]

Entering Perry's large office on the outer ring of the Pentagon, Gandy's attention was drawn to the Potomac River basin a few hundred yards away. He couldn't help wondering if some of the boats visible in the marina there were attacking Perry's office—and those of other top Pentagon officials, such as Les Aspin, the secretary of defense, with exactly the technologies he was about to describe to the under secretary. He made a note to himself to propose a "Red Team" microwave and optical attack, KBG-style, from the marina, in order to assess whether such attacks would work against Pentagon's defenses. If his Red Team attacks succeeded at the Pentagon and NSA headquarters—as he suspected they would—he wouldn't be a very popular man.

Oh, well, he had risen as high as he'd wanted to and didn't much care about popularity. But he cared deeply about what the KGB was getting away with, for sure in Moscow and probably on this side of the Atlantic as well.

It was funny what a trip to Moscow did to you, Gandy mused. He couldn't look at Route 32 or the Potomac River anymore and see just a road and a waterway: electronic danger lurked everywhere now.

Gandy reluctantly put thoughts of rivers, Russians, and Red Teams aside as Perry rose to meet him and shake his hand.

Gandy proceeded to highlight his findings to Perry, describing in detail the numerous security holes at the embassy (leaving out the part about the honey trap in the frilled peasant blouse).

Bespeckled and slender with dark, receding hair, Perry listened carefully to the details, asking insightful, highly technical questions that Gandy didn't usually hear from presidential appointees. Perry, a Ph.D. mathematician, had picked up a lot about SIGINT while running the defense company ESL, which he had founded.

When Gandy had finished, Perry said, "I'm concerned about the security in Moscow—and at our other missions, too, for that matter. What can I do to help?"

"You're doing it," Gandy answered, "just showing that you care."

"You don't need extra funding?"

Gandy smiled. "You've been more than generous already, and honestly, R9 has got a lot on its plate already, with more work coming in all the time, so money isn't my problem."

Perry regarded Gandy but didn't say anything for a beat. It occurred to Gandy that Perry, ever considerate, was too polite to ask what he was really thinking: *Then why did you come here?*

Answering the unasked question, Gandy said, "This could get ugly. I'm encountering the same resistance in the [intelligence] community to my ideas about the Russian threat that I have for the last decade. My Moscow trip evidently hasn't changed anything."

"Sounds like you could use some air cover."

Gandy nodded. "I like the way you put that," he said, rising to leave. "This *is* a lot like air warfare. When you're over the biggest targets, you catch the most flak."

Perry rose and shook Gandy's hand as he escorted him to the reception area outside his office. "I'll remember that one." Perry laughed. "I've never heard a better description of what it's like to get things done in D.C."

Gandy's prediction that things would get ugly and that he would take flak for pressing for action in Moscow proved accurate.

Despite Hathaway's seemingly genuine desire to find and plug leaks in Moscow, the rest of CIA, following the lead of the security group Gandy had met with after returning from Moscow, closed ranks and refused to act on Gandy's recommendation to swap out suspect equipment in Moscow for clean gear sent from the States.

Ditto for the State Department. Jon LeChevet later said that he "caught a lot of shit" for helping Gandy as much as he had on the recent trip. One senior diplomat in Moscow opined, in a thinly veiled attack on Gandy, "There is no place here for ne'er-do-wells who wrap themselves up in the flag of national security and pursue witch hunts." LeChevet's masters at State Diplomatic Security also ordered him not to help further with Gandy.

As the months wore on and it became clear that neither State nor CIA were going to cooperate with Charles's efforts to find and plug the Moscow leaks, Gandy considered his options.

He could send a cable to Hathaway, hoping that the man who had the most to lose by inaction would light a fire under his colleagues. But Gandy's long experience with CIA suggested that the most he would get would be a vague "We're working on it" response. Worse, the cable might aggravate CIA headquarters, who had already expressed their deep skepticism. Perhaps it was best not to tickle the dragon's tail, lest he get scorched.

But Gandy didn't want to give up. His whole life, obstacles had gotten in his way. Gandy's father, Carl, had been handed a crushing debt when a business partner embezzled most of their company's cash, and Carl had to pay the company's debt out of family funds. So although Gandy's father was a professional engineer with a good job managing a power plant, money was extremely tight, and Gandy had had to find inventive ways to pay for his ham radio and electronics hobbies. If he couldn't buy a part, like an induction coil, he would make it by hand from scraps.

But a far bigger obstacle was Gandy's reading disability.

It was hard enough to grind through his textbooks over and over again until comprehension seeped through, but he also had to cope with teachers who interpreted his "slow reading" as a lack of intelligence. It was an enormous effort to learn when the people teaching you didn't think you *could* learn.

But the early difficulties Gandy faced had been a blessing of sorts, because he had not only overcome them by sheer force of will but had learned a larger lesson that people without disabilities sometimes never get the opportunity to learn: that you *could* surmount enormous obstacles if you only looked hard enough for a way around them, just as when he would have his mother, and later Freda, read textbooks to him, because he was a quick study when the information came through his ears instead of his eyes.

Now, decades later, he had another towering mountain to climb—or go around: CIA and State's intransigence. He wasn't certain why they were digging in, ignoring overwhelming evidence of Russian successes in Moscow. Perhaps they were afraid of being criticized for having missed penetrations right under their noses or, with the twisted logic of D.C. bureaucracies, simply thought NSA was more of a threat to them than the Russians. *Or maybe,* an uneasy voice inside told him, *they're simply too arrogant to accept that the Russians could be that much better than we are.*

Recalling his deep suspicions about CIA counterintelligence chief James Jesus Angleton, Gandy even briefly considered, then discarded, the possibility that a KGB mole at CIA or State (or both) was working hard to discredit him.

Whatever the reason, whether well-considered, petty, or sinister, CIA and State were going to put up a fight on this one.

Gandy took pride at never having failed at anything he had set out to accomplish in his years at NSA, and he was determined not to give in to the growing opposition.

A no from a government bureaucrat, Gandy had come to believe, was really just a slow yes.

Gandy sometimes wondered what had made him so focused and persistent going around, boring through, or dynamiting obstacles in his life. Other people he knew persevered in the face of adversity, but he had rarely encountered anyone who was as allergic to failure as he was. Could it be that, at some level, he had spent his whole life trying to prove wrong the teachers who'd doubted him? Maybe, but it was also possible that a passionate, unquenchable curiosity—not a bad trait for an intelligence officer—drove him to be so persistent. Gandy found it difficult to keep a steady stream of clues, possibilities, and technical ideas from flowing into his head, and every day, before going to bed and after he awoke, he filled up three-by-five-inch index cards with these thoughts.

Regardless of his deep motivations, any reasonable person, in Gandy's view, wouldn't let the Moscow problem go. Lives were at stake.

The first strategy that Charles employed was to brief as many cleared security experts as he could in the Defense Department, FBI, State Department, and other intelligence agencies on what he had learned in Moscow. He took many trips down the Baltimore-Washington Parkway, his Kodak projector and two full 35 mm TOP SECRET carousels beside him. Perhaps he could build up a critical mass of support behind doing what needed to be done. At the very least, his national security colleagues would be warned about Russian capabilities and take steps to protect their own operations.

Mostly, his audiences were polite and asked an occasional question, but Gandy suspected that many of them either didn't really understand or didn't believe what he claimed the Russians could do. Part of the problem, Gandy knew, was that even Ph.D. scientists couldn't grasp the basics, but would feign comprehension, embarrassed to admit that they really had no clue what he was talking about.

More than once over Charles's career, a colleague who possessed more candor than tact had told Gandy that he was "too smart," that he saw things so clearly that sometimes he didn't understand what others *couldn't* understand. Gandy was a very visual thinker who saw lines of electromagnetic flux in his head, along with antenna gain patterns, eddy currents flowing in conductors, ground conduction effects, and other esoteric RF and electromagnetic phenomena.

Couldn't everyone?

No, everyone couldn't, he had discovered. Gandy had worked around his dyslexia, but how to overcome *other people's* problems, grasping concepts that came so easily to him?

He had worked hard at simplifying the complex but knew that he didn't always succeed.

Rumors had reached him over the years that some people he worked with thought that he left huge holes in some of his technical explanations, automatically and unconsciously assuming that his audiences would get things on the first bounce.

Perhaps that was one reason the concerns he was raising were not acted upon. Or perhaps people believed him but had other priorities.

One bright spot was that Gus Hathaway, who wielded considerable influence as Moscow COS, did not seem to share the perception of others at CIA that Charles's conclusions about the Russians were off the mark. Based on a thumbs-up from Rusty Williams, whom Turner had sent to Moscow to evaluate security, Hathaway had finally gotten the go-ahead from Turner to run Adolf Tolkachev as an asset (Gandy didn't know this at the time) and was doubtless eager to protect this valuable new asset from security leaks at the chancery. So in the fall of 1978, Hathaway put in a request for R9 to continue to investigate security at the Moscow embassy. Gandy complied, sending two of the colleagues who'd accompanied him on his first trip to gather more information about KGB activities from November 1978 through early January of 1979.

But R9's second trip to Moscow uncovered no new evidence of KGB penetrations, possibly, in Charles's estimation, because the KGB had become aware of his success on his first trip and laid low during R9's second visit. *The New York Times*, in 1987, said, "A team of investigators sent to Moscow in 1979 found nothing, according to the officials, who theorize that the Russians had been alerted."[5]

Gandy didn't dwell long on the failure of R9's second trip because his organization had a huge backlog of work.

Under Gandy's leadership, R9 constantly engaged in quick reaction capabilities (QRC) programs to solve one critical national security challenge after another.

Throughout 1978 and 1979, while Gandy continued to evangelize the Moscow problem, most of his time was spent fighting fires as trouble erupted around the globe. And where there was trouble, you would usually find NSA gathering information for policy makers and the military. America's ally in the Middle East, Israel, was enmeshed in a protracted, ugly war of occupation in Lebanon; Italian premier Aldo Moro was kidnapped and murdered, probably by left-wing terrorists such as the Red Brigades; terrorists killed 171 in a bomb attack in Beirut; Mauritania's government was toppled in a military coup; and so was Bolivia's. Worse, Marxist-leaning Sandinistas took over the national palace in Nicaragua, raising the specter of another Communist dictatorship in America's backyard. Back at home, the Camp David Accords between Israel and Egypt, presided over by Jimmy Carter, were conducted. Intelligence agencies, such as CIA and NSA, often supported diplomats in such negotiations, providing valuable insights about motivations and possible negotiating positions of different actors. Late in 1978, President Carter officially recognized China, meaning that a new embassy, and threats to that embassy, needed to be addressed.

Then the big bombshell hit in early 1979: after months of unrest and street violence, the shah of Iran fled his country, an Islamic revolutionary government came to power, and hostages were taken at the U.S. embassy. At the end of 1979, another huge challenge for the intelligence community, including NSA, was the unexpected Soviet invasion of Afghanistan.

In other words, R9—which, by 1978, had evolved into a break-glass-in-case-of-emergency response team—had its hands full responding to one global emergency after another. Gandy also assisted FBI in their counterintelligence efforts to find and arrest foreign spies illegally in the United States.

But throughout 1978, 1979, and 1980, despite the lack of results from R9's second trip to Moscow, Charles never stopped pressing for action in Moscow. He would have abandoned the apparently quixotic campaign if the evidence he'd accumulated in Moscow had been equivocal, but he was certain of his findings and their implications about how the Russians had destroyed CIA's HUMINT network in Russia.

In May 1980, support for Charles's campaign to find and plug security leaks in Moscow came from an unlikely source: a KGB major named Victor Sheymov.

Sheymov, who worked as an engineer and self-described troubleshooter in KGB's Eighth Chief Directorate—responsible for enciphering classified Soviet communications—defected to the United States after operating as a CIA asset in place for a short time. During his debrief in the United States, Sheymov warned that the KGB had plans to thoroughly bug the New Office Building (NOB) of the chancery that had begun construction in 1979. Some of the exploits that Sheymov warned that the KGB was inserting into the new building included technologies similar to those that Gandy had described in his slideshows.[6]

Possibly as a result of Sheymov's warnings, Hathaway, who by 1981 had moved up to run CIA's Soviet Eastern Europe Division (SE) in the DO, once again put in a request for Gandy to search the Moscow embassy for security leaks. Another reason for Hathaway's request could have been the mid-1981 arrest of Y. A. Kapustin, a CIA asset in Moscow. Thus, in August 1981, Gandy made his last trip to Moscow to find and plug technical penetrations of the U.S. embassy.

From Charles's point of view, the trip produced more smoking-gun evidence that the KGB were collecting text information from somewhere in the embassy, but CIA officials in Moscow, and many at CIA headquarters, remained unconvinced.

"I was never sure of Gandy," said Burton Gerber, CIA's COS during Gandy's 1981 visit. "He claimed in 1981 that the other side could read text using microwaves [MUTS], but he never produced any proof. It felt to me like Angleton [CIA's notorious chief of counterintelligence], who was always saying, 'If you knew everything *that I know,* you wouldn't argue with me,' but never produced everything he supposedly knew. . . . Gandy simply never proved a single thing he said. He was like a lot of technical people who raised alarms but, in the end, never any proof."

Asked about Hathaway's views of Gandy, Gerber, who was close to Hathaway and was Hathaway's subordinate in 1981, replied, "Hathaway thought Gandy was a genius, but even *he* wasn't convinced of Gandy's claims."

Despite these doubts, Gerber—a famous stickler for meticulous tradecraft—had given enough weight to the concerns about the KGB's ability to copy text that Gandy had raised on his 1978 trip, that when Gerber relieved Hathaway as Moscow COS in 1980, he ordered that all typewriters, both manual and electric, be removed from CIA's offices. "Pencils are pretty hard to compromise," Gerber observed.

Gerber, and others at CIA, however, still had their doubts. Another reason they weren't overly concerned about the KGB compromising text at the embassy was that any compromises of typewriters, printers, faxes, or other text machines had to be, in CIA's opinion, strictly those used by the State Department. Also, unlike State, CIA only shipped sensitive equipment through heavily protected channels. Finally, CIA operated inside of an RF-shielded SCIF that—in theory, at least—would not allow MUTS, or any RF signals from bugs, in or out.

By definition, in CIA's view (and Gandy's as well), State Department text and communications were essentially insecure anyhow because, well, State was clueless about security, letting foreign service nationals (FSNs) run all over the place, accepting KGB microphones as a fact of life, being careless with shipments into and out of the embassy, and so on. So even if Gandy were right about the KGB reading text, who really cared? Any lost text would be State's, which was probably lost anyhow due to State's lax security.

The bottom line was that Gandy's 1981 trip damaged his credibility at CIA because, in CIA's view, he never backed up his claims about KGB capabilities with demonstrations to DO case officers there.

Here was a classic breakdown in communication. Gandy had in fact demonstrated at Fort Meade that his claims were reasonable in 1978, then later in 1979 to CIA DS&T officers, but either those officers never passed along the information to DO officers such as Gerber and Hathaway, or they passed it along with the caveat that "Gandy might be able to do it, but the Soviets can't."

Gandy, for his part, assumed that Gerber and others would believe him precisely *because* of the multiple demonstrations he had presented to CIA officers at Fort Meade. It never occurred to Gandy that Hathaway, or even Gerber, didn't really believe him. Also, Gandy enjoyed a godlike reputation at NSA and was accustomed to people there taking him at his word.

Another difficulty that followed Gandy's 1981 Moscow trip came from the State Department.

"Gandy and State were in open warfare," Jon LeChevet said of the time following Gandy's 1981 trip, "because Gandy was going around saying that the Moscow embassy was compromised."

By 1982, this conflict had spread to the President's Foreign Intelligence Advisory Board (PFIAB), which started to investigate both

Gandy's assertions, including KGB access to the chancery, and troubling reports about bugging of the NOB in Moscow. Following up Sheymov's warning about the KGB bugging the NOB, a special team sent to study the NOB construction site discovered in May 1982 that prefabricated components of the NOB had listening devices embedded in them.

According to a declassified NSA report titled "American Cryptology During the Cold War":

> *In the early 1980s people on Reagan's National Security Council be-came concerned about the hostile foreign intelligence threat in general and about the security of the Moscow embassy in particular. So in 1982 NSA sent a team of people to look at technical penetrations in the Mos-cow embassy. They found the chancery honeycombed with insecurities, including cipher locks that didn't cipher and alarms that didn't sound. NSA alerted the FBI, which did its own survey and confirmed the prob-lems that NSA had found, plus others. [An unnamed NSA employee] teamed up with an FBI representative to brief President Reagan on the matter. The State Department, already suspicious of NSA "meddling" in embassy affairs [due to Gandy], was reportedly unamused.*[7]

Against this backdrop, the PFIAB, under Anne Armstrong, started asking State pointed questions about security at the Moscow embassy, especially the heavy use of FSNs in Moscow.

The State Department official who briefed PFIAB to justify the use of FSNs did not make State's life any easier when he confidently asserted that hiring KGB officers was actually safer than hiring Americans to do the same job. The official, Richard Combs, who was the deputy director of the Soviet desk, said that if the embassy hired Americans, they would be inevitable targets for KGB recruitment. Combs said it was safer to have known KGB employees than unknown security risks posed by cleared U.S. citizens who might be recruited by the KGB.[8]

Baffled by this logic, one PFIAB member came back at Combs, "By this reasoning, you would say that it would be best if *all* of our embassy positions were staffed by the KGB."

Together with Gandy's previous alarms about Moscow security and Combs's strange testimony before PFIAB the new NSA and FBI reports about embassy security in Moscow caused major headaches for both CIA and State. As early as May 1982, CIA director William Casey felt obliged to brief the PFIAB both on "CIA/State telecommunications" and renewed efforts to bolster counterintelligence against foreign intelligence threats.[9]

Secretary of State George Shultz, annoyed with the increasing attacks on the security of the Moscow embassy, particularly those originating from Gandy's work, told his diplomatic security staff that he was tired of hearing about Moscow security and didn't want to entertain further discussion on it unless someone could bring him a smoking gun proving a breach.

By late 1982, both State and CIA were irritated with NSA in general and Gandy in particular, ultimately leading to what Gandy would later refer to as "the worst phone call of my life."

According to Gandy, just after lunch on a Friday in the fall of 1982, his secretary, Nancy, popped her head into his office, saying, "The director for you."

As soon as Gandy picked up, Lieutenant General Lincoln Faurer said, "I've got some bad news."

"Okay." Gandy felt his stomach tense. In over twenty-five years at NSA, he'd never gotten such a call from an NSA director. "What happened?"

"We just got a memo from D/CIA [director of CIA] ordering us to 'cease and desist' all countermeasures activities outside of our core mission. We are directed to 'go back to making and breaking codes.'"

Gandy felt a heavy lump of lead sink to the bottom of his stomach as he digested that. "Countermeasures activities" was a veiled reference to his Moscow embassy work. Pushing down his anger and disappointment,

Gandy said, "Sounds like they're referring to me and all those alarms I've been raising."

"Sounds like it. You've been the lightning rod on these issues for a long time, and your slide presentations on the Russian threat must have finally really gotten to them."

"Yep," was all Gandy could muster, feeling numb.

"DCI claims he can't go anywhere without Cap [Secretary of Defense Caspar Weinberger] or someone from NSC [National Security Council] pestering him about Moscow embassy security, and it's become counterproductive. Apparently, State and CIA finally agree on something: they both don't like *you*."

Gandy could only look at his office wall in stunned silence.

Faurer went on, "I'm afraid we're going to have to go along with this, Charlie. Although we're part of DOD [Department of Defense], we report to D/CIA on diplomatic security, and we've got so many other problems with CIA right now, we can't afford to add this one to the pile."

Collecting himself, Gandy asked, "Do you think there's any chance they'll follow through in Moscow anyhow, without us?"

A curt laugh. "What do you think?"

"Okay," Gandy said dully. "It's not as if I don't have other things to do."

"Yes," came the response. "And for what it's worth, I think DCI, by taking this action, has done great harm to the nation. But we have to pick our battles."

Gandy sighed. "Yes, I guess we do."

After hanging up, Gandy cast his gaze out his office window. In a twenty-five-year NSA career, he had never once failed at any important task he had set out to accomplish, and this Moscow thing was about as important as you could get.

But now, for the first time in his working life, he had to swallow failure.

Locking away his papers in the office safe, Gandy put on his coat, turned off the light, and headed home early to dinner. Maybe Freda's seafood gumbo could wash away the bitter taste of defeat.

7. Who Hates Whom

Gandy's recollection that William Casey pressured Faurer to turn off his embassy countermeasures work with a cease-and-desist order remains controversial. When asked about the DCI's prohibition of NSA security work in embassies, Bob Gates, who was deputy director of CIA for intelligence (DDI) at the time (and later CIA director and secretary of defense), along with Burton Gerber, thought Casey never pressured Faurer on embassy security.

Gates suggested that someone below Casey at CIA might have pushed back on Gandy's constant harping about Moscow embassy security, but that Casey himself was too concerned about foreign intelligence threats to have taken such action.

And yet, Gandy vividly remembers the phone call from Faurer because "it was the first time in my entire career I had failed at anything. That phone call definitely happened, and I did abruptly cease all embassy countermeasures work. I even turned over all of my carousel slides to the technical security folks at CIA, hoping they might act on the information since I couldn't act on it anymore."

Gandy acknowledged that he never actually saw the cease-and-desist memo Faurer referred to, and, when recently told of Gates's and Gerber's doubts about Casey having authored it, speculated that someone below Casey might have contacted Faurer claiming to be carrying out Casey's wishes, or that Faurer, in order to take political heat off NSA, might have overstated CIA's position.

Certainly, both NSA and Gandy had no shortage of bureaucratic rivals who might have been making Faurer's life difficult.

By the time he got Faurer's call, Gandy had heard reports about Shultz's smoking-gun comment and was puzzled by it.

He *had* given both CIA and State more smoking guns about Moscow in 1981 on top of the original evidence from his 1978 trip. Then there was the chimney antenna, the constant MUTS bombardments, and the new stuff about KGB penetrations of the NOB. What did State think *those* were about?

A possible explanation for State's and CIA's lack of enthusiasm arrived in the form of a CIA report a few months later, sponsored by technologists in CIA's DS&T, describing CIA's analysis, among other things, of Charles's conclusions concerning KGB microwave attacks on the embassy.

The report contained a scathing rebuke of Gandy's conclusions, pointing out that the microwave signals probably were just jamming of U.S. receivers in the embassy, as the Soviets had argued. The report concluded that the KGB simply didn't have the technology or expertise to extract voice or data from the embassy in the way that Gandy said they could and even called into question the underlying physics of numerous demonstrations that Gandy and his team had presented at Fort Meade to prove that sophisticated KGB attacks were feasible. The report implied, but did not state outright, that such demonstrations had been "dry-labbed"—faked.

Gandy was appalled. Did those guys really believe what was in the report, or was the report just an instance of CIA pissing around their territory to keep NSA away? In an attempt at black humor, he placed two crossed Band-Aids on the report's cover before sending it around to his troops for review, signifying that the report was "damaged." In R9, the CIA document came to be known as the "Band-Aid report."

Word also came through the grapevine that CIA had analyzed the chimney antenna and concluded it was nearly worthless, with a high noise floor (ergo, low sensitivity to RF signals). What were those guys thinking? Had they treated it like a standard Yagi and completely missed the genius of the device, the way it plucked faint signals out of massive interference from TV stations? *Of course* the system had a high noise floor, in order to handle the extreme dynamic range (span of signal strengths) coming from multi-megawatt Moscow TV stations!

In late spring 1983, shortly after receiving the Band-Aid report, as Gandy puttered around with his ham radio gear in his home workshop in College Park, Maryland, he considered what to do about the resistance from CIA.

Gandy felt a strong urge to push back against CIA's pushback. If CIA had issued the cease-and-desist order based on the Band-Aid report and the erroneous analysis of the chimney antenna, perhaps he could, purely through technical arguments, get back into the Moscow ball game.

Ever since returning from his first trip to Moscow in 1978, concerned about the human cost of leaks in the Moscow embassy, Gandy had kept tabs on asset roll-ups and PNGs from the Soviet Union, mostly from press accounts because—for good reason—CIA did not share raw HUMINT-related information with NSA. As far as Gandy could tell from the newspapers and RUMINT (rumor intelligence), there had been a string of problems following the 1977 arrests of Ogorodnik and Filatov and expulsions of their CIA case officers Martha Peterson and Vincent Crockett, respectively. These problems included:

The expulsion of diplomat Donald Kursch in 1978
The conviction of a Soviet scientist "B. Nilov" for espionage in 1980
The expulsion of case officer Peter Bogatyr in August 1981 (which had occurred while Gandy was in Moscow)

The arrests for espionage, announced in *Moskovskaya Pravda,* of
four scientists in September 1982

The expulsion of diplomat Richard Osborne in March 1983

Later in 1983, two other case officers, Lon Augustenborg and Louis
Thomas, were also expelled. A senior NSA COMSEC (communications security) officer familiar with Moscow comms told Gandy that the
Soviets were so brazen about their penetration of the Moscow embassy that they tacitly told Ambassador Arthur Hartman about it during a heated exchange over the proposed Soviet gas pipeline to Europe.

When the Soviets pressured the Polish government to declare martial
law in December 1981, the Reagan administration showed their displeasure by imposing sanctions on the Euro-Siberian natural gas pipeline,
which was to bring a massive new supply of gas to Western Europe and a
major new source of revenue to Moscow. The sanctions, imposed early in
1982, prohibited the use of any American technology in the project. For
example, GE gas turbine engines, the preferred power source for pumps
for the pipeline, were embargoed by the sanctions.[1]

The American gas pipeline sanctions posed a major obstacle to the
project, so in 1982, the Ministry of Foreign Affairs began to pressure
Ambassador Hartman to persuade President Reagan to lift the restric-
tions. As a diplomat, Hartman didn't say no, merely, "I'll see what I can
do," but in fact took no steps whatever to do as the Soviets had requested.

During a face-to-face meeting in Moscow between Hartman and a
senior Soviet diplomat, when Hartman told the Russians, "I'm doing
everything I can to help you," and said he had sent a cable urging re-
consideration of the sanctions, the Soviet yelled (according to Gandy's
source), "You're a goddamn liar! I read everything you send back to the
States!"

To Gandy, this account, if true, was deeply troubling because it implied the Soviets were monitoring diplomatic traffic from the embassy
and they didn't *care* whether the United States knew it. Worse, the "I
read everything you send back to the States" remark implied that the

Soviets believed (correctly) Hartman would do nothing to investigate exactly how the Russians *knew* he was lying.

No, Gandy thought. *It's unacceptable that we sit on our hands while compromises in Moscow continue to risk the lives of assets who work for us and degrade the integrity of our sensitive diplomatic and national security communications. Who can I get to help me turn this situation around?*

Taking out a fresh piece of quadrille engineering paper, he diagrammed out the key players who might be shaping events. Perhaps by examining the motivations and relationships among these key players, he could figure out how to prove to someone with influence that closing holes in security at the Moscow embassy would be in their best interests. Maybe he could find an ally or two.

As he looked over the diagram he was creating, he remembered the old adage "The enemy of my enemy is my friend." Perhaps in the convoluted, ever-shifting web of relationships inside the beltway, he could find a friend or two.

Gandy had drawn the diagram with three types of lines. Gray lines identified different actors and what Gandy thought of as neutral relationships—that is, those relationships that were not particularly warm or antagonistic but more or less businesslike. The relationship between the Department of Justice and FBI, who served under them, was an example of a neutral relationship. There had been ups and downs between Justice and FBI, especially when Hoover was FBI director, but now attorney general William French Smith and FBI director William Webster got on well enough, so Gandy sketched a line between the two leaders in gray. Black lines denoted positive relationships, as between FBI and NSA. Gandy got on well with FBI special agents, helping them from time to time with their counterintelligence pursuits. True, he did call the clean-cut law enforcement colleagues "lawyers with guns," sometimes to their faces, but all in the spirit of good fun.

From press accounts,[2] he sensed that Caspar Weinberger, the secretary of defense, and William Clark, the national security advisor, also saw eye to eye on most matters. Both publicly advocated tough stances against the Russians, and Gandy was aware that steep increases in military spending under Reagan suggested that both the president and Congress agreed with Clark and Weinberger. So Gandy drew the connection between DOD to the national security advisor in black as well. NSA reported to Weinberger through several bureaucratic layers, but Gandy drew that connection in gray because of occasional friction between the secretary of defense and the NSA director, most recently over budgets. (The following year, Weinberger would fire Lieutenant General Lincoln Faurer for refusing to go along with budget cuts at NSA.[3])

On balance, the secretary of defense and national security advisor, who were hard-liners when it came to Russia, along with FBI, who chased Russian spies in the United States, might be potential allies in Charles's investigation.

But in Washington, such a strength can also be a weakness. With dashed lines denoting antagonism, Gandy connected State and DOD, and State and the national security advisor, who had locked horns over the U.S. foreign policy with Russia. Weinberger and Clark were adamantly opposed to any negotiations with the Soviets, on the grounds that the United States would, as it had in the past, come out on the short end of any deal due to the Soviets' superior ability to negotiate.[4] The Kremlin could decide exactly what it wanted in a negotiation and go for that objective with singular focus, but the United States was much more fragmented. The president had to get treaties he'd negotiated approved in the Senate, which often had a different agenda from the president's. It was tough to come out ahead in a negotiation when your adversary had its shit together and you didn't, Weinberger and Clark reasoned.

In contrast, Shultz and the State Department argued strongly for constructive engagement and negotiation with the Soviets across a broad range of issues, including arms control and human rights.[5]

As a result of these divergent agendas, State, DOD, and the national security staff had been waging increasingly open warfare with each other for the past year.

Thus, State might view anything that the national security advisor and

DOD advocated—and NSA was part of DOD—as an attempt to undermine diplomacy with Russia. Gandy's "witch hunt" for KGB penetrations at the Moscow embassy might be viewed from exactly this perspective. "Sure," a State executive might say, "NSA [and by extension DOD] found smoking guns in Moscow. What better way to scuttle diplomacy than to accuse the other side of bad behavior?"

Bottom line: the very fact that DOD and the national security advisor might be on Gandy's side could cause State to dig in its heels even deeper.

As Gandy fleshed out his chart with gray, dashed, and black lines, he found that he mostly sketched dashed lines after filling out the original set of actors and routine reporting relationships. State and CIA hated each other for many reasons, chief among them the fact that Bill Casey, who'd been Reagan's campaign chairman, had lobbied hard for Shultz's job back in 1981 and had had to settle for the consolation prize of CIA. Still believing that Reagan expected him to weigh in on foreign policy, Casey was constantly involving himself in foreign policy debates, much to Shultz's displeasure. State also had a long-standing, simmering resentment of CIA spying on the very people that State's diplomats were trying to make friends with.

Casey and Weinberger didn't get along very well, which was typical of CIA-Pentagon relationships since 1947, when CIA was established with the express purpose of developing intelligence assessments that were a counterweight against the typically dire threat assessments that the Pentagon used to justify its budgets.

Within the different agencies, there were also long-simmering disputes that Gandy drew in dashed lines.

State's black dragon diplomats looked down their noses at diplomatic security officers, who returned the ill will, and COS Moscow sometimes chafed under CIA headquarters control, as during the Turner-Hathaway years. But Gandy wasn't sure about the current relationship between COS and CIA headquarters, so he made the connecting line there gray. CIA's DS&T often felt bullied by the vastly more prestigious and powerful DO.

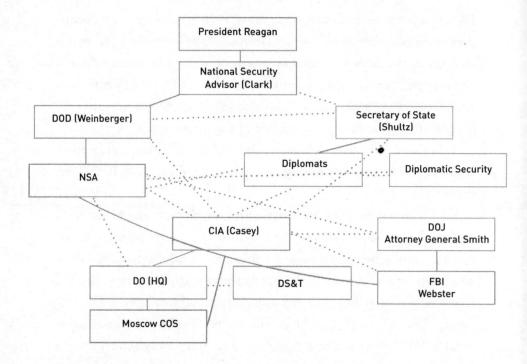

Maybe DS&T had authored the Band-Aid report to undermine DO as well as Gandy: stranger things had happened.

With a few exceptions, CIA and NSA were connected by dashed lines of enmity, as were CIA and FBI, who were about as culturally different as you could get. FBI agents were straight-shooter Eagle Scouts with a strong sense of right and wrong, who only wanted to put criminals behind bars and notch up convictions. To FBI agents, CIA DO officers *were* criminals, who bribed, blackmailed, conned, assassinated (before the intelligence reforms of the 1970s), and resorted to any other dubious or underhanded scheme to get a job done. From CIA's perspective, "Fat Boys Incorporated" agents were dull, unimaginative types who waited around for bad things to happen, while CIA was out in the field making sure bad things never happened in the *first* place.

Justice and NSA had butted heads in the past over allegations that NSA had collected information that they believed to be in the gray areas of NSA's legal charter. A few years earlier, attorney general Griffin Bell had stalked the corridors of NSA looking for Gandy to express his strong opinions about certain activities that he believed Gandy was involved in. So although FBI liked Gandy, their bosses at Justice sometimes did not.

It would later emerge that Gandy was not the only senior intelligence officer to take note of the parochialism and turf fighting that made mounting a serious effort against the Soviet technical espionage threat impossible.

Robert Gates, who was deputy director of CIA and eventually became CIA director, then secretary of defense, summarized the chaotic state of affairs in a memo to then CIA director Casey about problems with an interagency group, which included DOD, NSA, CIA, and the State Department, whose charter was to coordinate countermeasures against foreign intelligence technical threats.[6]

SECRET
28 April 1986

MEMORANDUM FOR: Director of Central Intelligence

FROM: Deputy Director of Central Intelligence

SUBJECT: Security and Countermeasures: Improving the SIG Process (S) [denotes SECRET]

1. We are under heavy pressure from the Senate Select Committee and the NSC Staff to make improvements in the security, counter-intelligence and security countermeasures arenas. They and others believe that these issues do not receive nearly enough attention of senior managers in government, including the Intelligence Community, and that those efforts that do exist are disconnected and proceed in isolation. They also believe that somehow shortcomings in these areas contributed to the rash of spies in the last year or so. They may be right. (S)

2. As a result of my examination of this problem, I believe their concerns, particularly in the security countermeasures arenas, are reasonably well founded; in addition, you and I perceive problems that others do not.

—Specifically, the division of labor between the Security Committee and the IG/Countermeasures is totally ambiguous. Essentially, there are two groups charged with responsibility for the same problems. Where there is not inaction, there is paralysis as a result of bureaucratic tugs of war and parochial viewpoints.

—The Security Committee has 10 subcommittees and half a dozen or so working groups all involving people at the working level. As noted above, parochialism dominates in this area (more so than in any area I have ever seen).

—Moreover, there is little contact or coordination among the committees—that is, across security disciplines (computer security, personnel security, physical security, etc.)

—The leadership of the Security Committee is competent but not very aggressive and lacking a charter to attack some of the more difficult problems.

—Simultaneously, the leadership of the IG/CM is weak and provides little leadership or coordination.

—A variety of ad hoc groups have sprung up, some from within the Intelligence Community, others at the instigation of the NSC Staff or others, to try and work around these problems. Mary Lawton's group on personnel security is an excellent example.

—The relationship between organizations in the Intelligence Community or the SIG and non-intelligence organizations (such as NTISSC) is ambiguous, and as a result there is little contact, consultation or coordination.

—There is no Intelligence Community organization to identify and act upon leaks. (S)

3. In sum, the bureaucratic underbrush has grown so high it is straining efforts in the security/countermeasures area to address some of the problems we face. There is a lack of coordination and sharing of information, a prevalence of bureaucratic turf fighting, and a general passivity in the entire structure. (S)

4. By contrast, all are in agreement that there has been significant progress in the counterintelligence arena, particularly in the 16/31 chaired by Judge Webster [FBI director]. He has provided effective leadership and as Director of FBI and a member of the SIG has the clout to make things move. In addition, there is now a group of people leading the counterintelligence effort in the various agencies—especially in CIA and in NSA—who are much more willing to collaborate with their colleagues. In short, this is an area that I think is working reasonably well. (S)

5. I suggest the following changes in structure and procedure to address some of the problems above:

—First, abolish the Security Committee and restructure its activities under the auspices of the SIG.

—Second, split the IG for Countermeasures into one that deals with physical and personnel security and another that deals with technical surveillance countermeasures, COMSEC, etc.

—Third, consolidate the various committees and subcommittees under SECOM into five or six broader committees operating under the auspices of the appropriate 16 for Countermeasures. These committees should be chaired by a senior line manager from the agency that has the largest equity involved in the subject (or the best expertise) and the membership of each committee should be comprised of, again, senior line managers from agencies that have a useful role to play. The key is to involve senior line managers who can make commitments for and deliver their agencies so that the committee structure is not just a staff undertaking.

Fourth, restructure the Intelligence Community Staff elements involved in these issues to create a Counterintelligence and Security Countermeasures Staff that would provide staff support to the three IG's, house the Unauthorized Disclosure Analysis Center, and the analytical capability to continue to perform such ad hoc responsibilities as you assign as well as the Annual Hostile Threat Assessment. This Staff will have the additional responsibility of ensuring not only support for each of the committees under the two Countermeasure 16's but also that the results of each committee's work are shared with the other committees and that there is a continuing consultation and coordination among the various disciplines. This will require a far more aggressive staff chief and staff than has been the case in the past.

Fifth, the Chairman of NTISSC should be a member of the SIG to ensure that issues on telecommunications and computer security going beyond the Intelligence Community are coordinated with efforts being taken within the Community. (S)

Recommendation.

1. That you [CIA director William Casey] approve the above measures.

2. That you sign the attached memorandum forwarding these pro-
posals and associated organization chart to SIG principals for their
consideration.

3. That we schedule a SIG for the end of this week to get these recommendations blessed.

4. That within a day or two of the SIG the new structure be imple-
mented.

Attachment: As Stated (S)

SECRET

Two of Gate's most noteworthy comments in the memo that echoed
Charles's frustration were:

"Where there is not inaction, there is paralysis as a result of bureaucratic tugs of war and parochial viewpoints. . . ." Parochialism dominates in this area (more so than in any area that I have ever seen).

And the kicker: "There is no intelligence community organization to
identify and act upon leaks."

So Gandy, filling out his chart in 1983, was merely anticipating
Gates's memo, not the first—or last—time that people at the working
level discovered problems long before leaders at the very top did.

After sketching the gray line between Moscow Station and CIA
headquarters, Gandy's fingers began to cramp with all the drawing, so
he put down the pencil.

Surveying his work, he decided there was no point to continuing. The
political landscape that he had just sketched was one in which no one,
from top to bottom, could afford to show weakness, lest a determined
opponent attack them in that weak spot. And no one could afford to cooperate with him.

State couldn't admit any security problems because it would give

DOD, through its henchman NSA, carte blanche to uncover still *more* problems and further sabotage diplomatic efforts with the Soviets. CIA headquarters couldn't admit they needed NSA's help because that would put them at a disadvantage in their eternal struggle for supremacy with FBI and NSA in matters of overseas counterintelligence and technical countermeasures. DS&T had to issue the Band-Aid report to prove they were on top of things to the ever-critical DO.

And if Gandy were honest with himself, NSA was not pure as the driven snow either. Historically, NSA had pushed against CIA to increase its own power and prestige. Then there were the reports that NSA was withholding intelligence from CIA in order to get credit with the president for big scores. Gandy didn't know if these reports were true, but, well, senior executives usually got where they were at NSA, as elsewhere, by being competitive. You couldn't expect competitive people not to compete, could you?

A deep, bone-numbing fatigue settled over Gandy. This stuff was way above his pay grade, involving death struggles between heavyweights like Weinberger, Casey, and Shultz.

Attempting to recruit allies was pointless in a city where every new ally came with one or more new enemies.

He thought about crumpling up the paper he now came to think of as the who-hates-whom chart, but he thought better of it. Might come in handy down the road. In this town, you never knew.

Turning off the light in his work shed, Gandy went to his living room to relax in front of a Baltimore Orioles game. Opening up his favorite soft drink, Diet Coke, and taking a sip, he was grateful that real baseball was a lot more understandable, and rewarding, than the hardball played in D.C.

8. A Trip to the Oval Office

French Embassy, Moscow, January 1983

One of several teleprinters that transmitted highly classified diplomatic communications to and from the embassy jammed, prompting the code clerk who operated the printer to call in a repairman. The teleprinter was part of the Myosotis system of French diplomatic communication, named after the *Myosotis* flower for reasons known only to the French.

Opening up the machine and probing it carefully, the repair technician discovered several nonstandard components, which, upon closer inspection, seemed to have no obvious function in printing documents. This puzzling find led the technician to suspect that he had stumbled upon implants from a foreign intelligence service, so he proceeded no further with his repairs and immediately informed his superiors of the anomalies he had discovered.

When the printer was put into the secure diplomatic pouch and sent back to Paris for closer inspection at the French counterintelligence service, the Direction de la Surveillance du Territoire (DST), engineers there made a troubling discovery: a stealthy optical device connected to the printer's data bus was wirelessly transmitting all messages sent to or from the printer.

Further investigation revealed that the teleprinter had also been fitted with RF remote control circuits, which would cause the optical device to generate burst transmissions, exfiltrating stored message traffic in extremely hard-to-detect, ultrabrief transmissions.[1]

French intelligence was astonished at the technical sophistication of the implants. The teleprinters had been installed in the embassy in 1976 and 1977, when optical communication devices (which use technology similar to modern TV infrared remote controls) were just becoming widely available. Ultracompact digital memory to store messages for later burst transmission was also considered high-tech in 1976.

Most troubling of all, DST realized that even state-of-the-art TSCM could not detect the optical burst transmissions, because the teleprinter implants radiated infrared energy rather than RF signals that conventional TSCM gear sensed.

If the teleprinter had not jammed, the French never would have discovered that someone, almost certainly KGB, was collecting ultraclassified cable traffic between Paris and Moscow.

The teleprinter implant discovery raised many troubling questions. First, how many of the embassy's printers had been compromised? A quick follow-up survey established that every one of them sported optical implants.

Second, how had the KGB gotten their hands on the teleprinters to modify them? An investigation revealed that the Soviets had almost certainly hijacked the modified printers during shipment from Paris to Moscow. KGB defector Victor Sheymov later said that the KGB had a special facility at Sheremetyevo International Airport for "inspecting" such equipment and a "factory" in Moscow for quickly installing implants.

Finally, how were the optical transmissions escaping the embassy where Soviet infrared receivers could pick them up? The rooms where the teleprinters operated had painted-over windows that blocked all light. Was infrared energy somehow leaking out through gaps in the room?

Embassy employees had been known to scratch small holes in black-painted security windows so that they could see what the weather was like outside. Was IR energy getting out through such a hole? Or did the optical devices transmit ultrashort bursts when the door to the teleprinter room opened so that receivers *elsewhere* in the embassy could pick them up and relay them to a nearby KGB listening post?

Was it conceivable that optical energy could escape the embassy through unpainted windows in the embassy when code room doors were opened? Even if there were no windows across from the room where the teleprinter operated, infrared signals could bounce off embassy hallways, turning corners and eventually finding a window where the signals could escape to the outside world. (Point a TV remote at your forehead instead of the TV and observe that you can change channels with IR energy bounced off your head.)

If the French found the answer to how the IR signals made their way to the KGB, they never revealed it. But the KGB would probably not have gone to the trouble and expense of installing the devices if they weren't able to receive data from their optical implants.

Indeed, Victor Makarov, who worked in the KGB's Sixteenth Chief Directorate (SIGINT) from 1980 to 1986, confirmed that the KGB *was* reading all French diplomatic traffic during that time period.[2]

French president François Mitterrand was outraged when informed of the KGB operation and, even though he was a left-leaning socialist, retaliated by expelling forty-seven Russian diplomats, most of them undercover KGB officers, from France.[3]

The French knew exactly which Soviets to PNG, because they had their own asset inside Russian intelligence, Colonel Vladimir Vetrov (codenamed *Farewell*) of the KGB's T group, who named individual KGB officers to DST.[4]

When the Soviet ambassador to France protested the expulsions, a

French official showed him KGB classified material provided by Vetrov, proving that the expelled diplomats were indeed spies. (Incidentally, the French official who revealed Vetrov's "product" to the Soviets probably doomed Vetrov, because KGB counterintelligence used the material in the leak to trace it back to its source. Colonel Vetrov, who was already serving twelve years for murder, was then tried and executed for treason.)[5]

Normally, the French, like any nation that had been compromised by a foreign intelligence service, would keep a discovery such as the teleprinter implants to themselves. Not only was such a KGB penetration highly embarrassing, but allies, such as other members of NATO, might not trust the French with sensitive information if they knew how insecure French communication channels were.

However, in order to embarrass the Soviets, and to deter them from future espionage, French officials leaked information to the French press about KGB successes, along with detailed descriptions gathered from Colonel Vetrov about Soviet efforts to steal technology from France and other Western powers. The French press ran with the scandalous stories, stoking anti-Soviet sentiment.

Possibly because the Franco-Russian espionage spat played out in the press, the French government decided there was little harm in sharing the teleprinter find with allies. And sharing such information with allies, such as America, might induce those same allies to return the favor if and when they found their *own* clever KGB implants. So in mid-1983, a French general who had served with Lincoln Faurer at NATO when the NSA director was stationed in Europe sent a note to Faurer describing the teleprinter discovery and inviting him to send experts to France to study it. Faurer in turn called Gandy and asked that he send someone from R9 across the pond to conduct a detailed examination and to report back on the implant and its implications for U.S. communications security. Gandy got in touch with one of his top deputies, who promptly got on a plane to France.

Linthicum, Maryland, February 1983

Gandy sat at his desk at NSA's Friendship Annex, near Baltimore-Washington International Airport, reading and rereading the report that his deputy, an engineer whom we'll call Brad, had prepared describing the teleprinter implant after his inspection in Paris. The report was well organized, thorough, and troubling. The KGB had, in addition to an optical device, fitted the teleprinter with a cleverly disguised power line exfiltration system that relayed messages typed on the teleprinter through the Moscow power grid directly to KGB listeners. Such a "belt and suspenders" approach was typical KGB tradecraft, ensuring that if one exfiltration method failed due to adversary countermeasures, such as power line filters or efficient optical blockers, a backup system could do the job.

From his two trips to Moscow, Gandy had become familiar with State Department TSCM methods, and he doubted they would be able to find such a device if the KGB had gotten it into the embassy.

That meant that a sophisticated implant like the one found by the French might, at that very moment, be relaying classified information to the Soviets. Maybe that was what those mysterious clicks he had heard on both trips to Moscow represented.

While he was considering what to do about the threat posed by the teleprinter device, Walt Deeley, one of NSA's deputy directors, strode into his office unannounced.

Although Gandy did not report to Walt, the deputy director was a couple of notches higher in the NSA management chain, reporting directly to Lieutenant General Faurer. So Gandy was not surprised that Walt had felt no need to schedule the visit in advance or to knock before entering.

Walt, a blunt, aggressive, profane executive, was not big on formalities. Without being invited to sit, he pulled up a chair next to Gandy's desk and lit up a cigarette without asking if he could smoke. Walt was coatless, with a canary-yellow short-sleeved shirt and light brown tie sporting multiple food stains and a small hole where a hot ash from a cigarette had burned through.

Gandy couldn't be certain, because most of Walt's ties looked similar, but he believed the cigarette burn on this particular tie was new.

"Well, hello there," Gandy said.

Walt did not return the greeting. Instead, from his back pocket, he produced a folded-up, coffee-stained version of the same report Gandy had just been reading and waved it at Gandy. Taking a deep drag on his cigarette, then exhaling, Walt asked, "Did you read this fucking thing?"

"Just finished it."

Walt had smoked his cigarette down to a small nub and looked around for an ashtray. Gandy, who kept one in his top right drawer for Deeley's visits, pulled out a white ceramic ashtray proclaiming UN, a souvenir from a trip to New York, and pushed it across the desk.

Walt snuffed out his butt in the ashtray and lit up again, squinting through the smoke. "Goddamn Frogs were lucky to find this sucker. Normally they can't find their asses with both hands."

Gandy said nothing to that. Walt would not have cared for Gandy's opinion of the French even if he had been foolish enough to offer it. Walt had strong opinions about nearly everything and was not known for listening to contrary views. "My way or the highway" was one of his most-used phrases around his offices. He was about as different from other NSA executives as it was possible to be.

Where most NSA leaders were college educated, often with Ph.D.s, Deeley had risen to the highest levels at the agency after joining it as an army sergeant with only a high school diploma. Walt was a brilliant linguist who spoke seven languages fluently, including Russian, Chinese, German, and Korean, but he was the opposite of polished. In an NSA culture that avoided face-to-face confrontations, Walt was a stab-you-in-the-chest-not-in-the-back sort of manager whose favorite threat to subordinates who displeased him, which happened often, was "I'll cut your balls off."

Walt had spent years at the pointy end of the SIGINT spear. His first stint overseas was in Korea during the war on the peninsula, where he commanded a small, mobile squad of army "cryppies" (cryptologists) who traveled back-mountain roads in radio-equipped jeeps, dodging enemy fire while performing low-level intercept of unencrypted Chinese military voice communications. Remaining in the army after the Korean armistice, Walt transferred to Berlin, where he went up against East Germans and Russians for six years.

Returning from Berlin, Walt joined NSA in 1960 as a linguist and steadily climbed the management ladder, ultimately becoming the deputy director of NSA in charge of communications security in 1983. The job came with heavy responsibilities, including protecting the president's most sensitive communications and nuclear launch codes, as well as all military and defense communications.

Born dirt poor in Flint, Michigan, and moving to Boston, where he grew up in working-class Irish Catholic neighborhoods, Walt was a street fighter who used his mental toughness to bully subordinates and outmaneuver bureaucratic NSA rivals—almost always introverts—who shied away from open conflict.

Gandy's private name for Walt Deeley was "Junkyard Dog." The Junkyard Dog had a slight build, wore thick-rimmed, dorky glasses, and was inches shorter than Gandy, but he somehow managed to fill up any room he entered with unquestioned alpha maleness.

One of Walt's traits, which had endeared him to a string of NSA directors, was that he didn't seem to care what anyone thought of him. So NSA directors often picked him to lead unpopular projects that more image-conscious NSA managers avoided at all costs. One such "radioactive" project was the investigation of the USS *Liberty* incident.

In June 1967, during the six-day Arab-Israeli conflict, Israeli jets attacked the NSA-controlled SIGINT collection ship USS *Liberty* cruising off the Mediterranean coast, possibly to prevent the ship from relaying back to Washington ultrasensitive communications between Israeli military commanders that Israel believed the *Liberty* had collected. Israeli leaders considered the content of the communications (rumored to involve severe mistreatment of Arab prisoners) so damning that it could undermine Western support of the country. Therefore, Israel decided that intercepts of the communications could not, under any circumstances, leak out. Or so early reports from the *Liberty's* survivors suggested.[6]

Digging into the politically charged incident, which both the Johnson administration and the Israeli government attributed to a tragic case of mistaken identity, was a career killer. If Walt found that a key U.S. ally had intentionally killed twenty-seven of its sailors, higher-ups in D.C. who wanted Americans to continue supporting Israel would crush him; if he went along with a cover-up, colleagues at NSA who knew what really happened would come for him with a vengeance.

Yet Deeley managed to skillfully navigate the political land mines in the *Liberty* review and issued the highly regarded "Deeley report" on the incident, most of which remains classified to this day. (So rumors about the true Israeli motive for the attack remain rumors.) As a result of his virtuoso performance on the delicate *Liberty* investigation, a series of NSA directors subsequently overlooked Walt's abrasive, combative personality and continued to make him the go-to guy for many thorny problems.

And the French discovery of a teleprinter implant in Moscow, was, by any definition, a thorny problem. If NSA ignored it, the KGB might continue to intercept classified U.S. diplomatic traffic using a stealthy, previously undetected variant of the French embassy implant. But if NSA actively investigated the possibility of a similar device in the U.S. embassy, it invited the wrath of both George Shultz and William Casey.

Deeley smoked in silence, periodically flicking ashes from his pants as he appeared to work through the dilemma. Emerging from his reverie and locking eyes with Gandy, Walt said, "Here's the problem as I see it with the teleprinter thing: although the Frogs are a third-rate power, the other side has chosen to target them with some truly high-tech shit."

"Why is that a problem?" Gandy asked.

Walt stood and began to pace. "Because *we* are the Soviet's grade-A, number-one main enemy, yet we haven't found anything even close to this sophistication in our place in the Moscow embassy. Why? For sure, Sixteen [KGB's Sixteenth Chief Directorate, roughly equivalent to NSA] is going to throw their best shit at us before screwing has-beens like the French with it."

"Maybe our State Department security is better than the French's and we've kept Russians best at bay," Gandy said in a somber voice.

Walt stared at Gandy in astonishment for a few seconds, then realized Gandy was being sarcastic. "Right. Hand me that ashtray, would you?"

Gandy emptied the ashes in a trash can beside his desk and handed Walt the empty tray. Walt snuffed out his smoke, extracted another cigarette with his lips, flicked on his BIC lighter, and lit up again. Walt continued, "You had me going there for a second, but you know as well as I do, those security pukes over at State suck. So odds are, the bad guys have slipped something in on us over there that we haven't found."

Gandy let Walt's observation pass without comment.

Walt scowled at Gandy. "You and your guys have been over there, what, three or four times. Did you see any evidence of something like the teleprinter thing in your TSCM work? Anything show up optically, in the RF spectrum, or on power lines?"

"Optically, no. But I guarantee the other side is getting text from one or more of our machines through RF. A teleprinter, code machine, maybe a typewriter or two." Gandy went on to describe the other smoking-gun evidence he had collected and had reported.

"Oh yeah. Now I remember. Jesus H. Christ. And State and Langley sat on their hands?"

"Pretty much."

Walt stopped pacing and sat down again. "Okay. This French thing tears it. If I believe you, and I do, we're fucked. Royally. We've got to get over there and stop this shit."

Gandy's eyes were beginning to sting from Walt's smoke, but windows at NSA didn't open for security reasons, so he pushed back from his desk to avoid the worst of the smoke. "But we have a cease-and-desist order from CIA telling us to stay out of countermeasures. It's officially not our job to find and fix leaks in embassies. Moscow COSs have had us over in the past, but we can't just invite ourselves over there."

"Bullshit. It's national security communications, isn't it?"

"Of course, but it's not DOD or military."

"Who the fuck cares? What's our name here? The *National Security Agency*. If compartmented comms out of Moscow aren't national security, then nothing is."

"You're preaching to the choir, Walt, but that cease-and-desist memo was targeted specifically at me. If I stick my fingers into the pie uninvited, I'll get them chopped off."

The two men regarded each other, thinking. Whereas the majority of NSA officers spent their careers working either defense (making codes to protect information) or offense (intercepting information and breaking codes to gather intelligence), both Walt and Gandy had spent many years working *both* missions, sometimes simultaneously. Both were intimately familiar with how offensive operators such as the KGB worked, because, well, that was the way they *themselves* sometimes worked. Thus, although neither man would have thought of his present role responding to the security threat implied by French bug finds in Moscow in exactly these terms, Gandy and Deeley were essentially two experienced burglars who now needed to burglar-proof the U.S. embassy in Moscow.

Walt's deep understanding of what could be done offensively to a target had motivated him to revolutionize protection of military and intelligence communications, out of a belief that these communication channels were highly vulnerable. Deeley said that when he took over the COMSEC organization,

I was appalled. Within weeks I told Faurer [NSA director] that I would rank the United States in the top half of the Third World countries when it comes to protecting its communications.[8]

Deeley later testified to Congress that

the United States is in jeopardy because it does poorly protecting its vital communications. . . . As a nation so far, we have not made this commitment.[9]

Thus, shortly after Walt ascended to the role of top COMSEC official in the United States, he introduced a campaign he called "a new way of doing business," in which communications systems, such as secure telephones, would have encryption and decryption embedded in them, rather than relying on vulnerable links to external encryption.

After thinking about the dilemma that Gandy had encountered—where NSA would be hurt if it did react to the French find and NSA and the nation would suffer if it *didn't* react—Walt said, "I heard something about Shultz telling his guys he needed a smoking gun. We don't want both him and Langley jumping down our throats." Walt stroked his chin, thinking. "Okay, so what would it take to get us back in the game?"

"That's easy," Gandy answered, tongue in cheek. "Get the president to overrule State and CIA." Gandy had offered the comment to illustrate the futility of pressing the issue of embassy security and so was surprised at Walt's response.

Walt jumped to his feet. "Okay. I'll take this to Reagan and have him lower the hammer on those motherfuckers."

Gandy said, "You're joking, right? That would short-circuit DIRNSA [NSA director], SECDEF [secretary of defense], and Poindexter [Reagan's national security advisor]."

"So?" Walt came back. "What's your point?"

Realizing that Walt actually *did* intend to go to the White House to reignite the stalled Moscow embassy investigation, Gandy said, "Well, my point is . . . good luck!"

Three days later, while Gandy was conducting a meeting with a small group of his direct reports, the light over one of his phone lines lit up with an incoming call. Almost immediately, his secretary stepped into the office. "Mr. Deeley for you. Sounds urgent."

"Could you give me a minute?" Gandy asked his staff, who rose and filed out. The last one out the door closed it gently. Gandy picked up the call and heard a slow intake of breath as Walt inhaled smoke. "Gandy," he said.

"Got it," Walt said.

"Excuse me. Got what?"

"Letter from the boss green-lighting Moscow."

Gandy felt a thrill of excitement. "By 'boss,' do you mean who I think you mean?"

"Fuckin' A. POTUS [president of the United States] himself."

"How did you pull that off?"

Deeley laughed. "I practically *live* at the White House. Who do you think does the football [the briefcase containing nuclear launch instructions and codes] and Secret Service comms? Who does the White House COMSEC and pen [penetration] testing? Wasn't that hard for me to convince Poindexter to give me a few minutes with his boss when I suggested the Evil Empire might be eating our lunch. Lots at stake over there. SALT treaties, Pershing missiles in Europe, tons of heavy shit POTUS cares a whole lot about goes in and out of the Moscow embassy."

Gandy asked, "What does the POTUS letter say?"

The sound of rustling paper came over the line. "Let's see," Walt said, reading. "'NSA is hereby authorized to take whatever measures necessary to resolve the question of Moscow embassy security one way or another.'"

Holy mackerel! Gandy thought, hoping Walt would not get fired for going over so many of his bosses' heads.

"There's more," Walt said. "POTUS signed out a separate eyes-only memo to Shultz—I think Poindexter actually wrote it, but who gives a shit?—directing State to cooperate. I understand Shultz is penning a note to Ambassador Hartman as we speak, ordering him to give us what we need and to tell no one, absolutely no one, about our project."

"Not even CIA?"

"*Especially* not CIA. I told Reagan, who incidentally I don't like much and didn't vote for, that CIA would obstruct us, and he seemed to understand. Bottom line: we've got a blank check . . . sort of."

"Mind if I ask what 'sort of' means?"

"'Sort of' means 'get on with it but don't take forever.' Reagan was sympathetic, for sure, but he didn't want to seem to take sides. Has to keep peace in the family and all that. My sense, reading Reagan's body language, is that we've got a month or two, three tops, after we get our hands on the gear. Then he'll step in and put an end to the squabble unless we find something compelling."

While Gandy was thinking that over, Walt added, "You know the lay of the land over there. Can you organize what needs to be done?"

"Sure, but it'll take some work. This is like a chess game against two opponents at the same time. We can't tip our hands to either the KGB or CIA."

"Agreed. I remember the safe thing. And CIA will shove this up our butt in a heartbeat if we step on our dicks."

Gandy knew that what Walt meant by "the safe thing" was a Russian implant that had been discovered in a code machine years earlier at a sensitive U.S. operation in Europe and stored in a safe overnight in a SCIF for NSA to pick up the following morning. But when an NSA man opened the safe as planned the next day, the device and its implant had vanished. The KGB apparently had learned of the discovery and managed to get into a tightly secured room to recover their device without being detected. Or maybe CIA, for their own opaque reasons, had removed the compromised code machine.

As leaky as the Moscow embassy was, the chances that the KGB—or CIA—were going to learn about the operation that Reagan had just approved were excellent. A scary thought. If, after raising such a big stink in the White House, NSA came up short in Moscow because the KGB got to their implants before NSA did, NSA's prestige would plummet, CIA's posture in the never-ending game of one-upmanship with NSA would go through the roof, and both Walt and Gandy would be headed for early retirements.

"Okay," Gandy said, "I'll work up a plan. But I can tell you the first step already. We need to send someone over there ASAP to do a thorough inventory so we know what to replace when we swap out suspect gear over there for clean stuff we prepare over here."

"Who did you have in mind?"

Gandy said, "You know that guy who works for you, always sits in the back of meetings and never says anything. Except when, once in a blue moon when he does speak up, it's always right on target?"

"Yeah. I think I know who you mean." Walt supplied a name. "I call him Wallflower. You hardly know he's there."

"That's the guy. Keeping his mouth shut is Wallflower's default mode. If anyone can keep State and CIA off the scent, he can."

"You got him. I'll send him over to you this afternoon."

Gandy was about to thank Walt and hang up when Walt said, "One more thing. We got to have a name for this thing."

"I suppose. We'll need to create a compartment and bigot list [short list of NSA employees who would be read in to the project]. We can't have a compartment without a name. What do you suggest?"

"Well," Walt said slowly. "Shultz did say 'bring me a smoking gun' or stop our bitching about Moscow, right?"

"So I heard."

"Then we're going to give Herr Shultz the smoking gun he asked for. We're calling this GUNMAN. Project GUNMAN." Walt hung up without saying goodbye.

Gandy put down the receiver and let out a deep breath. Over five years had gone by since his first trip to Moscow, and he had encountered nothing but obstacles and foot dragging. "Who hates whom" had won out over "who helps whom."

Now, the hand of God had magically swept all those obstacles away.

9. Project GUNMAN

Linthicum, Maryland, March 1984

Gandy sat in his office looking across his small conference table at the man Deeley had described as Wallflower. We'll call this NSA officer Wally.

Wally was of average height, average appearance, and average weight and outwardly seemed unremarkable in every way. The kind of person you'd pass on the street and never notice.

But Gandy knew Wally was anything but average. Possessed of a sharp mind, maturity, and good judgment, Wally had sat through countless meetings Gandy had attended, keeping silent as others argued, postured, and jockeyed for position, until Gandy asked for Wally's opinion.

Wally's opinion was invariably insightful and on point. It was easy to underestimate such a person, which was precisely why Gandy had sent him to Moscow the previous week: no CIA or State Department employee could imagine, in Gandy's estimation, that Wally was carrying out a mission directly authorized by the president of the United States.

"Welcome back. How'd it go?" Gandy asked.

Wally pushed a thick three-ring binder across the table. "Well enough, sir. There's my inventory."

As Gandy opened the binder and leafed through it, he said, without looking up, "Please call me Charlie."

"Yes, sir."

Gandy sighed. NSA was a highly stratified, heavily military organization where it was hard for many junior intelligence officers like Wally to relax and act informally around civilian seniors (equivalent to brigadier generals and up in the military) such as Gandy. Scanning down the columns of entries, which described the model and serial number of every piece of electronics in the Moscow chancery, Gandy said, "Very thorough. How much gear in total are we talking about?"

"Ten to eleven tons, in all, counting copiers, faxes, printers, teleprinters, computers, OCRs, code machines, and typewriters."

Gandy closed the binder and looked up. "That sounds like what I remember. We've got a huge task ahead finding replacements for all this gear and swapping it out without arousing suspicion."

"Yes."

Gandy was amused at Wally's economy of expression. "Speaking of suspicion, how'd it go with the locals?"

"You mean CIA and State?"

"Uh-huh."

"Well, they tried," Wally offered.

"To learn what you were really up to?"

"Many times. It seems the cover story from Lamb [assistant secretary of state for diplomatic security] authorizing my inventory didn't sit well with them. No one had ever done it before."

"How'd they come at you?"

Wally thought for a moment. "Different ways. The State guys kept asking who I worked with back home, like they didn't believe I was an NSA equipment control person and wanted to know why I was really there."

"What'd you tell them?"

"New on the job, didn't know anybody back home except my boss, didn't know the reason for the inventory, only there to do as I was told, et cetera, et cetera. I was a broken record. Eventually, the State guys gave up."

"What about the CIA folks?"

A grin slowly spread across Wally's face, one that Gandy had never seen before. "That was fun, actually."

"Really? I've had many encounters with them but can't remember any that were particularly fun."

"This one was. They dragged me to a party and tried to get me drunk, or laid, or both drunk and laid to loosen my tongue. Vodka was flowing like a river, and there were plenty of very friendly young ladies—if you know what I mean—all of them Russian, as far as I could tell."

Gandy was about to comment when Wally added, "And the stereo kept playing 'What's Love Got to Do with It,' you know, Tina Turner's latest, like they were trying to hammer home a subliminal message that cheating on my wife was okay. What happens in Moscow stays in Moscow, that sort of thing."

Gandy thought about telling Wally of his own steamy encounter with the honey trap in Moscow but thought better of it. Instead, he said, "I'm guessing that you escaped Moscow with your virtue intact."

"Pure as the driven snow. I nursed one vodka all night, just for appearances. Eventually, the guys gave up on me."

"Thanks. I knew you were the right man for the job. Anything else to report?"

"Just one. If you go back, accept any invitation to a party like the one I got."

Gandy's eyebrows raised in an unspoken question.

"Oh, I didn't mean booze and women," Wally said hastily. "I meant food. Blini, piroshki, smoked salmon, caviar. So much better than the embassy snack bar, only decent calories I took in the whole trip."

Using Wally's inventory as a guide, Walt Deeley's organization undertook the daunting task of quickly obtaining eleven tons of electronics to pack up and ship to Moscow, and to box up everything and then return to Fort Meade with all the suspect equipment from the embassy. It was imperative to examine the Moscow embassy equipment at Fort Meade instead of in Moscow, because there were too many ways for the KGB to uncover and compromise any investigation on their own turf.

Also, NSA had more sophisticated tools for examining equipment at Fort Meade.

Some of the equipment to be exchanged, such as code machines, faxes, and computers, was already available at NSA, but there were 250 IBM Selectric typewriters at the embassy. Where to get that many IBM machines on such short notice, especially ones modified to operate on Soviet 210-volt power?

The IBM plant in Lexington, Kentucky, could supply only fifty new machines, so Gandy and Walt decided to settle for the fifty to replace those used in the most sensitive areas of the embassy, then to ship over additional machines to less critical areas as they became available. Walt reminded Gandy that, although President Reagan had set no hard time limit on Project GUNMAN, his body language during Walt's briefing at the White House had said, "Don't fuck around."

Apart from time pressure from the White House, the longer the equipment swap took, the more opportunities there would be for the State Department, CIA, or the KGB to discover what NSA was up to and to interfere. Although State and CIA could only throw bureaucratic hurdles in NSA's way, KGB opposition could take much more lethal forms: in the past, the KGB had poisoned, beaten, or harassed technicians from NATO countries sent to look for bugs in Moscow embassies.

Given that the entire reason for the equipment swap was to hunt for bugs that were compromising sensitive embassy communications, NSA had to assume that the KGB would intercept any messages sent to or from the embassy about the equipment swap-out itself. Thus, only two State Department officials—Secretary Shultz himself and Under secretary Lawrence Eagleburger—were told the full details of the operation, while at CIA, only Director William Casey was informed. U.S. ambassador to the Soviet Union Arthur Hartman would be informed of the ultrablack operation behind the equipment swap by a note hand-carried by an NSA officer once the shipment arrived safely in Moscow.

Although Gandy and Walt assumed that if the KGB had bugged embassy equipment, the modifications most likely were made either in Russia or while the equipment was in transit from the United States to Moscow, they couldn't rule out the possibility that the Russians had managed a "supply chain" operation that modified equipment at its point of origin in the United States. So Gandy and Walt arranged for each piece of new equipment to be x-rayed for bugs, then carefully tested, as well as adding some new secure countermeasures and tamper-evident and authentication technologies to make sure all the equipment would work in Moscow the way it was intended to (and not have to undergo a shipping-and-repair process that would create new opportunities for the KGB to tamper with the equipment).

One particularly vexing challenge, given the compressed schedule, was to find enough anti-tamper sensors, tags, and technologies to place on each and every box, PC board, and connector of every piece of equipment shipped to or from the embassy. Mindful that the Soviets had pervasive access to the chancery, Gandy and Walt assumed that the KGB would quickly learn about new equipment arriving and make every effort to compromise the new equipment as soon as it arrived. So, in addition to all those anti-tamper sensors, tags, and sensors, which Gandy obtained from various operational sites, Gandy and Walt organized guard details to watch over equipment coming in and out of the embassy 24-7. The concern was that the KGB, given the chance, would insert "gifts" into the new equipment and remove monitoring devices on old equipment before it could be shipped back to NSA to cover their tracks. As an added security measure, Gandy directed that these special anti-tamper sensors, tags, and technologies be placed inside *every* sensitive device and case, such as those for code machines and OCR devices, in addition to sensors attached to shipment boxes.

By April, all the new equipment, except for the two hundred IBM

Selectric III typewriters, had been bought, x-rayed, tested, packaged, and tamper-proofed, then placed into secure containers. Also, each container was wrapped in burlap, signifying it was part of the diplomatic pouch, which, by treaty, would not be inspected by Soviet customs authorities. The Armed Forces Courier Service then transported the entire shipment to Dover Air Force Base in Delaware in unmarked semitrailers.

A glitch arose at Dover Air Force Base when the NSA officers accompanying the shipment found that no crane was available to load the shipment on its designated cargo plane. Rather than leave the containers at Dover while a military crane could be found, NSA rented a commercial crane so that the shipment could depart on schedule.

Once in Frankfurt, NSA supervised the transfer of the shipment to a guarded warehouse.

From Frankfurt, NSA chartered special Lufthansa flights to Moscow in stages, which fit the State Department's normal procedure for shipping new equipment by diplomatic pouch to Sheremetyevo International Airport.

At Sheremetyevo, the large, sealed CONEX boxes (sea/rail shipping containers) filled with replacement electronics were loaded onto flatbeds for transport to the embassy. Guards accompanied the shipment because the KGB had been known to follow trucks carrying sensitive equipment, insert skilled operatives into the cargo section of the moving trucks—*Mission: Impossible*-style—and to modify or replace sensitive equipment without the driver of the cargo truck in question ever sensing that anything was amiss.

One factor that helped conceal the true reason behind the April equipment shipment was that the U.S. embassy normally waited until midspring to receive new equipment each year, because the embassy's heavy equipment lift was normally frozen—literally—during subzero Moscow winters.

The first day of unloading the equipment and hoisting it up to the attic for storage went without incident, but on the second day, the Soviets cut off power to the equipment hoist, causing the NSA techs to carry, by hand, most of the heavy boxes ten stories from the courtyard up narrow stairways to the attic.

Why the Soviets disabled the powered hoist has never been established, but one reason could have been that a U.S. diplomat in Moscow, outraged at the unannounced work disruption from a complete equipment swap, sent an irate cable back to Washington, D.C., demanding to know what was going on. If the Soviets were monitoring such communications through bugs that might have been implanted in sensitive communication equipment, they would have been tipped off that the arrival of new equipment was not a routine spring upgrade.

Proceeding on the assumption that the KGB would now try to compromise the new equipment, NSA technicians ran wires from the tamper sensors on boxes in the attic down to the Marine guard station on the sixth floor, where the boxes could be monitored 24-7. As an added measure, NSA arranged for round-the-clock guards for the attic itself.

Over the next ten days, NSA techs systematically emptied the new boxes they had stored in the attic, filled each of those boxes with corresponding equipment that was being replaced, then reengaged the tamper sensors.

The swap complete, NSA ran the shipping operation in reverse, transporting the old equipment in guarded CONEX containers to Sheremetyevo via diplomatic pouch, from Sheremetyevo to Frankfurt, Frankfurt to Dover, and ultimately Dover to Fort Meade, Maryland.

By early May, all the equipment was back safe at Fort Meade, and the frantic hunt for bugs was on.

Fort Meade, Maryland

The first Monday after the equipment arrived, as the morning shift began at NSA, twenty-five handpicked security specialists from Walt Deeley's organization stood shoulder to shoulder in one of the trailers that had been rolled into the parking lot of the NSA motor pool, waiting for the big boss, Deeley, to show up. The spring weather was cool, but the air inside the cramped trailer quickly grew hot and stuffy.

Each of the techs had been read into the GUNMAN compartment and had been given stern warnings to tell no one of the project, even— for those in the group who were married to cleared NSA employees— their spouses.

Walt didn't keep the group waiting long. Climbing into the trailer by stepping on a large spool of wire that served as the trailer's stepladder, he took one last puff on his cigarette, threw it into the parking lot, faced his troops, and got right to the point.

"We're meeting here in this fucking shit hole because I don't want any rubber-neckers in OPS3 [the main information security building] getting curious. You've all been told this project is VRK [very restricted knowledge], right?"

There were nods and murmured yeses everywhere.

"You know what *VRK* really means?" Walt didn't wait for an answer. "It means I'll cut your fucking balls off if you breathe a word about what you're doing to anyone, and I mean anyone." Walt pointed to the open door and uttered the words everyone in the audience knew were coming. "You do this my way, or it's the highway."

The group did not wait for Walt's inventible "Got it?" to start nodding.

"Okay, so here's the deal," Walt continued. "We're dividing the gear into two groups; the accountable stuff [e.g., cipher machines that had to be carefully tracked] will be looked at in our labs in OPS3, while the rest ['unaccountable' equipment that processed uncoded plaintext, such as faxes, teleprinters, copiers, and typewriters] will be examined here. Each of you has been given a specific assignment by your supervisor, and work starts the second I leave here."

Walt surveyed the room, then continued, "Just so you know, I had to pull lots of strings very high up to make this happen, and for better or worse, NSA's reputation will be riding on how well each of you does your job." After letting that sink in, Walt said, "And we don't have forever to get the job done. The longer we take finding whatever exploits the other side has slipped in, the more chance that we're gonna get fucked by assholes at State, at Langley, or by the Russians."

Walt paused to light up another cigarette, then took a deep drag. "Accordingly, to speed things up, I'm offering $10,000 to the first one to find a smoking gun."

An excited murmur spread through the group—$10,000, equivalent to $25,000 in today's dollars, was a sizable fraction of most NSA employees' yearly pay.

Walt looked around the room. "Any questions?"

There were none.

"Okay," Walt said, "then get to work." With that, Walt climbed out of the trailer, stepped down from the wire spool, and headed back to his office.

Whether the electronic device in question was accountable or unaccountable, the procedure for checking it was the same. Walt's techs would perform a careful visual inspection, then prepare the device for x-ray using emulsion films. Some devices could be x-rayed directly, while others, such as copiers, had to be partially disassembled so that the x-rays could penetrate each and every component. Once the x-rays were developed, they were compared against x-rays of safe equipment of the same model that had been previously filmed.

The work was slow and exacting. Based upon the craftsmanship and stealthiness displayed by the KGB implant inside the French teleprinter, techs were instructed to pay exquisite attention to detail, taking note of and photographing the slightest anomaly.

Walt directed that his techs start with equipment that processed the most sensitive information from the embassy, such as code machines, along with teleprinters and computers used for classified information.

As the first full week of the bug hunt turned into the second, x-rays piled up by the hundreds, then thousands. But no implants were discovered. By the end of the third week, several thousand x-rays failed to reveal anything amiss. Walt stopped by each survey location in the trailers and OPS3 once a week, chain-smoking, looking over shoulders and getting quick status updates, but by the end of the fourth week, despite painstaking examination of over five tons of equipment from Moscow, all the equipment appeared normal, so far.

Gandy stopped by from time to time when other business took him to Fort Meade, growing nervous after the sixth full week and over ten thousand x-rays had produced nothing. After the end of the eighth week, all the accountable equipment, and a significant portion of the less sensitive gear, had been thoroughly investigated with the same result: nothing.

Gandy was baffled. His smoking-gun information, collected on multiple R9 trips to Moscow, made him certain that the Soviets had been transmitting text of some sort from inside the U.S. embassy text-processing machines for at least the past six years. Had the KGB somehow managed to remove the bugging device, or devices, before NSA's swap-out team had arrived in Moscow? Given the lax security at the embassy and the number of Soviets with access, the possibility could not be ruled out. Although only two people at the State Department and one at CIA knew in advance about GUNMAN, one of those three individuals might have purposely or inadvertently leaked the operation to someone who then relayed the information to the embassy, where the KGB could have picked up on it.

Word had filtered back to NSA through the rumor mill that although George Shultz obeyed the direct order from the president to cooperate with GUNMAN, Shultz's reaction to NSA having free run of the embassy to recover possibly bugged equipment was, "We're letting the fox in the henhouse."[1]

Gandy thought that if the secretary of state believed in his heart of hearts that the "fox in the henhouse" was NSA, not the KGB (who really did have free run of most of the embassy), how hard would State try to hide GUNMAN from the Soviets? Especially when the number-one

State Department official in Moscow, Ambassador Arthur Hartman, had been the one who'd referred Gandy as a "ne'er-do-well" who wrapped himself in the flag of National Security and is doing great harm to our relationship with the Soviets.

After an additional two weeks went by and all but a few low-priority classes of equipment had been exhaustively studied with nothing to show for it but tens of thousands of x-rays and ten tons of disassembled equipment, Gandy and Walt found themselves in a meeting unrelated to GUNMAN. They exchanged worried glances across the large conference table.

Gandy was not looking forward to the three-day weekend, just a day away from starting, and by the look on Walt's face, he wasn't either.

Although Gandy didn't know it, ten straight weeks of no results, with just a few pieces of equipment to go, had taken an emotional toll on Walt. Walt normally arrived home at nearby Catonsville, Maryland, a suburb of Baltimore, after his family had finished dinner, and he either had a light snack and a beer, watched TV with his wife, Patricia, and youngest children, Sean and Kathleen (the only two of Deeley's eight children still living at home), or simply went to bed.

But for the last couple of weeks, as it became clear GUNMAN might fail, Walt's home life started to change. Each night, he would arrive exhausted, usually after 8:00 p.m., grab a beer or two, retreat into his study, and turn Gershwin's *Rhapsody in Blue* up on the stereo, a signal to his family that he needed solitude. For over an hour, Walt would sit in his study, nursing his beer, playing the same Gershwin piece at high volume, over and over again, as if the music could cleanse him of toxins.

At NSA, watching Walt chain-smoke at a faster pace than usual in the meeting they were both attending just before the weekend, it occurred to Gandy that he was looking at a man whose improbable career, which had taken him from a lowly army sergeant to a deputy director of the agency, was about to come to an abrupt end. If GUNMAN failed, Gandy's reputation would take a severe beating, for sure, but Walt had gone over the heads of the NSA director, secretary of defense, CIA director, and the national security advisor to get to President Regan. There was no way Walt would survive having been wrong to do so.

NSA would need a scapegoat for the embarrassing GUNMAN spectacle, and Walt's take-no-prisoners approach to moving up the career ladder had left him with plenty of powerful enemies both inside and outside NSA.

Gandy also felt compelled to consider the impact of GUNMAN's failure on NSA's standing in the national security community. After raising such a stink and not-so-subtly impugning both State and CIA's abilities to keep the embassy secure, while keeping them in the dark about the GUNMAN operation, the hit to NSA's reputation might take decades to recover, especially given that CIA had recently pushed hard to keep NSA out of embassy countermeasures work.

But careers, reputations, and NSA's prestige hanging in the balance were not Gandy's main concern that Friday afternoon: whether the techs found any bugs or not as GUNMAN wound down, Gandy knew for certain that the Moscow embassy *had* been penetrated and that Soviets working for America had died in the past because of the penetration, and more would likely die in the future if the leak were not found and plugged through GUNMAN.

If GUNMAN failed, embassy security in Moscow would stay firmly in State and CIA's hands—for decades, if not forever—leaving the embassy with the same security it had always had: crappy.

U.S. intelligence gathering in Russia, as a result, would continue to limp along, occasionally grinding to a halt as it had under Admiral Turner. On top of these worries, Gandy believed that the KGB would continue to know in advance U.S. positions on nuclear weapons treaties, human rights issues, foreign policy, and a host of other sensitive national security information flowing into and out of the Moscow embassy.

Gandy found it difficult to concentrate on the meeting he was in as he realized that time was fast running out on his best, and possibly last, chance to stop the Russians from eating America's lunch in Moscow.

As the long meeting wrapped up and participants filed out, Gandy stayed behind to chat with Walt about GUNMAN.

But when the two NSA executives were alone, they just looked at each other and realized there was little to talk about. The techs would either find something in the next couple of weeks, or they wouldn't. Walt would survive to fight another day at NSA, or he wouldn't. Gandy's six-year odyssey for validation would end in success or infamy.

What else was there to say?

Walt put out his half-smoked cigarette in an overflowing ashtray in front of him and simply nodded to Gandy as he left.

Gandy nodded back and headed out of the building for the most agonizing three-day break in his long career.

10. A Wife in the Wrong Place at the Right Time

Motor Pool Trailer, Fort Meade, Maryland, July 20, 1984

Of the twenty-five security specialists that Walt had handpicked to hunt for bugs in the Moscow embassy equipment, none was more motivated than twenty-five-year-old Mike Arneson. Mike had grown up in a poor Minnesota family with a mother who had five boys and three girls before she was thirty-one and a father who worked as a machinist. Mike thought of his father as a workaholic who spent most of his spare time with friends at a favorite bar, away from the constant arguing with Mike's mother.

Mike said his parents weren't very good at giving recognition to any of their offspring, because they'd become parents immediately after high school and had eight kids before they were both thirty-two. No matter how well Mike did in school or sports, or how clever he was inventing gadgets (he had sold greeting cards from the back of comic books in order to buy a pair of walkie-talkies that he souped up to get a much longer range), young Mike Arneson never felt appreciated by either parent.

During the separation and divorce of his parents, Mike, who was the oldest boy, had to become a proxy father to his younger siblings. Mike observed that his father's disengagement from the family had left him with a "permanent hole, with the constant need for recognition, that I would never achieve until much later in life."

This unquenchable need drove Mike to "work harder than everyone else" and to be the first person in his family to go to college. But in 1974, when he approached his father about college, his father just laughed and said, "The only way to college for you is through Saigon," meaning Mike would have to enlist in one of the armed forces to get the GI bill benefits if he wanted a college education.

So, with his parents' approval, when Mike graduated from high school at seventeen, he enlisted in the U.S. Air Force. Mike tested high in mathematics and electronics, so the air force put him through security electronics training at the Electronic Security Command after he completed boot camp.

Mike then went to Camp Bullis for advanced field and survival training, but he never went to Vietnam because the war was fast drawing down. Instead, Mike shipped off to Aviano Air Base in Italy.

After serving six years in the air force, with tours in Turkey, South Korea, and Japan, Mike served his last tour of duty in Denver, Colorado, at the Aerospace Data Facility.

While in Denver in 1979, just before leaving the air force, Mike noticed an executive secretary at NSA named Joan. Joan had also noticed Mike, and one morning at the start of the work shift, she asked him out on a date.

Mike knew from asking around that Joan was seven years older than he was, but he accepted her offer anyway and went out with her that night. On the date, Joan told Mike she was a Baltimore girl from the little village of Dundalk and that she'd worked at NSA since 1968 after graduating high school.

Within a year of that first date, Joan and Mike were married.

When Mike left the air force, he joined Hughes Aircraft Company as an engineering technician, working in Denver.

In early 1984, Joan had to curtail her work in Denver because her mother experienced kidney failure and needed dialysis. To help Joan's mother, Joan and Mike moved to Maryland, where Mike hired on at NSA as an engineering specialist, a low-level technician.

When GUNMAN began later that year, Mike had earned his two-year engineering degree at night school while working full-time, but despite "working my ass off" and leading a research-and-development team of about a dozen technologists, developing many highly classified programs (including biometrics, liquid crystal technology, and holographic tamper protection tags/pouches), Mike was still effectively invisible in an agency loaded with Ph.D.s and fully degreed engineers.

Each of Mike's supervisors told him he'd never get promoted because he didn't have a bachelor of science in electronic engineering (BSEE) degree and that he would always be a tech and *only* a tech.

The only NSAers who got promoted, it seemed to Mike, were the ones who constantly took time off to get second master's or Ph.D. degrees, while doing no "real" work to fulfill NSA's mission. Mike said that "underlings like me, who carried so much of the workload that they had no time for vacation, never got promoted."

Despite experiencing powerful career headwinds, Mike wanted to be the first "non-degreed engineer to make it to the Senior Executive level" (i.e., as high as Gandy) and was still looking for the recognition he never got from his parents. NSA, by failing to recognize Mike's contributions, was replaying the awful dynamic of Mike's family: *Excel as much as you like, but we're never going to praise you.*

In other words, NSA, by failing to acknowledge his good qualities, was pushing all of Mike's buttons, and pushing them hard.

Thus, Mike was highly motivated to be the one to find a bug in the Moscow embassy equipment first. "Most of the other guys were just putting in their time, watching the clock," according to Mike, but Mike continued to stay late, work weekends, and "do whatever it took." Another reason Mike wanted to find the bug was that, after learning of what GUNMAN's purpose was, he was "pretty pissed off at the Russians for trying to screw us."

This same passion for recognition and achievement would serve Mike well later in life. Upon leaving NSA in 2000 at the age of forty-two and after twenty years of service when a "controlling asshole boss ticked me off for the last time," Mike gave up all of his government retirement. He then went on to found multiple start-ups (Matrics1, Matrics2, and Innurvation), authored over 150 patents or patent applications, won two prestigious IEEE best paper awards, and played a key role in developing important technologies such as USB thumb drives and ultralow-power RFID chips. Mike's first start-up sold for over $230 million.

But back in July 1984, Mike was just an anonymous, lowly tech without even a bachelor's degree, who was focused on winning Walt's $10,000 prize and the recognition that—finally—would come with it.

Mike worked nights and weekends in the stifling, hot trailers, wearing just shorts and flip-flops to keep cool because there was no air-conditioning and, for security reasons, he and the other techs needed to keep the doors closed. The trailers smelled of "nasty body odors and grease."

To ease the tension, Mike and the other techs would play Trivial Pursuit at lunchtime and throw a baseball around the motor pool, then plunge back into the stiflingly hot trailers, don their lead aprons, and start snapping more x-rays. Mike observed, "It got to the point where most of the guys thought they were going to be glowing in the dark after all the hundreds of thousands of x-rays they took."

About once a week, Walt would drive up to the trailers smoking a cigarette with an ash nearly an inch long in what Mike described as "a big light-colored boat that actually was Walt's '70s-era Cadillac."

"Find anything yet?" Walt would ask. Mike's answer was always the same "No," and Walt's loud response was invariably the same "Fuck!"

Part of Mike's strategy for winning the $10,000 was to take a different approach from that of the other handpicked techs who were working only on the most likely places where the Russians might have planted bugs—within the code machines, which processed the most sensitive information.

So Mike decided he didn't want to work on the code machines, because he figured that the Russians would have to have broken NSA codes to exploit them, so he started first on x-raying the optical character recognition (OCR) equipment that had converted the classified and unclassified text/handwriting to digital text. The OCRs had huge electronics boards with thousands of wires running everywhere—"a perfect place to hide an implant," according to Mike.

But after what Mike called "two fricking months of donning a lead apron, snapping x-rays, developing the film, and looking and evaluating each and every x-ray film" on a light table, Mike had found nothing.

Finally, Mike turned his attention to "all those lonely IBM Selectric III embassy typewriters, which nobody wanted or cared to even look at."

Those typewriters were the least "sexy" of all the equipment because they were ubiquitous. When originally shipped to Moscow, the IBM machines were not even sent by diplomatic courier or pouch because they were not considered that sensitive. However, Mike knew that every classified telegram from the embassy, from TOP SECRET on down, had to be typed by the secretaries before being scanned into crypto-equipment or via the OCRs. *If I were a Russian spy,* Mike thought, *why spend all the extra money on hacking U.S. crypto when I can have it free in plaintext [typed on the IBM Selectrics]?*

One challenge of the large IBMs was that, in order to get a clear eight-by-ten-inch x-ray, Mike had to take each of them apart so that one part of the complex machines would not block another on the x-ray film. But after snapping tens of thousands of x-rays on GUNMAN, NSA had run out of Kodak x-ray film, causing delays in the time-pressured bug hunt. This film shortage forced Mike and the other techs to preserve film by taking fewer shots of larger "chunks" of equipment, which Mike said "wasn't optimal for spotting anomalies."

Most nights, Joan would wait in the car for Mike to finish, reading one of her Danielle Steel novels. Although Joan had a very high security clearance, she was not "read in" to the GUNMAN compartment and therefore was not allowed in the trailers or even to know about the project's existence.

But Mike didn't feel right leaving Joan alone in the parking lot, so early in the evening on the Friday of a three-day weekend, he broke the rules and brought Joan into the trailer, where he had just begun to inspect the ambassador's secretary's IBM typewriter (Mike's theory was that if there were any implants in these typewriters, they would be placed in the machines of the highest-ranking diplomats).

Another good reason for having Joan join him was that she typed classified documents all day every day on the same type of Selectric III typewriter that Mike was about to inspect, and she might have some useful insights about what was normal versus abnormal.

Joan, who, against protocol, had already learned about GUNMAN from her husband, handed Mike his favorite drink, a Mr. Pibb, found a chair at the far end of the trailer, opened her Danielle Steel novel, and let Mike get to work. There was little chance Mike and Joan's security violation would be found out, because all the other techs had left early for the long weekend.

That evening, after weeks of taking, developing, and examining thousands of x-rays of dismantled machines, Mike had ruled out implants in all but four components: a transformer, the typing keys themselves, the power switch, and a solid aluminum bar that held the typewriter together. Donning his lead apron, Mike began the next tedious process of x-raying each of those parts.

Three hours later, as Mike was inspecting a freshly developed x-ray of the aluminum bar, he grew confused over the images on his light table. There, in the middle of what should have been a solid piece of metal, were "six dark circles." He had x-rayed "normal" typewriters earlier and had never seen anything resembling such circles, nor did he recall there being any electronics or devices inside a solid piece of aluminum.

His first impression was that the six circular objects resembled "can" (metal-shielded) resistors with three faint wires leading from them. He thought, *What possible reason could there be for any electronics to be embedded deeply inside a purely solid structural aluminum bar?*

Mike looked up from the light table. Motioning to Joan, he said,

"Mind taking a look at this? Isn't the bar across the front of the type-writer supposed to be solid?"

Joan put down her novel, keeping her place with a bookmark, and traversed the length of the trailer. Mike pointed to the x-ray. "You use these, right?"

"Yes," Joan said. "Everyone in the office does. Why are you asking?"

Pointing to the six circular smudges, Mike said, "There's electronics in there. It could be that we've just won $10,000, or it could also be that this is some new kind of Selectric model, maybe one that could read memory cards." A few years earlier, IBM had introduced a precursor to the word processor with a magnetic memory card that stored informa-tion typed on IBM Selectric IIIs.[1] "Do you have any models like that?"

"No. None of these had memory cards that I know of."

Mike looked at his wife. "Holy fuck! I found it!"

Working feverishly, Mike unpacked and x-rayed seven other machines and found the same anomalies in all of them. He also noted that a power switch in some of the eight machines contained what looked like a trans-former coil. Studying electronic engineering in night school to get his bachelor's, Mike knew of no reason for such a coil to live inside a simple on-off switch. Perhaps that coil, which wasn't supposed to be there, was a hidden transformer to power electronics that *also* weren't supposed to be present within that "solid" aluminum bar.

Mike could only guess how the stealthy electronics were sensing and transmitting typed information, but on that Friday night, it didn't matter. He, Mike Arneson—lowly, unrecognized, associate-degreed tech—had just found the most sophisticated implanted Soviet bug in all U.S. his-tory.

After a lifetime of seeking recognition for his abilities, appreciation—along with a nice check—was about to come to him. Mike later said, "Joan was so sure I had found the smoking gun, she was already spend-ing the $10,000."

At 10:00, when Mike had finished x-raying eight more machines, he was desperate to tell someone—anyone—about his discovery. But late Friday night before a three-day weekend was the worst possible time for contacting his superior or any other boss. Mike phoned his office, but no one answered. His immediate two bosses were out of town or on vacation, and he was "too low on the totem pole" to get the NSA operator to give him Walt Deeley's home number.

Frustrated and angry at having to keep the news bottled up inside and to wait for vindication that had been a lifetime coming, Mike reluctantly shut down the equipment, locked up, and drove home with Joan for the longest three days of his life.

He'd just have to wait for NSA to open for regular business on Tuesday.

The weekend was very hard on Mike. "I couldn't sleep," he said. "I was so excited. I tried to keep occupied doing yard work, grocery shopping. washing the car . . . anything. I don't think I slept the entire three days." When he wasn't working around the house to distract himself, he sat like a zombie in front of the TV, not really watching, just thinking about his discovery.

At long last, when Tuesday arrived, Mike rushed into Fort Meade early, hoping to find someone to tell about his discoveries. But many of his coworkers had extended the three-day break into a longer holiday, and there was not one employee who was GUNMAN cleared with whom he could share his news.

Frustration building, Mike finally found a coworker who had Gandy's home number.

"Gandy was way above me in rank, in the stratosphere. But I had been told that R9, who did all the spooky shit, reverse engineering and stuff, were the only ones authorized to dig deep into implants. So although I had never met him and only heard of him through his blacker-than-black program reputation, I called Gandy at home. But I couldn't just tell him what I'd found, because it was an unclass [open] line."

About 7:30 a.m., Mike reached Gandy. "Sir," he said, bursting with energy and pent-up frustration, "I think you should stop by the trailers on your way into work this morning."

Gandy, hearing the excitement in the young tech's voice, simply said, "I'll be right there."

"I hadn't even finished dressing or eating breakfast," Gandy later explained. "But I went right to Freda [an accomplished artist] and asked, 'Can you quickly make up three awards with ribbons and gold seals [like the ones artists get for prizes at art shows]?'"

"Okay," Freda said as she pulled on a bathrobe and went for her supplies. "But why three?"

"Well," Gandy said as he quickly got dressed, "I want one for the guy who just called me and one each for his bosses. Nobody buys into anything at Fort Meade unless they get credit for it, and I need this young man's bosses to get plenty of credit for his discovery to stick."

Shortly after Gandy finished dressing and had gulped down a cup of coffee, Freda presented him with three awards. "Perfect," Gandy said, putting the awards into a manila file folder and heading for his car.

The drive from College Park to Fort Meade went faster than usual, as many federal employees had extended their three-day holiday. Heading north on the Baltimore-Washington Parkway at an unusually brisk clip, Gandy felt a sense of triumph building inside. The young tech who'd called him would not have taken the risk of calling someone as senior as Gandy at home without an excellent reason. The excitement in the boy's voice had said it all, and the excitement had infected Gandy.

Six years of hard work, bureaucratic fistfights—including the big one he had lost with the cease-and-desist order from CIA—speculation, endless arguments about smoking-gun evidence . . . with one phone call from a tech in a trailer, all of that was about to come to an end.

Gandy let out a long breath, allowing himself to savor the win. In his mind, there was zero doubt that GUNMAN had just unearthed an indisputable, inarguable smoking gun that *this* time could not be explained away. He had known it was there all along, but that feeling had been a lonely one.

Now Walt would be able to keep his job, NSA would keep their reputation, and CIA assets in Russia might now get to keep their lives.

Gandy parked his car in the motor pool, jumped out, and stepped briskly toward the trailer where Mike Arneson was working. He heard loud voices throughout the trailer's thin wall, arguing.

"It's just a new mod," one of the voices said, angry. "Nothing there to get excited about."

The response, in a voice Gandy recognized as Arneson's, said, "How can you say that? Look! Have you ever seen a power switch in your life with a coil hidden inside it?"

When Gandy climbed up on the spool of wire that served as the trailer's doorstep and knocked on the door, the door quickly flung open, revealing a young man with a mop of brown hair that he assumed was Mike Arneson.

"Come in," Mike said. "You can settle this."

Gandy shook Mike's hand, then that of an older man, presumably the one arguing with Mike, and went into the trailer, pulling the door shut behind him.

Mike walked Gandy over to the x-ray light table and pointed at the x-ray of a power switch showing what looked like solenoid coil wrapped inside of it. "I say that's an implant, but he," Mike said, motioning to the other man, "says it's just a rivet of some kind."

Gandy, still holding the manila folder, peered at the x-ray.

"There." Mike pointed again at the coil in the power switch.

After studying the x-rays for fifteen seconds, Gandy asked, "Can you show me the machine itself?"

Mike walked Gandy over to the disassembled typewriter and pointed at that particular switch.

Gandy experienced a cocktail of emotions looking at the typewriter switch. His dominant feeling was elation, because he agreed with Mike that there could be no innocent explanation for a coil hidden in a simple power switch. Gandy knew this because very recently, on an unrelated project, he himself had been working on the problem of how to retrofit a transformer into an ultraconfined space and had been unable to manufacture the added space needed for such a transformer. But whomever had modified the IBM power switch had succeeded where Gandy had failed, cleverly taking advantage of the "unused" space inside a power switch to embed the coil.

So, on top of feeling exhilarated at Arneson's find, Gandy felt humbled and a little embarrassed that he had given up on his own transformer problem too early.

Straightening up as he turned toward Mike, Gandy opened his folder and took out one of the awards Freda had made. "Well, I can settle your argument here and now. Got something to pin this on?"

Mike took the award. "Does this mean you believe me?"

"Oh yeah," Gandy answered. "That's exactly what you think it is: an exploit. It's a transformer coil that converts 210 volts into something much lower, probably 5–12 volts."

Gandy didn't mention that he was also inwardly kicking himself for not having thought of this packaging idea for his own project.

"How can you be so sure those are not just normal IBM mods or upgrades?" asked the man who'd been arguing with Mike.

Gandy thought Arneson was bright and seemed to catch things on the first bounce, but this other guy seemed to lack imagination or even common sense. But ever polite, Gandy asked with no rancor or sarcasm, "Can you give me any reason why IBM would build a transformer into a power switch? They have plenty of space. Why go to all the trouble of modifying a switch? And why use expensive nonstandard parts?"

The other man, not having ready answers and evidently realizing who he was talking to, kept silent.

"So," Gandy continued, "I think Mike here has solved the mystery of the information leaks in Moscow. This transformer is powering some hidden electronics that are reading and transmitting keystrokes to a KGB listening post."

Gandy, remembering the clicks he had heard six years earlier in Moscow through the chimney antenna, realized that the clicks were probably burst transmissions containing recorded keystrokes from the device he was looking at or one just like it. Gandy pointed to the IBM device and looked at Mike. "Where did this one come from?"

"The ambassador's office," Mike said. "That's why I started with it. I thought it would be the most likely one modified."

Gandy nodded in admiration of Mike's achievement. "Then it could have been the same one that the chimney antenna was listening to all those years ago. Everything typed by the ambassador's secretary or the ambassador himself, and possibly the deputy chief of mission [DCM] was going straight to Moscow Center [KGB headquarters]."

Gandy thought, but did not say, *And if the ambassador or DCM had ever sent TOP SECRET cables written on this machine containing the identities— or clues to the identities—of either CIA case officers or their human assets, the implant that Mike had just discovered could have triggered the arrests and executions of our assets in Moscow . . . and God knows what other supersensitive information they got.*

The man who had been arguing with Mike when Gandy had arrived in the trailer, apparently finding his nerve after Gandy's earlier gentle put-down, said, "But that antenna was removed six years ago. Wouldn't that make the typewriter worthless to the Russians?"

"Not at all," Gandy said. "Those guys have backups for everything that they do, and backups to their backups. If they didn't have some other way of listening to this device—and probably others in the chancery—it would be a first."

As Mike Arneson watched this interchange, a wide grin appeared on his face. He held tight to the award Gandy had given him. Maybe the paper-and-ribbon award was a little cheesy, but no less than the head of spooky shit, Charles Gandy, had just given it to him. Gandy's outfit was so black, so spooky, that Mike had been told before GUNMAN that he couldn't even *talk* to anyone from R9, let alone its leader.

To Mike, at that moment, Freda Gandy's hastily assembled award was far more than a couple of ribbons glued to a piece of paper cut with serrated edges to look like a gold seal: it was the first fatherly recognition he had ever gotten in his life.

And, man, did it feel good. Not just the $10,000 check he would be getting soon, but something far, far more precious. The unfillable hole left by unappreciative parents, at least for the moment, had been filled.

After the skeptical man, who Gandy later learned was Mike's supervisor, left the trailer, Gandy asked Mike if he could use the gray phone—the classified line.

"Sure," Mike said, pointing to one of two phones in the trailer.

Gandy went to the phone and dialed his office, getting his secretary, Nancy, on the first ring. "Could I get you to cancel all my meetings today? Something urgent has come up."

Replacing the receiver, Gandy removed his coat jacket and draped it over the back of a chair, loosened his tie, and unbuttoned and rolled up his sleeves. He knew that, as a very senior executive, he should delegate the detailed investigation to the talented engineers who worked for him, but here was the most exciting find of his long career. There was no way he was going to turn all the hands-on work over to anyone else. This investigation was going to be more fun than, well, thinking of Freda . . . *almost* anything he had ever done before in his life.

He asked Mike, "Do you have one of those new Simpson volt ohm meters [VOMs]?"

Mike opened a drawer and handed a new VOM, which was used to measure voltages, currents, and resistances, to Gandy. Accepting the instrument, which had one black and one red lead running from it, Gandy glanced at the probes and asked, "Got any leads with fine-needle probes?"

"Sure." Mike quickly retrieved a set of probes with ultrafine points and handed them to Gandy, who swapped them for the duller probes that had been originally attached to the VOM.

"Okay," Gandy said, "let's do some detective work." Gandy experienced a flutter of excitement in his chest that he always felt when performing TSCM work. He was about to embark on an incredibly exciting hunt, matching his wits against those of world-class KGB adversaries. He had asked for the needle-point probes because he strongly suspected that the KGB engineers had gone to great lengths to hide the implant from the kind of inspection he was about to perform and would need to make ultraprecise placement of his probes.

Clamping the black lead on the chassis's ground of one of the typewriters where Arneson had discovered a modified power switch, Gandy held the red probe, guiding the tip along push bars embedded in springs leading away from the power switch. Presumably, the springs around the push bars helped the on-off key on the keyboard operate the switch, which was located almost a foot away from the on-off key, linked by a complex set of pivoting mechanical bars that moved the switch's toggle arm from on to off (or the reverse) when the on-off key was depressed.

The mechanical links from the on-off key on the keyboard to the switch toggle seemed unremarkable, so Gandy traced the connections of the switch to the structural aluminum bar.

Because Mike had shown Gandy the six circular smudges in an x-ray of the bar, it was likely that the bar concealed some kind of electronics that would need power—of the kind that could theoretically come from the concealed transformer inside the power switch—so Gandy's first thought was that what looked like a purely mechanical anchoring mechanism, in which the springs from the power switch toggle "anchored" to a lug under a screw attached to the aluminum bar, probably was a disguised electrical power connector. In other words, in Gandy's estimation, the "spring" was not a mechanical spring at all but a power conductor.

If that were the case, the spring connecting from the power switch toggle would be hot with electrical power, and the screw that secured the lug that held the spring to the bar would also be hot, floating from the typewriter's electrical ground so that a voltage difference between the power source and ground could provide current to any electronics hidden in the aluminum bar. (If the spring, lug, and attachment screw did not float with respect to ground, no voltage could be developed to power hidden electronics.)

But when Gandy used the VOM to check the resistance between electrical ground and the head of the attachment screw that secured the spring from the power switch toggle, he found a direct short, indicating that there were no hidden electronics present.

Perplexed, Gandy put down the probes and considered his next steps. He felt certain that the power switch transformer must be providing low-voltage AC to hidden electronics, probably secreted within the aluminum bar, but the ohmmeter didn't lie: a short was a short, and you couldn't power electronics with zero voltage through a short.

Staring at the baffling attachment screw, it occurred to Gandy that maybe a short wasn't a short after all. Picking up the needle probe again, he poked at the head of the attachment screw securing the lug and found that it was as hard and unyielding as he would expect with bare metal. But when he probed the lug that held the spring from the power switch toggle, he was surprised to feel some give beneath his needle probe.

Examining the lug closely with the loupe, he saw that the lug was not bare metal but insulated with a clear, rubbery coating. Placing the red needle probe on the lug's coating, he saw, with satisfaction, that the lug did indeed float from ground.

Now he was getting somewhere! But how the heck did current from the power switch transformer pass through the insulated lug, through a screw shorted to ground into the electronics presumably hiding inside the aluminum support bar? The screw being shorted to ground was like a deep moat surrounding a castle: nothing could get past.

Unless, by analogy, there were a hidden tunnel under the moat.

Removing the spring from the lug and unscrewing the lug from the attachment screw, Gandy inspected the lug ring through which the attachment screw passed and saw that the clear insulation that protected most of the lug had a neat, circular gap in it running all the way around the ring of the lug.

Okay, Gandy thought. *That's how current gets out of the insulated lug. But how does it get through a solid metal screw without shorting to ground?* On its face, the idea seemed impossible.

But careful inspection of the screw revealed that the KGB had milled a circular groove in the underside of the screw head and installed a floating metal conductor ring, which, when tested with the ohm meter, proved to be perfectly isolated from the main body of the screw itself. Thus, current could flow out of a gap in the ring of the lug, into the floating conductor ring in the screw head.

Turning the screw on its end, examining the threaded tip under his loupe, Gandy discovered that the screw had a tiny insulated core that contained a conductor connected to the isolated conductive ring on the bottom of the screw head.

That was how the KGB got power into the bar through an "impossible" short to ground.

Gandy put down the loupe and reflected on his discovery. His admiration for the Russian mind that had conceived of this concealment transformed into something far deeper than admiration: Adoration? Affection, even? After a moment, Gandy pinpointed the emotion: kinship.

The fraternity of elite intelligence officers who did what Gandy did was exceedingly small, so there were very few people with whom he could—or should—share his passion for ultrasophisticated surveillance technology. Looking at the virtuoso piece of engineering in front of him, though, Gandy felt that he was, in a weird way, communicating with a kindred spirit, someone who got it, someone he could respect and understand.

And who could understand *him*.

But as much as he admired and respected the adversary who had crafted the marvel in front of him, a nagging thought tugged at the edge of his consciousness.

Something was wrong here.

By this stage of his career, Gandy had developed a savant-like sixth sense about electronics in general and surveillance technology in particular, and this sixth sense was telling him that something didn't fit.

Moving to another machine that had been disassembled but still had the power switch linkage firmly attached to the aluminum bar, Gandy pushed the on-off switch on the keyboard on, off, on, off through multiple cycles, thinking as he watched the linkage move each time he hit the on-off switch.

Then it hit him. Transferring electrical power through separate mechanical linkages was a hit-or-miss proposition because parts that moved with respect to one another—as the linkage between the toggle switch and aluminum bar did—did not maintain a perfect, continuous electrical connection but momentarily made and broke electrical contact as the parts moved.

Over many on-off cycles, with mechanical wear, the electrical connection would get ever more tenuous. Such an intermittent, unreliable system could not be relied upon.

And yet the Soviet engineers, who were obviously hypercompetent, had done it anyway.

Why?

Shifting back to the bugged IBM machine where he'd discovered the insulated lug and insulated-core attachment screw, Gandy looked at the lug ring more closely.

And there they were!

Subminiature pins in the inner part of the lug ring, probably made of a hard, corrosion-resistant conductor such as rhodium, were pushed by tiny springs to maintain a snug connection between the grounding lug ring and screw.

These spring-loaded pins ensured a good electrical connection during and after movement of the linkage.

The whole assembly was . . . incredible! The KGB had anticipated that someone looking for a bug would try to trace power into the aluminum bar and had literally covered up the insulated power conductor inside the screw, both by insulating the lug and hiding an insulated, conductive core inside an attachment screw.

Satisfied that he was on the right track looking for the electronics that constituted a bug, Gandy turned to Arneson. "Let's take the aluminum bar completely out of the machine. We need to get inside this thing."

Arneson, who had been watching Gandy's detective work, removed the aluminum bar.

Inspecting the aluminum bar through the loupe, Gandy noticed a line of dark marks, each less than a millimeter wide, along the bar's underside. Using a needle probe, he poked at dark marks and immediately discovered that there were dabs of grease that concealed machined holes.

"Mike, can you find me some solvent?" Gandy asked, now the surgeon giving instructions to a skilled scrub nurse.

Again, Mike found what Gandy needed.

Gandy cleaned the dabs of grease away with the solvent and peered into one of the machined holes, which appeared to taper to a point. There, near the bottom of the taper in one of the holes, he saw two miniature slots.

Straightening from his work, Gandy put down the loupe and rubbed his eyes, recalling something he heard Winston Churchill say about Russia: "It is a riddle, wrapped in a mystery, inside an enigma."

The multilayered hiding of intent that Churchill referred to was certainly evident here. The twin slots were probably spanner caps that hid a set screw that secured the cover of the supposedly "solid" aluminum bar to the body of the bar, which in turn must be hiding electronics. An insulated lug connected to a screw with a hidden insulated center conductor, now, a dab of grease had hidden a spanner cap that in turn probably hid a set screw.

Man, were these guys good at hiding things!

Gandy asked Mike, "Can you find me some precision calipers to measure these drill holes?"

Arneson rummaged around and found what Gandy needed, and he watched as the older man carefully measured the diameter of the small holes and jotted down his measurements.

Gandy took the pad on which he'd written the measurements to the gray phone and called the R9 machine shop. "Gandy here," he said to his lead machinist. "I'm fixin' to undo a custom cover and need you to make me a special miniature spanner wrench to these dimensions." He then read off the dimensions he needed and asked, "When can y'all have it? An hour? Super. Thanks."

Hanging up, Gandy looked at his watch. Four hours had slid by since he had entered the trailer. He asked Mike, "Can I buy you lunch?"

After lunch, Gandy collected the custom miniature spanner wrench from his machinist, who had driven it to Fort Meade as soon as he was finished making it, and returned with Mike to the trailer.

Inserting the small fork of the wrench into the miniature slots at the bottom of one of the holes in the aluminum bar, Gandy gently turned, removing the threaded spanner from the hole. Through the jeweler's loupe, he confirmed that a subminiature, flat-head jeweler's screw was at the bottom of the hole. Arneson, who had been looking over Gandy's shoulder, handed Gandy a set of fine jeweler's screwdrivers. Selecting a screwdriver he thought was the right dimension, Gandy then unscrewed the tiny jeweler's screw, turning the bar over when he was done and dropping the now-loosed screw into a jar.

Using the special spanner wrench and jeweler's screwdriver, he quickly removed all the hidden screws, slid an X-Acto blade into a barely perceptible hairline seam that had emerged when all the screws were removed, and, with great difficulty because the near-perfect machining created a vacuum-like seal, lifted the cover off the "solid" aluminum bar. Gandy was stunned at the magnificent craftsmanship of the bar. The many small, hidden jeweler's screws secured the bar's cover so snugly to the main body of the bar that no seam could be detected visually—before the screws were removed—even with a jeweler's loupe.

Gandy and Mike leaned over, looking at the inside of the aluminum bar. The first thing that the two men noticed was that there were small wires attached to a circuit board, densely packed with microelectronics, and six dark round circles lay in front of them. But the wires were unique for such a circuit because they were colored red, white, and blue (instead of red, white, and black).

Mike's first comment upon seeing America's colors in the electrical wires inside a Soviet bug was, "Ain't that sticking it right in our face? Maybe the fricking CIA did this just to fuck with NSA." Mike paused to consider what he'd just said, then added, "Naw. CIA is way too incompetent to create something this good."

Letting Mike's comment pass, Gandy pointed to the dark circles, which Mike had originally assumed were can resistors. "Those are magnetometers, almost for sure," he said. "They must sense the movement of the latch interposers, which probably have some ferrous or magnetic material embedded onto them and when they pass over the bar on that felt pad there, and thus register which key has been struck."

When a typist depressed any key of the IBM Selectric III, that key, through a complex set of mechanical links, in turn moved a set of six latch interposers in different combinations, which the Selectric decoded to determine which character to type. The ends of all six latch interposers passed forward and back over the aluminum support bar in which Arneson had discovered the magnetometers.

Mike said, while pointing at the interposers that moved back and forth over the bar, "Wouldn't that mean there must be tiny magnets embedded in the ends of those interposers?"

Gandy smiled at Mike's perceptiveness. "Yep. Now I need to ask if you have any Magnaflux."

Mike said, "You mean that ferro-fluid that traces out magnetic lines of flux?"

"That's what I mean."

"Not here in the trailer," Mike said.

Gandy called his R9 lab and asked that the special fluid be couriered over to him.

While they were waiting for the fluid, Gandy said, "I'm going to spray some of it on the end of the interposer, and it will show us exactly where the magnets are and what type of magnets they are. It has microscopic particles that align with magnetic lines of flux." As he spoke, Gandy examined the ends of the interposer with a loupe where they passed over the bar. The ends of the interposers looked completely solid, with no sign of a gap or milling marks or seam where magnets might be concealed.

When an R9 staffer delivered the Magnaflux, Gandy placed a clear plastic sheet over the interposer and quickly sprayed it over the end of the interposers, expecting to see curved lines of flux, denoting the presence of hidden permanent magnets underneath.

Gandy scowled as he and Mike looked at the fluid. Where a clear pattern should have been there was instead a random collection of speckles. No magnetic field was present in any of the interposers, implying that there were no magnets inside.

That simply couldn't be. Why have the magnetometers in the bar if there were no magnets in the interposers?

Mike asked, "Could the magnetometers be sensing something else?"

"No way!" Gandy answered more loudly than he had intended, squinting at the random particle pattern of the Magnaflux. "There simply *have* to be magnets in there somewhere. Can you take the interposers out for me so we can lay them out on the table?"

Getting his tools, Mike did as Gandy requested.

Gandy took one of the freed interposers and laid it flat on the workbench at a right angle to the way it normally sat in the Selectric, then covered it with plastic and sprayed the Magnaflux on it again.

This time, a horseshoe pattern of lines quickly appeared. "I knew it!" Gandy exclaimed, pointing at the lines of flux. "That there is what you'd expect with horseshoe magnets, with the north and south poles right next to each other."

"Why didn't we see it on the top of the interposers?" Mike asked.

"Because the other side is diabolically clever. With a tiny horseshoe magnet, you're never going to see any net lines of flux because, in the vertical orientation, with one pole on top of the other, the fields will appear to cancel each other. The only way to spot the magnets is to turn the interposers on their sides where you can see the magnetic field lines exiting and entering the poles."

Man, oh, man, Gandy mused. The KGB designers were fighting his efforts to diagnose what they had done at every turn. A power switch hid a transformer. Supposed mechanical springs meant to anchor the switch toggle were actually conductors that attached to a lug screw that hid its true purpose with a thin insulated cover and floating inner conductors. Grease spots hid holes, which hid spanner covers, which hid set screws, which clamped the bar's lid so tight that a razor-thin seam was hidden even to a jeweler's loupe.

Gandy looked at Mike and said, "What we're looking at here is what happens when smart people who take security very, very seriously are given a free hand. They went to extreme lengths to prevent us from finding these implants, even with thorough inspections. You've got to take your hat off to them."

Mike asked, "Want to dig into the end of those interposers to find the horseshoe magnets?"

"Oh yeah," Gandy answered and went to work doing just that.

Five hours later, he had found and removed six tiny horseshoe magnets that had been secured inside milled-out cavities in the ends of each interposer. "You do realize the genius of these things," he told Arneson. "Flipped vertically, the horseshoe magnets have both north and south poles pointed toward the magnetometers so that when they pass over the magnetometers, they generate two signals, one signal for both north and for south. Redundant, and I'm sure, extremely reliable. This thing is nothing less than a work of art."

At that, Gandy looked at his watch. "Oh, wow. Where did the time go?" he said to Mike. "I should let you get home to supper."

Mike nodded and let Gandy out, locking up the trailer. Even though it was July, darkness had fallen, and stars filled the eastern Maryland sky. Gandy looked up at the sky, patted Mike on the shoulder, and said, "You are one of those now, Mike. A star."

The two men parted, each to his own wife and own supper, and each to his own reward.

The next day, when Mike heard that Walt Deeley had returned to work, he and one of his bosses, a man named Herb, asked for and got an appointment to see the big boss to inform him of the typewriter finding. On the walk over, Mike was bursting with excitement. *Yeah,* he thought. *I knew I'd be the first one to find this sucker! Yeah!* Mike had hardly slept the night before, anticipating the reception the head honcho was going to give him, running the expected encounter repeatedly in his head.

Walt Deeley didn't keep Mike and Herb waiting in his reception area—as NSA top executives usually did—but had them shown into his spacious office as soon as they arrived.

Mike, who had never set foot in the office, looked around the cavernous space in awe. Glass bookshelves were filled with exotic mementos from Walt's many travels around the globe. The view was spectacular, the whole setup radiating the awesome power of Deeley's position as an NSA deputy director.

A feeling of euphoria came over Mike as Walt rose to shake his hand. Mike felt that he had well and truly just changed the world and was about to be recognized for it.

But Walt didn't congratulate Mike, thank him, or say, "Well done." When Mike and Herb had sat in two chairs in front of Walt's desk (without being invited to take seats) and had given Walt a brief account of the typewriter find, Walt said to Mike, without removing the cigarette from his mouth, "Okay, you'll be getting the $10,000 check."

"Thank you, sir. But I want you to know it was truly a team effort. We all worked hard."

Deeley squinted at Mike through a thick cloud of smoke. "Split it with whomever the fuck you want. I don't give a shit. But you're paying the fucking taxes to the fucking IRS on the full $10,000." (Perhaps Walt was focused on the IRS because he not only got to keep his job but got his own $50,000 check for his role in GUNMAN.) Walt then looked down at some paperwork on his desk, the meeting evidently over.

Herb and Mike looked at each other, rose from their chairs, then left the office.

Mike's euphoria seeped away, replaced by a feeling that he likened to losing his virginity: Is that all there was?

As far as Mike Arneson's technical work was concerned, it quickly became clear that yes, that *was* all there was.

Although he was passionately curious to learn more about the bugs he had discovered, the next day, unmarked trucks—presumably from R9—showed up, and some techs Mike had never met—also presumably from R9—removed all the typewriters and took them "behind a green door." (A *green door* was NSA slang for an ultrablack-burn-before-reading operation). To Mike, everything at R9 was behind a green door.

But the authority to reverse engineer enemy tech rested with R9 and others in Walt's COMSEC organization, not Mike's organization, so Mike would be shut out of any follow-up discoveries or insights. He'd been fortunate to see as much as he had when Gandy had spent the previous day with him.

As a reward for finding what came to be known as the GUNMAN implant, Mike was eventually promoted, given a check and plaque at an NSA assembly (for achievements, according to the presenter, that "cannot be talked about"), and earned a trip to Moscow in the fall, where he joined the team inspecting the new embassy building for listening devices. But as far as the typewriters went, he'd just have to learn what he could from RUMINT, along with everyone else at NSA.

But Mike wasn't like everyone else at NSA. In his mind, everything in life happens for a reason, and he had been put on the planet for many things, including finding the GUNMAN bugs.

And he had not disappointed whomever had put him on the planet to do that.

11. Behind the Green Door

Gandy was a hands-on leader who spent hours each week at a workbench in R9 laboratory spaces, working alongside his employees on electronics. Soldering, probing, measuring, adjusting, fabricating, and testing. A player-coach, this time Gandy was not going to delegate away all the investigation of the most exciting discovery of his career.

He was going to do some of the work himself.

He organized teams to x-ray, probe, disassemble, and test each of the twenty-five typewriters that had come back in the first shipment from Moscow, assigning to himself some of the work.

R9 would later examine additional IBM machines from Moscow, Leningrad (now Saint Petersburg), and U.S. embassies throughout the Warsaw Pact nations, along with stateside machines from high-level U.S. government facilities, including the White House.

But that July, R9 focused first on the eight machines in which Mike Arneson had found implants.

Using the x-rays as a guide, Gandy and his team carefully took apart each piece of each machine and subjected the parts to rigorous visual, mechanical, RF, and electronic investigation.

Building on Gandy's and Mike's discoveries that first day in the trailer, it became apparent that the A team at the KGB had designed and built the typewriter bugs. The workmanship, technical sophistication, stealthiness, and sheer genius of the system were, in Gandy's view, nothing short of jaw-dropping.

To fully understand the cleverness of the KGB exploit, an understanding of the IBM Selectric typewriter itself is essential.

IBM first introduced the model in 1961, completely revolutionizing the way electric typewriters worked. Whereas the first electric typing machines were simply motorized versions of manual typewriters, where each letter had a dedicated swinging lever arm that typed on paper moving on a carriage, the Selectric had one ball that moved on a carriage, leaving the paper stationary (except for line advance).

The Selectric permitted much faster typing because it was impossible for multiple letters to type simultaneously, jamming against each other. Instead, all letters and characters were on a single ball that contained four rows of twenty-two columns, with small letters on one side of the spherical ball and capital letters on the opposite. By simply changing one type ball for another, different character fonts or special scientific and mathematical characters and languages could be typed.

Each character on the ball had a unique position such that tilting and rotating the ball a precise amount would bring a particular character into the correct position for typing. Thus, the typewriter sensed, or selected (ergo the name Selectric), which key had been struck, then rotated and tilted the ball exactly the amount that would bring that character into the typing position. In total, each ball had eighty-eight possible characters.

An elaborate linkage mechanically encodes 7 bits of information that uniquely define 128 possible ball positions (40 more than needed to specify 88 unique characters, but 6 bits would only have defined 64 unique characters, 24 too few for the full character set on each ball).

Six of these bits were for character selection, while the seventh bit was used for sensing shift and special characters. Thus, when each key was pressed, seven mechanical latch interposers would move into one of a total of 128 possible combinations of positions, which controlled the amount of movement on two pulleys that tilted and rotated the type ball: a tilt pulley that moved into one of four possible positions, and a rotation pulley that moved the type ball into one of twenty-two possible columns.

The entire assembly built upon design concepts for mechanical calculators that preceded the first fully digital calculators of the late 1960s (remember, IBM stands for *International Business Machines,* which originally were mechanical calculators).

Looking at one of the IBM machines on his workbench, Gandy remembered the cleverness of the horseshoe magnets and other concealments and wondered how many other hides he would find. (In the business that Gandy was in, the clever masking of the presence of a bug was sometimes called a hide.)

Six years earlier, while listening through the chimney antenna in Moscow, he had encountered another hide: the placement of the exfiltration signal (which turned out to have been from transmitters embedded in the Selectrics' aluminum bars) in the intermodulation region of two Moscow TV stations, such that a TSCM receiver would interpret any signal coming from the typewriter bug as a normal artifact.

In all, R9 ultimately discovered that the GUNMAN typewriter implants had eighteen different hides, some of which have been revealed while others remain classified.

In addition to the insulated lug and cored-out attachment screw, the grease, the spanner cover, the snug fit that hid the seam in the aluminum bar, the horseshoe magnet, and intermodulation hides, the modified typewriters included these other hides:

- The machines had to be disassembled before x-rays could be used to detect the implants. Jon LeChevet did x-ray one of the bugged typewriters in 1978 (his own) but did not detect the implant because he did not first take it apart.

- The springs that connected the on-off switch to the on-off button on the keyboard, in addition to being power conductors, were actually disguised induction coils that "loaded" the bug's transmitter and receive antenna to operate at the desired frequency (30, 60, or 90 MHz). The electrical conduction path from the modified power switch to the transmitter/receiver in the aluminum bar actually served four functions: spring, delivering power, acting as an RF transmit antenna, and serving as a receive antenna for remote controls (to command burst transmissions). To make the antenna portion of the spring linkage function properly, each spring had to be cut to extremely accurate dimensions. Gandy's team discovered that the springs in each IBM machine had been custom cut, or tuned, to account for slight variations in the antenna properties of the spring linkage system from machine to machine.

- The RF signals themselves frequency-hopped, making them harder to detect and decode by U.S. TSCM receivers.

- The captured keystrokes were stored in a memory chip, then transmitted in ultrashort bursts that were also very difficult for TSCM gear to differentiate from normal click artifacts from light switches and even toilets flushing. These were the clicks that Gandy originally heard through the chimney antenna in 1978.

- The transmissions were further protected via encryption so that even if TSCM receivers did manage to intercept them, code-breaking technology would be needed to read them. (Gandy speculated that the KGB had encrypted transmissions from the bugs mainly to protect them from their *rival* intelligence agency, the GRU—Soviet military intelligence—so that the KGB could get full credit for the take from the keystroke loggers. The Soviets, it turned out, had their own version of the who-hates-whom chart, pitting one directorate of the KGB against another, Communist party apparatchiks against the military, and the KGB writ large against archrival GRU.)

- As an added protection, the bugs did not sense all seven bits of information so that uppercase and special characters had to be reconstructed. In addition, the KGB had reduced six bits to four bits, decreasing the power that transmittal needed (making the signals harder to detect) and requiring sophisticated computer algorithms to reconstruct the text.

The stealthiness of these hides—and others—meant that the security scans that were performed at U.S. diplomatic facilities in the Soviet Union and its allies in the Warsaw Pact had not only missed the typewriters but might also be missing *other* types of bugs with equal sophistication.

Lieutenant General Lincoln Faurer, NSA director when the GUNMAN implants were discovered, commented on the sophistication of Soviet tradecraft after Gandy described R9's conclusions from studying the Selectrics:

I think people tend to fall into the trap of being disdainful too often of their adversaries. Recently, we tended to think that in technical matters we were ahead of the Soviet Union—for example in computers, aircraft engines, cars. In recent years, we have encountered surprise after surprise and are more respectful. Most folks would now concede that they have enormously narrowed the gap and have caught us in a number of places.[1]

Aside from the scary prospect that the Soviets were collecting invaluable intelligence from other "undetectable" bugs, the GUNMAN project had other deeply troubling results.

Although the bug in the IBM machine taken from the ambassador's office had gotten power from the typewriter's normal AC power (and down-converted it via a transformer hidden in the power switch), other, earlier versions of the bug (there turned out to be five different configurations that had been inserted into the U.S. embassy over a period of eight years between 1976 and early 1984) used batteries. These batteries were connected to an external connection that would allow a KGB employee at the embassy to quickly test battery status and to replace the battery if needed.

For this battery test-and-replace feature to make any sense, the KGB had to have believed they could get easy and repeated access to the machines, some of which were in sensitive locations, such as Jon LeChevet's security office and the ambassador's office.

Gandy was disappointed and worried by this development, but not surprised. The buxom honey trap and her escort, along with the KGB watchers who had left their cigarettes in neat rows on the staircase landings, had certainly had no trouble getting around the embassy.

The presence of batteries in early versions of the typewriter bug answered a question that had been bothering Gandy ever since Jon Le-Chevet's team had discovered the chimney antenna six years earlier: Why did the KGB need to put a receive antenna so close to the ambassador's office? The amount of data transmitted from the bug was relatively low, so that an entire payload of stored text could be packaged in a low-power signal that could be easily sensed by antennas in KGB listening posts across the street from the embassy. Taking the risk of placing an antenna in U.S. territory, where it could be discovered and removed, seemed unnecessary.

Unless, Gandy realized, the KGB had to set the transmit power of the bug to a very, very low level in order to preserve battery life. With extremely low transmit power coming out of the bug, the KGB would need to place an antenna as close as possible to the bug's transmitter—ergo the chimney placement.

Two other questions troubled Gandy. How had the KGB gotten their hands on the typewriters to modify them in the first place, and how had the Soviets *known in advance* that they could easily get their hands on them? The GUNMAN implant design was so clever, so thoroughly engineered, that it must have taken the KGB a lot of time and money to design, test, and manufacture the implant devices. It was inconceivable to Gandy that the KGB would have spent all that time and money—probably a few years before the first bugged typewriter went into the embassy (in late 1976, a records search discovered)—if they had not been extremely confident that they could intercept the IBM machines and modify them.

Although NSA, CIA, and State never learned exactly how the IBM Selectric intercept was accomplished, Victor Sheymov, a KGB defector, said that inasmuch as the machines were not shipped by diplomatic pouch because they were not deemed that important, during supposed customs inspections at Sheremetyevo International Airport, the KGB probably shipped the machines to a special KGB factory in Moscow, where they were modified prior to being returned to the Americans.

Burton Gerber of CIA, who served as both Moscow COS and later as head of the DO's SE division, asserted that the typewriter shipments had probably been intercepted not in Moscow but in Helsinki, Finland.

However the typewriters had been intercepted, ultimately, R9 discovered that a total of 16 out of the 250 IBM Selectrics at the embassy and at the U.S. consulate in Leningrad had been bugged.

R9's investigation took over fourteen weeks, but Gandy felt that the discoveries were so important to evangelize around the IC that he issued highly classified weekly reports summarizing each week's findings and conclusions. On several occasions, the KGB had so thoroughly masked what the GUNMAN bug was doing that Gandy and his team reached erroneous conclusions about how the bug worked because the typewriters had so many hides layered inside other hides.

The errors in R9's reporting caused by the KGB's sophisticated misdirections had to be corrected in subsequent news releases to the small group of security experts read into GUNMAN, causing some embarrassment to NSA, but Gandy believed embarrassment was a small price to pay for helping others in the IC—and the State Department—look for similar exploits that might be sending classified information to Moscow Center.

When R9 was finished, they collected all their findings and forwarded them to Walt Deeley's organization, who in turn put together NSA's complete, official summary of the GUNMAN investigation.

In a typical in-your-face move, Deeley had two crossed .45-caliber pistols printed on the cover of the report, with smoke rising from each of the pistols' barrels.

All by itself, the cover Deeley had designed proclaimed loudly to NSA's doubters—most prominently George Shultz, who had demanded to see a smoking gun from the Moscow embassy—"You wanted a smoking gun? *Here's* your fucking smoking gun!"

12. Putting the Smoke Back in the Gun

According to Jon LeChevet, as soon as George Shultz received the in-your-face GUNMAN report, he summoned his top security officers, including LeChevet, up to a conference room near his office.

LeChevet said,

We went into the meeting room, and Shultz was standing on the other side of the table with the Blue Report with the crossed .45s in front of him. There were no preliminaries—Shultz just stood there and asked if any of us knew anything about the report or if we had ever seen it before. He picked it up and slammed it down, and I think there may have been a profanity or near profanity uttered. It was a very short meeting and we were dismissed. I did not get to see the report until a couple of weeks later.

(In late 2017, when directly asked about this account, George Shultz did not recall the meeting that LeChevet referred to but said it would not have been like him to utter a profanity.)

Although it's not clear what Shultz was thinking right after he left the meeting LeChevet described (Shultz said he has very little recollection of the entire typewriter incident), later official statements from the State Department suggest that the KGB bugs had done no damage whatsoever.

The level of concern was apparently so low that there is no evidence that an official damage assessment from the typewriter bugs was ever done. Shultz, LeChevet, and other State security officers reached for comment did not recall seeing such a report.

FBI did try to reconstruct which typewriters had been used, when, and by whom, but the Moscow embassy routinely destroyed such records and did not keep close tabs on the machines in the first place. So both FBI and NSA concluded that a rigorous damage assessment was impossible.[1]

The State Department said that it did modify its embassy equipment shipping, maintenance, and inventory procedures after the GUNMAN discoveries and also asked Admiral Inman in 1985, who was chairing a panel on embassy security convened after the Beirut embassy bombing, to add electronic espionage to his list of study subjects.[2]

But an official State Department comment on the typewriter bugs,[3] issued after CBS News broke the story in 1985, said that there was "no evidence that the Soviets ever acted on information obtained from monitoring the compromised typewriters."

Senior State Department officials also claimed that none of the bugged typewriters were ever used in the ambassador's or DCM's offices. Asked to comment on this assertion, a senior member of the PFIAB who reviewed the GUNMAN finds in 1985 said, "Well, they're just big fat liars, aren't they?" For his part, Gandy thought the State Department's claim that no GUNMAN implants were ever near the ambassador's office didn't square with the placement and orientation of the chimney antenna. "Why else would they go to all the bother of hiding an antenna where they did, and use the roof as a perfect waveguide from the chief's office, et cetera?"

Ambassador Arthur Hartman, who famously issued a memo to the State Department titled "Counterproductive Counterintelligence," complaining about Gandy's activities and those of other countermeasures experts in Moscow, was especially unconcerned, according to a diplomat who worked with Hartman.[4]

"He [Hartman] *wanted* the Soviets to hear 95 percent of what he had to say—when he briefed a congressman, for example," the diplomat said. "This was one way he had of getting his ideas across to the Soviets. For the other 5 percent, you had the secure rooms." (Virtually all the GUNMAN-implanted typewriters were *not* in secure, RF-shielded rooms that protected the "other 5 percent," so presumably Hartman regarded information typed on them as either relatively unimportant or also worthy of sharing with the Soviets.)

When asked about whether Hartman and other diplomats actually wanted the Soviets to learn what was typed—as well as spoken—in nonsecure areas of the embassy, Jon LeChevet said,

> *I am an old Cold War warrior and don't see how you can make State look good if the bottom line is that they would be willing to let the Soviets read our mail to achieve a big-picture goal, but this is the culture of State. The attitude among many black dragons [career diplomats] was that the job of diplomacy was paramount and intelligence was a sideline that should not be a function of an embassy (grudgingly tolerated at best).*

The bottom-line result from the GUNMAN discovery was that State Department diplomats (but not security officers, such as LeChevet) regarded it largely as a nonevent.

Deeley, Gandy, and the rest of NSA may have thought they'd discovered a smoking gun, but the State Department had done their best to put the smoke right back in the barrel.

Many at CIA were equally unconcerned about the GUNMAN discovery. According to Burton Gerber, Moscow COS from 1980 to 1982 and later head of DO's SE Division, no CIA assets were ever compromised through the GUNMAN implants for the simple reason that all of the GUNMAN typewriters belonged to the State Department, and

State diplomats, almost without exception, never learned of CIA's assets' identities.

Gerber and other former CIA officers who served in Moscow also wryly observed that State Department security in areas under their control was so lax—with heavy dependence on FSNs—that the KGB had redundant access to information typed on IBMs and may not have gotten that much extra value from the GUNMAN implants. One CIA officer observed, "Heck, why would they need GUNMAN when KGB officers or informers were doing a lot of the typing in the first place!"

In belated recognition of this problem, George Shultz made an announcement, a full four years after the GUNMAN discovery: "In Eastern Europe, we are establishing core areas of the embassies where no one but cleared Americans are allowed. Our aim is to ensure that classified material is processed in areas free from all foreign nationals or other uncleared personnel."[5]

Another CIA officer, a DS&T employee who went to NSA to look over the GUNMAN implants, went much further discounting GUNMAN. "I think that Gandy faked the whole thing to look like a hero," the DS&T officer told an NSA staffer. "The only reason the so-called discovery took three months was in order to allow time for Gandy to hire a U.S. contractor to design and build the bug, so that Gandy's crew could then 'discover it' to justify their wild claims and get bigger budgets." (This is an ironic theory given that Arneson briefly considered the possibility that CIA had installed the GUNMAN bugs to "fuck with NSA.")

Just how many others at CIA shared this view is unclear, but CIA's view of the GUNMAN incident seemed to range from "Yes, there was a smoking gun, but who cares?" to "There was no smoking gun in the first place."

So in the end, did the GUNMAN typewriter implants do any real damage to U.S. interests? Did Gandy's six-year odyssey to find and plug leaks in the Moscow embassy, which culminated in the discovery of the GUNMAN implants, make America securer? And did the GUNMAN discovery achieve the most important goal of all, according to Gandy, of saving the lives of Soviet citizens who risked everything to gather intelligence for the United States?

Let's start by looking at what was actually typed on the GUNMAN implanted machines.

The History of the Diplomatic Security Service addressed this question:

Security Engineering Officer George Herrmann recalled that the news [of the typewriter bugs] was "terrifying," because nearly every telegram generated by the Department was prepared as a machine readable document on an IBM typewriter, and then carried to the post communications center.[6]

(A few telegrams, like those Hathaway sent, were handwritten on special forms, then converted into digital text via an OCR, then transmitted over one of the embassy's encrypted communications links.)

What kind of typed State Department telegrams were sent from Moscow, and what did they contain?

Ironically, the first clue to that question can be found in the cables that went from Moscow to Washington, D.C., when the chimney antenna was discovered. If George Herrmann was right that essentially all telegrams out of Moscow were typed on IBM machines, then the telegrams that Jack Matlock sent, reproduced in chapter 4, to State in D.C. about the "technical penetration" were typed on IBM machines that the KGB had implanted. As mentioned earlier, the placement and aim of the chimney antenna (directly at Toon's and Matlock's offices) suggested that the KGB was exploiting those very machines.

This means that the Soviets were almost certainly listening to the State Department describe the chimney antenna of the very KGB collection system that was the subject of Matlock's cables.

Similarly, Matlock's and Toon's regular cables to D.C. about the

TUMS and MUTS measurements (such as the one included in chapter 3) *also* were typed on compromised machines, so the Soviets were monitoring—through the GUNMAN bugs—the U.S. monitoring of Soviet microwave monitoring.

True spy-versus-spy stuff.

It seemed that the Soviet official who, in an argument with Arthur Hartman over the gas pipeline, had claimed in 1982 to "read everything you send back to the States" was actually telling the truth.

Declassified State Department archives provide other hints about what the KGB read coming out of the U.S. embassy in Moscow. Here are examples of cables typed on IBM machines that were almost certainly compromised.

This first cable from DCM Matlock, titled "SOVIET MAN REPORTEDLY FRUSTRATED BY SITUATION IN POLAND," citing an unnamed Soviet citizen, describes KGB activities in Poland. The classification of the document has been blacked out, but given the subject (the KGB and confidential informants whose relationship with the United States had to be kept away from the Soviets), it was probably TS (TOP SECRET).[7]

FM AMEMBASSY MOSCOW

TO SECSTATE WASHDC 3793 I

SUBJECT: SOVIET KGB MAN REPORTEDLY FRUSTRATED BY SITUATION IN POLAND

1. (TS) ENTIRE TEXT) D C

2. SOVIET KGB OFFICERS STATIONED IN POLAND ARE REPORTEDLY FRUSTRATED OVER THEIR INABILITY TO CARRY OUT SUBVERSIVE ACTIVITIES AGAINST SOLIDARITY LEADERS, ACCORDING TO A MOSCOW REFUSENIK SOURCE. THE SOURCE, C WHO IS WELL KNOWN

TO EMBOFF [embassy officials] BUT WHOSE INFORMATION CAN NOT ALWAYS BE CONFIRMED, CLAIMED TO HAVE HEARD THIS ASSESSMENT FROM AN ACQUAINTANCE WHO IS SEEKING TO JOIN THE KGB AND WHO REPORTEDLY SPOKE RECENTLY TO A KGB OFFICER JUST RETURNED FROM POLAND. ACCORDING TO OUR SOURCE, THE KGB MAN TOLD THE POTENTIAL RECRUITEE THAT "THINGS WERE A MESS" IN POLAND, AND THAT THE KGB WAS NOT ABLE TO WORK EFFECTIVELY THERE NOW. HE REPORTEDLY SAID THE KGB HAD CONSIDERED BUT THEN ABANDONED PLANS TO KIDNAP OR PHYSICALLY INTIMIDATE POLISH UNION LEADERS BECAUSE THEIR PERSONAL SECURITY PRECAUTIONS WERE "TOO GOOD." HE ALSO CLAIMED THAT SOVIET KGB WORKERS STATIONED IN [redacted] POLAND HAD A "MORALE PROBLEM" BECAUSE THEY WERE BEING KEPT ON THE SIDELINES, WITHOUT A CLEAR SENSE OF WHAT THEY WERE SUPPOSED TO BE TRYING TO DO.

3. COMMENT: WE DO NOT KNOW HOW MUCH CREDENCE TO GIVE THIS ADMITTEDLY THIRD-HAND ACCOUNT BUT REPORT IT AS POSSIBLY REFLECTING THE ATTITUDE OF A LOW LEVEL CADRE PROBABLY USED TO OPERATING MORE DIRECTLY WITH LESS RESTRAINT END COMMENT

MATLOCK

The next cable, read by the KGB and probably also classified TOP SECRET, is intriguing because it includes the instructions in paragraph three (PROTECT) to protect the fact that the Polish ambassador was speaking freely to the United States, although the Polish ambassador himself, according to Hartman in paragraph ten of the cable, assumed that the Soviets were eavesdropping on the conversation and was making certain statements for the benefit of "listening Soviet ears."

If the Polish ambassador had in fact assumed the KGB would learn of the conversation, he had been correct.[8]

FM AMEMBASSY MOSCOW

TO SECSTATE WASHDC PRIORITY 9120

1 (S) ENTIRE TEXT

2. SUMMARY POLISH AMBASSADOR TO MOSCOW OLSZEWSKI WAS PESSIMISTIC ABOUT EVENTS IN POLAND AND TOOK A TOUGH, SOVIET-SOUNDING LINE IN A MEETING WITH AMBASSADOR HART-MAN NOVEMBER 17. IN ADDITION TO PAGE 02 MOSCOW 15919 01 OF 02 171829Z BEMOANING THE DROP IN POLAND'S INDUSTRIAL OUT-PUT, OLSZEWSKI ATTACKED SOLIDARITY, DERIDED THE IDEA OF THREE-WAY POWER SHARING, PRAISED SOVIET ATD, AND CRITI-CIZED WESTERN RADIO STATIONS—IN SHORT, HE HEWED TO A LINE THAT WOULD PLEASE SOVIET EARS, WHICH MAY WELL HAVE BEEN LISTENING. FOR WHATEVER REASON, OLSZEWSKI'S PESSI-MISTIC VIEW CONTRASTS SHARPLY WITH THE TOLERANT, HOPE-FUL LINE ANOTHER POLISH EMBASSY OFFICER HAS BEEN PURVEYING TO US AND OTHER WESTERN DIPLOMATS THROUGHOUT THE CRISIS.

3. POLISH AMBASSADOR KAZIMERZ OLSZEWSKI (PROTECT) BEGAN BY DISCUSSING AT LENGTH HIS COUNTRY'S ECONOMIC AND POLIT-ICAL DIFFICULTIES EXT OF TELEGRAM B1MOSCOW015919. EXHIB-ITING LITTLE SYMPATHY FOR THE CRINGES THAT HAVE COME ABOUT IN POLAND DURING THE PAST FIFTEEN MONTHS, HE AT-TACKED SOLIDARITY—WITHOUT MENTIONING THE UNION BY NAME—FOR THE DETRIMENTAL EFFECT HE SAID IT HAD HAD ON THE COUNTRY'S ECONOMIC AND POLITICAL WELL-BEING. HE NOTED THAT IN THE COURSE OF ONE YEAR, POLAND'S INDUS-TRIAL OUTPUT HAS DROPPED BACK TO THE LEVEL OF 1968'S AND "NOT A DAY PASSES" WITHOUT A STRIKE BEING CALLED SOME-WHERE IN POLAND.

4. OLSZEWSKI BEMOANED THE POLISH GOVERNMENT'S DECI-SION TO CONSULT WITH SOLIDARITY AND THE CATHOLIC CHURCH, SAYING THAT THE GOVERNMENT'S WILLINGNESS TO SHARE POWER WITH THE CHURCH WAS REMINISCENT OF THE MIDDLE AGES, WHEN POWER IN POLAND WAS—INEFFECTIVELY—SHARED BY THE KINGS THE SLECHTAS AND THE CHURCH. THE ONLY OTHER STATE IN THE MODERN WORLD IN WHICH THE RELI-GIOUS AUTHORITIES HAVE SO MUCH POWER, HE SAID WAS IRAN. THUS HE CONTINUED THERE ARE THREE CENTERS OF POWER IN POLAND, NONE OF THEM WITH ANY POWER. HE SAID THAT THE GOVERNMENT HAS DONE NOTHING BUT TALK, YET NOBODY LISTENS. DISCIPLINE WITHIN SOLIDARITY IS COLLAPSING, AND THE NEW POLISH PRIMATE, ARCHBISHOP GLEMP, SAYS ONE THING, WHILE "HIS SUBORDINATES DO QUITE ANOTHER." IN SHORT, HE SAID THERE IS "NO END IN SIGHT" TO THE CURRENT CRISIS.

5. AMBASSADOR HARTMAN ASKED ABOUT PLANS FOR STABILIZING THE SITUATION IN POLAND. OLSZEWSKI SAID THERE ARE TWO PLANS, ONE ECONOMIC AND THE OTHER POLITICAL. THE ECO-NOMIC PLAN, HE SAID, CALLS FOR REFORMS IN MANAGEMENT OF INDUSTRIAL PRODUCTION'S "EXTREME" DECENTRALIZATION OF DECISION-MAKING POWER, AND THE ESTABLISHMENT OF GREATER INCENTIVES FOR WORKERS. THE POLITICAL PLAN CALLS FOR AVOIDING THE USE OF FORCE BY THE GOVERNMENT AGAINST THE TRADE UNION MOVEMENT AND CREATION OF A FRONT OF NA-TIONAL AGREEMENT, TO ACCOMPLISH POWER-SHARING WITH THE CHURCH AND THE UNION

6. ASKED BY AMBASSADOR HARTMAN ABOUT THE REACTION OF POLISH WORKERS TO "ADVICE" THEY MIGHT GET FROM THE IMF TO INCREASE WORKER PRODUCTIVITY, OLSZEWSKI DECLARED "THEY OF COURSE WILL NOT LIKE IT" BUT THEY WILL NOT HEED IT ANY

MORE THAN THEY CURRENTLY HEED THE GOVERNMENT OR, IN-
CREASINGLY, THEIR OWN UNIONS.

7. ON THE QUESTION OF SOVIET AID, OLSZEWSKI CLAIMED THAT
WITHOUT IT ~ POLAND WOULD BE COMPLETELY BANKRUPT IN "TWO
OR THREE DAYS" CITING THE 1982 PLAN, HE SAID THAT IF THE SO-
VIET UNION INSISTED ON A "BALANCED EXCHANGE, WHICH THEY
ARE ENTITLED TO DO UNDER THE TERMS OF THEIR AGREEMENTS
WITH POLAND," THEN THE USSR COULD LEGALLY DELIVER, ON THE
AVERAGE, LESS THAN ONE HALF OF THEIR COMMITMENTS OF OIL
AND PETROLEUM PRODUCTS, NATURAL GAS, AND COTTON, TO SAY
NOTHING OF GOLD, INDUSTRIAL DIAMONDS, AND SO FORTH. GIVEN
THEIR SIGNIFICANT ECONOMIC STAKE, IT IS ONLY NATURAL THAT
THE SOVIETS ARE SO INTERESTED IN WHAT IS HAPPENING IN PO-
LAND, OLSZEWSKI SAID.

8. AMBASSADOR HARTMAN ASKED OLSZEWSKI IF HE THOUGHT THE
SOVIETS REALLY BELIEVED THEIR OWN CHARGE THAT THE WEST ~
AND PARTICULARLY THE U.S. WAS INTERFERING IN POLAND'S
INTERNAL AFFAIRS, OR IF THE ACCUSATIONS WERE SIMPLY PRO-
PAGANDA. OLSZEWSKI REPLIED "IN ALL HONESTY" THAT IF ONE
LISTENED TO THE WESTERN RADIOS ESPECIALLY RADIO FREE EU-
ROPE, AS HE CLAIMED HE DOES "CONSTANTLY," ONE WOULD HAVE
TO CONCLUDE THAT THESE BROADCASTS CONSTITUTE "DIRECT IN-
TERFERENCE IN POLAND'S INTERNAL AFFAIRS, "AND THAT MANY
OF THEM CONTAIN "DIRECT INSTRUCTIONS" TO CERTAIN ELE-
MENTS ON "WHEN AND WHERE TO ACT." AMBASSADOR HARTMAN
OBJECTED, STATING THAT HE KNEW THESE BROADCASTS WERE
CAREFULLY EDITED TO AVOID APPEARING TO INTERFERE IN THE
CRISIS, AND THAT THEY CONTAIN FACTUAL STATEMENTS ON THE
SITUATION IN POLAND. OLSZEWSKI REJOINED THAT HE DID NOT
HAVE IN MIND THE NEWS PROGRAMS, BUT RATHER COMMENTAR-
IES AND EDITORIALS, AND THAT HE STOOD BY HIS CHARGE.

9. IN CONCLUSION, OLSZEWSKI EMPHASIZED HIS COUNTRY'S IN-TEREST IN AN IMPROVED RELATIONSHIP BETWEEN THE U.S. AND USSR, AND STATED HIS HOPE THAT HARTMAN WOULD BE SUCCESS-FUL IN HELPING TO BRING THAT ABOUT.

10. COMMENT: LIKE MANY POLES THESE DAYS BUT UNLIKE AT LEAST ONE YOUNGER MEMBER OF HIS OWN STAFF, OLSZEWSKI HAS A DESPERATE TONE. I HAVE MET HIM A NUMBER OF TIMES OVER THE YEARS AND HAVE ALWAYS FOUND HIM A PRAGMATIC INTEL-LIGENT FELLOW; SOME OF WHAT HE SAID, I BELIEVE, WAS IN-TENDED FOR LISTENING SOVIET EARS. OLSZEWSKI HAS BEEN HERE [Moscow] SINCE 1978 AND SEEMS TO HAVE BEEN LEFT REL-ATIVELY UNTOUCHED BY THE HISTORIC EVENTS OF 1980-81. HE TOLD ME THAT HE AND HIS WIFE HAVE "MANY FRIENDS: DOCTORS, PROFESSORS, ARTISTS AND ACTORS, "BUT THAT NOW, WHEN THEY GO BACK TO WARSAW, "WE FIND WE CANNOT TALK WITH THEM." OLSZEWSKI SAID THAT HE WAS "EXILED" TO MOSCOW BECAUSE OF A FALLING OUT WITH THE OLD REGIME (GIEREK). LIKE MANY POLES BEFORE HIM, HE HAS A HANKERING FOR THE STRONG-MAN SOLU-TION. SINCE HE DID NOT ONCE MENTION JARUZELSKI, EXCEPT TO SCOFF AT "TRI-LATERAL" GOVERNMENT, I CAN ONLY CONCLUDE THAT HE DOES NOT SEE HIS PRESENT LEADER AS THE SOLUTION. END COMMENT.

MATLOCK

Aside from tipping off the KGB about the existence and identities of U.S. sources, such as Refuseniks (Jewish Soviet citizens who wanted to emigrate but were denied exit visas) and Warsaw Pact ambassadors, the KGB's bugs in IBM typewriters that prepared classified cables also gave the Soviets invaluable insights about U.S. negotiating positions and strat-egies on issues such as nuclear arms control.

A 1981 cable from Jack Matlock in Moscow to the State Department in D.C. provides an example of the kind of insights the Soviets gleaned about U.S. thinking. This cable was originally classified SECRET. Note Matlock's assessment of the negotiating strategy that the Soviets were likely to take, along with his detailed recommendations about tactics to handle expected Soviet positions. (Numerous paragraphs have been deleted for brevity.)[9]

MOSCOW, SEPTEMBER 8, 1981, 1337Z

12552. FOR ASSISTANT SECRETARY EAGLEBURGER FROM CHARGE.

SUBJECT: GROMYKO AS AN INTERLOCUTOR. REF: STATE 237032.[2]

1. (SECRET—ENTIRE TEXT).

4. TACTICS FOR THE BILATERAL [discussion on arms control with the United States]: GROMYKO'S PRINCIPAL OBJECTIVE WILL BE TO MOVE THE U.S. INTO NEGOTIATION OF ARMS CONTROL ISSUES, PARTICU-LARLY SALT AND TNF, WITHOUT MAKING CONCESSIONS IN OTHER AREAS. HE WILL HAMMER HARD AGAINST LINKAGE, AS HE DID WITH THE SENATORS. HE WILL PROBABLY COME ON AS THE "WOUNDED PARTY," WITH REPETITION OF SOME OF THE THEMES HE PLAYED TO CRANSTON AND MATHIAS: THE U.S. ILLOGICALLY SUSPENDED THE SALT PROCESS, THE U.S. IS AN UNRELIABLE PARTNER WITH CHANGES IN POLICY EVERY FOUR YEARS, SOVIET INTENTIONS ARE PURE AND IT IS THE U.S. WHICH IS FLEXING ITS MUSCLES DANGER-OUSLY, HEIGHTENING TENSIONS AND FANNING A WAR PSYCHOSIS.

5. SUCH AN APPROACH HAS THE OBVIOUS TACTICAL AIM OF PUT-TING THE SECRETARY ON THE DEFENSIVE, IN EFFECT CHALLENG-ING HIM TO "PROVE" U.S. GOOD FAITH AND RELIABILITY BY MOVING TOWARD THE SOVIET POSITION THAT ARMS CONTROL SHOULD BE NEGOTIATED WITHOUT REGARD TO OTHER ISSUES. NOT ALL OF IT WILL BE SHAM, HOWEVER. GROMYKO AND THE SOVIET LEADERSHIP ARE SERIOUSLY CONCERNED WITH THEIR INABILITY TO GET A

LONG-TERM "FIX" ON U.S. POLICY; THEY GENUINELY FIND THE MA-
JOR U.S. POLICY SHIFTS THAT THEY EXPERIENCE EVERY FOUR
YEARS A PERPLEXING AND FRUSTRATING EXPERIENCE.

THEY PROBABLY ALSO HONESTLY SUSPECT THAT CURRENT U.S.
POLICY AIMS AT STRATEGIC SUPERIORITY AND HAVE GENUINE
DOUBTS (WHICH THEY ARE TOO CAGEY TO ADMIT) THAT THEY COULD
MATCH US IN AN ALL-OUT ARMS RACE.

6. GROMYKO WILL BE A MASTER OF HIS BRIEF AND WILL MAKE
EVERY EFFORT TO CHANNEL THE DISCUSSION INTO THOSE AREAS
OF PRIMARY INTEREST TO THE SOVIETS. ALTHOUGH HE IS CAPABLE
OF EMPLOYING FILIBUSTERING TACTICS (AS HE DID WITH THE SEN-
ATORS), I DOUBT THAT HE WOULD INSULT THE SECRETARY WITH
EXCESSIVELY LONG WINDED LECTURES. BUT HE WILL BOLSTER HIS
PRESENTATION WITH FREQUENT EXAMPLES WHICH CRY OUT FOR
REFUTATION, AND IT WOULD PROBABLY BE A MISTAKE TO RISE AU-
TOMATICALLY TO THE BAIT, SINCE THIS WOULD IN EFFECT ENABLE
HIM TO DETERMINE THE AGENDA OF THE DISCUSSION.

7. I BELIEVE THE SECRETARY CAN BEST COPE WITH THESE TACTICS
BY INSISTING ON A FULL DISCUSSION OF THE PRIORITY ITEMS ON
OUR AGENDA. IF GROMYKO CHOOSES TO PLAY THE "OFFENDED
PARTY" ROLE, THE SECRETARY SHOULD COUNTER IN KIND WITH A
CLEAR EXPOSITION OF THOSE SOVIET ACTIONS WHICH HAVE
BROUGHT US TO THE CURRENT UNSATISFACTORY RELATIONSHIP.
(THIS SHOULD BE DONE IN ANY EVENT, BUT THE TONE AND CON-
TEXT MIGHT BE ADJUSTED TO THE EMOTIONAL LEVEL GROMYKO
CHOOSES TO ADOPT.)

8. ONE FAVORITE GROMYKO TACTIC IS SIMPLY TO IGNORE SIGNIFI-
CANT POINTS RAISED BY HIS INTERLOCUTOR, AND TO TALK ABOUT
OTHER THINGS UNTIL TIME RUNS OUT. THE SECRETARY SHOULD

NOT LET A SENSE OF POLITENESS DETER HIM FROM RETURNING REPEATEDLY TO POINTS OF INTEREST TO US IF GROMYKO PROVES EVASIVE IN RESPONDING TO THEM.

9. AS THE SECRETARY'S AGENDA IS WORKED OUT, IT WOULD BE WELL TO BEAR IN MIND THAT THE SOVIETS WILL TAKE IT AS A CLEAR SIGNAL THAT ANY SUBJECT OMITTED IS SECONDARY TO THE ONES RAISED, IN OUR ASSESSMENT OF PRIORITIES. THIS DOES NOT MEAN THAT THE SECRETARY MUST PROVIDE A DEFINITIVE CATALOG OF ALL OUR DESIDERATA—WHICH WOULD BE QUITE IMPOSSIBLE IN ANY CASE—BUT SIMPLY THAT IF HE DOES NOT TALK ABOUT (FOR EXAMPLE) COMPLIANCE ISSUES OR MENTION THAT WE STILL EX-PECT MORE ON SVERDLOVSK, THE SOVIET INFERENCE WILL BE THAT OUR CONCERNS ON THESE MATTERS ARE NOT REALLY VERY ACUTE. FOR THOSE SUBJECTS RAISED, THE SOVIETS WILL BE AT-TENTIVE TO SUCH MATTERS AS THE LENGTH OF TIME SPENT ON THEM AND THE VIGOR OF THEIR PRESENTATION AS DIRECT CLUES TO U.S. PRIORITIES. PERFUNCTORY MENTION OF A SUBJECT CAN BE INTERPRETED AS SIGNALING LOW PRIORITY SINCE THE PRE-SUMPTION WOULD BE THAT IT WAS READ INTO THE RECORD MERELY TO SATISFY SOME INTEREST GROUP OR COTERIE.

10. IF ANY PORTION OF THE MEETING IS CONDUCTED ONE-ON-ONE, THE OPPORTUNITY SHOULD BE USED TO CONVEY OUR MOST IMPORTANT POINTS AS DIRECTLY AND POINTEDLY AS ELEMEN-TARY POLITENESS PERMITS. GROMYKO, LIKE MOST RUSSIANS, CAN TAKE STRAIGHT TALK IN PRIVATE. INDEED, THEY PRIZE IT, AND THE SIGNALS GIVEN AT SUCH A MEETING—SHOULD ONE BE HELD—WILL BE THE MOST IMPORTANT HE WILL BRING BACK TO MOSCOW WITH HIM (ASSUMING GROMYKO DOES NOT MEET WITH THE PRESIDENT).

MATLOCK

Although very few TOP SECRET cables from Moscow outlining U.S. negotiating positions and strategies have been declassified, from George Herrmann's assertion that virtually *all* cables were typed on IBMs, it is safe to assume that, from 1976 through 1984, when the GUNMAN bugs were active, the KGB collected a significant amount of information on U.S. positions in TOP SECRET Moscow-to-D.C. cables on nuclear arms negotiations, such as SALT (Strategic Arms Limitation Talks), START (Strategic Arms Reduction Treaty), and INF (Intermediate-Range Nuclear Forces Treaties) that were discussed during that period.[10]

Whether the KGB's possession of that sensitive information resulted in more favorable terms for Russia in various nuclear arms agreements—advantages that persist to this very day—is unknowable, but it's hard to imagine that the Soviets knowing about U.S. negotiating goals and tactics prior to arms negotiations *helped* U.S. interests.

But what about Gandy's original reason for traveling to Moscow in 1978: Hathaway's concern that leaks in the embassy were exposing CIA assets and CIA case officers to the KGB? Is there any evidence that the GUNMAN implants played a role in these compromises or that putting an end to KGB collection of typed information made CIA case officers and their assets safer?

In addition to asserting that the GUNMAN bugs compromised no human assets, Burton Gerber went on to say that each and every asset roll-up or case officer PNG between 1976 and 1984 had been fully explained by factors unrelated to GUNMAN. Ogorodnik, for example, had been betrayed by a Czech double agent named Koecher.[11] while Richard Osborne, Peter Bogatyr, Lon Augustenborg, and Louis Thomas were expelled either because of rare examples of flawed tradecraft or, more often, successful dangles, where the KGB entrapped the CIA men with Soviet "volunteers" under KGB control.

Asked about the arrest for espionage of Soviet citizen B. Nilov in 1981 and four Soviet scientists that the Soviet newspaper *Moskovskaya Pravda* (*Moscow Truth*) claimed were arrested for spying for the CIA in 1982,[12] Gerber replied, "There were no such assets. Don't believe everything you read in the Soviet press." (Gerber's skepticism is well-placed, because the Kremlin insiders sometimes publicly claimed that political dissidents, or merely those who'd fallen out of political favor, were spies in order to discredit them.)

The dangle explanation of CIA case officer expulsions, however, raises the question of how the KGB knew to target those CIA men in the first place.

Here we encounter a potential flaw in the assertion that GUNMAN implants in IBM typewriters played no role in HUMINT compromises in Moscow from 1976 through 1984.

Although CIA and State Department operations were kept separate, and the CIA station was much securer than the rest of the embassy, as Burton Gerber stated, CIA case officers in the embassy were officially U.S. government employees. This meant that, when new CIA case officers were sent to foreign postings, the State Department in D.C. had to know who they were and had to communicate their identities to the ambassador and DCM. In addition, when CIA deployed officers for temporary duty (TDY), that information also had to be transmitted to senior embassy officials. These D.C.-to-Moscow communications were not compromised by GUNMAN implants, but the embassy's *response* to those communications, through something called *the Roger channel*, was almost certainly compromised, because Roger-channel telegrams were typed on IBM Selectrics.

The recently declassified U.S. Department of State classification guide describes the Roger channel this way.[13]

> *Roger Channel messages are controlled by the Assistant Secretary, INR [Head of State Department Intelligence]. They are used to report sensitive intelligence matters and have very limited distribution. Roger Channel should normally be classified SECRET for a duration of 25 years, or marked 25X1-human if they reveal the identity of a human intelligence source. (Inclusion of information here on Roger Channel does not constitute authority to initiate messages in*

this channel. This will normally be done by an OCA [Original Classification Authority].)

Essentially, the Roger channel was a State Department–controlled sensitive communication channel that was intentionally separated from CIA's classified communication channel in the embassy so that, among other reasons, State's diplomats could communicate with the State Department in D.C. about CIA *without CIA being aware of it.* For instance, if any ambassador wanted to complain to his bosses about CIA's COS, he would do it away from CIA's prying eyes through the Roger channel.

Returning to the question of how the KGB learned the identities of case officers such as Boagtyr or Augustenborg, one obvious source was the bugged IBM typewriters that typed Roger-channel messages acknowledging the original deployments of these officers.

While acknowledging that information typed on IBM Selectrics might have informed the KGB of CIA case officer identities, Jon Le-Chevet said the KGB had many other ways of figuring out which embassy officers were legitimate versus intelligence officers:

> *Spotting station [CIA] personnel was a no-brainer and was often the topic of conversion among State/AID, etc., people. Most of the time the gossip was correct, so it would also be a no-brainer for the KGB to determine who was in the Station using the locals in the Embassy (who handled all travel, car bookings, vacations, cultural events, etc.). The fact that the KGB knew exactly who was an intelligence officer was a given, not a mystery—we were tightly controlled by the local employees who all reported to the KGB. No need to read our traffic to identify IC personnel, it was given to the KGB through the employment of locals in service and support positions.*

Based upon LeChevet's observations (later corroborated by KGB counterspy Yuri Totrov),[14] the GUNMAN typewriter implants and Roger-channel responses may have aided the KGB's efforts to unmask

CIA case officers but were only one of many different ways the KGB had of doing this.

But even if the GUNMAN bugs helped identify CIA case officers, these unmaskings did not necessarily tip the KGB off to the identities of those case officers' assets. Case officers were rigorously trained in countersurveillance (e.g., shaking off tails), covert communications, and many other types of tradecraft, such as dead drops and brush passes, and were held accountable for scrupulously protecting the identities of their assets. Thus, with normal tradecraft, case officers rarely made mistakes that informed the opposition who their assets were.

With normal tradecraft.

But in 1984, a KGB officer and CIA asset named Sergei Vorontsov told CIA that the KGB had for years been covertly sprinkling "spy dust" on CIA case officers (probably through FSNs under KGB control in the embassy) that allowed the KGB to not only track case officers after they slipped their KGB tails but to identify Soviet citizens who came in contact with the case officers.[15] The chemical nitrophenyl pentadienal was invisible but glowed under ultraviolet (UV) light in very small quantities and normally transferred from one person to another through contact or exchange of objects (such as microfilm containers and cameras).[16] Thus, even with flawless tradecraft, CIA case officers, identified through GUNMAN bugs in typewriters—or the other sources LeChevet referred to—could have led the KGB straight to their assets.

Taking all these factors into consideration, it seems likely that the GUNMAN typewriter implants were somewhat helpful—although far from necessary—to the KGB in unmasking CIA case officers and that it's further possible, although far from certain, that some of these unmaskings led the KGB to some CIA human assets through spy dust or other means.

Presented with the weak, circumstantial evidence linking GUNMAN implants to human asset roll-ups in Moscow, Gandy said in 2018, "Well, Hathaway told me about other roll-ups [excluding Ogorodnik, Filatov, Nilov, and Kapustin] that Hathaway worried *were* lost through text [typing], although before Project GUNMAN, I thought we were losing text through MUTS. Remember, I told Hathaway from the very start I thought the problem was text, and he *did* invite me over there three separate times [twice in 1978 and once in 1981], and his main concern all along was HUMINT losses."

One final piece of evidence that indicates how much damage the GUNMAN implants did to U.S. national security was the very existence of the GUNMAN system itself. Although the Soviets put a high priority on intelligence gathering, Russia was (and is) a poor country that was not in the habit of focusing scarce resources on unproductive pursuits.

The typewriter implant itself cost a lot to design and manufacture, especially with the eighteen different ultrasophisticated hides that NSA uncovered. GUNMAN implants also required staffing at listening posts, maintenance, analysis, and other activities that cost rubles. Gandy estimated that over the eight years GUNMAN was known to operate, the KGB operated six listening posts around the chancery, each with a crew of three officers.

Moreover, the KGB invested in four technical upgrades to the system after its original introduction in 1976. Bottom line: the Soviets believed the GUNMAN system was worth the investment over an eight-year period. Would they have felt this way if reading typewriters in the U.S. embassy *didn't* compromise U.S. national security in a meaningful way?

So, how much damage did the GUNMAN implants do, either on compromised arms negotiations or human intelligence gathering in Moscow?

Either a little or a lot, depending upon whom you choose to believe.

13. Lessons About the Russians for Today

Annapolis, Maryland, Early Spring, 2018

I sat in Charles and Freda Gandy's spacious house overlooking the water, marveling at the spectacular view and sipping the second Diet Coke Gandy had given me. I had been running draft chapters of this book by Gandy for months and often stopped by his house to discuss the drafts. I also frequently shared source material for the book with Gandy, especially Russian-language accounts of the embassy typewriter bugging and microwave attacks that I had translated for his benefit.

Gandy shook his head, a sad look playing on his usually cheery face as he read one of these translations, a 2005 article, "Moscow's Sensitive Ears," in *Independent Gazet* by Dimitry Prokhorov, who has written extensively on Russian and Israeli "special services."

> *In 1984 masters from the 16 Department [of KGB] mounted bugs in 30 new typewriters intended for the US Embassy in Moscow and US Consulate General in Leningrad.*[1]

"We only found sixteen," Gandy said while he read and reread the translated document. "That means we missed fourteen or that there was a fifth generation that went undetected."

"How was that possible?" I asked.

"Don't know. Perhaps the other side knew we were doing a swap in '84 and held some back so that we'd *think* we got them all, or maybe they slowly slipped them in one at a time after the swap. They [KGB] were sophisticated like that, and patient. They also had free run of the chancery until after the Marine guard scandal in '87 and endless opportunities to put in new machines, or do swaps during maintenance." (Several Marine guards at the Moscow embassy had confessed to being seduced by KGB honey traps employed at the embassy, potentially compromising secure areas and leading to congressional investigations and the ultimate expulsion of all but a few FSNs from the Moscow embassy.)

"So it might be true? There really could have been another fourteen?"

A faraway look came over Gandy as he looked out at the large sailboat at his backyard dock, still protectively wrapped for the winter. "Could be. I'm sitting here kicking myself for not thinking of it. I was so busy doing other things at the time and let others take over. After GUNMAN, Deeley's organization was renamed INFOSEC [information security] from COMSEC [communications security] to expand NSA's charter from com links to things like computers and typewriters, and NSA was given much more responsibility over there [for embassy security in Moscow]. But I moved on." Gandy sighed deeply.

"So after all that Sturm und Drang with CIA and State, after your tortuous six-year odyssey, the cease-and-desist from DCI, Deeley, Reagan, Arneson . . . all of it, the KGB might have just kept going?"

Gandy said, "Well, maybe those extra fourteen [undiscovered GUNMAN implants] mattered, and maybe they didn't. I do think we put at least a temporary dent in their operation, because right after we pulled the typewriters in '84, they dug trenches all around the compound and buried coax cables to improve the sensitivity of MUTS [microwave attacks on the embassy] so that they could gather text, and maybe voice, too, that way. They wouldn't have gone to all that extra trouble with the trenches, I think, unless they'd lost some important access."

"Okay," I said slowly, "but what you're telling me is that even if the Russian journalist is wrong about the extra fourteen GUNMAN machines, the KGB made up for the loss of GUNMAN by beefing up MUTS."

"Well, sure," Gandy said, brightening. "They never stop."

As I digested that, I ran the phrase *they never stop* over and over in my head. I said, "So it's a safe bet they're going strong against us right up till today."

Gandy smiled as he used a phrase he'd picked up from one of his grandkids. "Well, *duhhh.*"

"Okay," I said, feeling sheepish for asking such a dumb question. "Does GUNMAN teach us anything useful for today about the Russians? Does it have some value in 2018?"

"I'm not sure I follow you," Gandy answered.

"Well," I said, "did GUNMAN play a role in getting us to where we are today with the Russians? For instance, did we teach them back then how to treat us? Think about it. They leaned *way* forward, took a huge risk invading our embassy, and in the end, what did we do when we finally caught them? We took six years, all the while denying, finger-pointing, and fighting each other. Ultimately, we did nothing to the Russians to hold them accountable for what they did to us. Sounds a whole lot like the 2016 election and its aftermath to me."

Gandy leaned forward in his stuffed chair and said, "You'd have to go much further back than GUNMAN for the 'we taught them how to treat us' thing. They bugged the Great Seal in the '50s, and we found a hundred microphones in the embassy in the '60s, and all that time, up to the present as far as I know, they've been hammering us with microwaves. And throughout all of that, they [Russia] suffered no consequences."

I said, "So what we're seeing today with the hacking, election meddling is business as usual. If you're the Russians, as long as you stay away from kinetics [overt military warfare] and invasions . . . take your best shot at America, and nothing bad will happen to you."

"Yeah. I don't imagine they are too worried about sanctions."

As Gandy spoke, I thought back to his who-hates-whom chart. "It occurs to me," I said, "that we have very little influence over the Russians, but we do have some control, at least in theory, over ourselves."

Gandy said, "Go on."

I opened the printed draft of the book to the who-hates-whom chart. "We've got one of these right now, you know. Different boxes—different players, maybe—but not a whole lot different. CIA and DOD still despise each other. Ditto for FBI and CIA; State still doesn't like CIA; and the White House is in conflict with plenty of key players. The only new box for your chart is ODNI [Office of the Director of National Intelligence that oversees all seventeen U.S. intelligence agencies], and I can tell you from firsthand experience as a DNI guy, *everyone* hated us as meddling, micromanaging, incompetent bean counters."

Gandy chuckled.

"So it seems to me that now, as then, the Russians may instigate bad things, but we inflict most of the damage on ourselves by fighting each other after the Russians do to us what the Russians always do."

"I can't argue with a single thing you said," Gandy answered, "but what do you propose to do about it?"

I answered, "That's a tough one. When you think about it, three of the key actors in GUNMAN—you, Hathaway, and LeChevet—were not turf defenders who battled other agencies on principle. You three did cooperate—a lot—to get to the truth, but it wasn't nearly enough to overcome the enmity of your respective organizations. LeChevet, for example, was stepped on hard by his masters for helping you, and you were squashed by CIA. If it weren't for Walt Deeley saying, "Screw everyone, we're going to solve this," and going directly to the president, the typewriter bugs would never have been found."

Gandy got up to get me another Diet Coke. On the way back from the refrigerator, he said, "Yeah, Walt was the real hero of GUNMAN. But there sure aren't many like him."

I pondered that. If the U.S. intelligence community couldn't overcome its internal friction without a Walt Deeley—someone willing to risk everything to do the right thing—then the future didn't look so rosy because leaders like Walt Deeley's only came along once in a generation. Or a century.

I stared at the who-hates-whom chart, mentally superimposing new names, boxes, and links into it to bring it up to date. I tried to imagine the current set of actors—or indeed any set of actors past, present, or future—putting aside politics, turf wars, and tribal Washington hatreds to unite against the Russian threat. The 2016 election episode taught the Russians that, when they get caught conducting active measures to destabilize America, America wouldn't do much to retaliate but *would* spend years tearing itself apart.

Considering this, I wondered how the current inhabitants of the who-hates-whom chart would react when Russia, encouraged by 2016, tested America further through a crippling cyberattack on U.S. banks, the stock exchange, or even the power grid. The Russians would deny the attack, of course, knowing that some of the players on the modern who-hates-whom chart would accept their denial, thereby spawning a protracted conflict with those on the chart who *wanted* to retaliate against the Russians.

For the Russians, it would all be good. The damage to the United States from the cyberattack would be nice, but the recriminations, finger-pointing, and bitter political disputes that would follow the attack would be far, far better. Going all the way back to Lenin, dividing Russia's enemies has not just been a means to an end for the Kremlin but a desired end all unto itself.

At length, I said to Gandy, "Boating season will be here soon, right?"

"Yep."

"Well," I said, putting away the chart and standing up, working the kinks out of my legs, "let me help you get the boat ready and rigged for spring. Could be stormy weather ahead."

Author's Note

This work was derived from declassified U.S. government documents, interviews, press accounts, books on the period, and publicly available technical documents, mostly from Russian-language sources, on technical surveillance. No classified information was used in the book, and all documents marked SECRET or TOP SECRET in the book have since been declassified. Neither NSA nor CIA, who approved release of the material as unclassified, acknowledges the accuracy of any of the accounts.

Nothing in this work represents validation, based upon my service as a U.S. intelligence official, of any of the claims described in the book from public literature—such as Russian-language literature on technical surveillance techniques—regarding the technical viability of techniques described or their use by any U.S. government entity, including NSA. For instance, possible ways that Gandy may have gained confidence in 1978 that Russian intelligence was reading text from machines in the U.S. embassy were speculation on my part and not based upon any information from either Gandy or from any U.S. government sources.

The conversations described here were based upon the recollections of at least one participant in each of the conversations, and multiple participants, where possible.

In searching for completely unclassified sources for technical surveillance techniques discussed in the book, I made an intriguing and, to me, disturbing discovery. Techniques such as radar flooding (microwave attacks) and microphonic exploitation (recovering voice signals from vibration of electronic circuits) are widely described in entry-level Russian-language textbooks on information security under the heading of "leakage of information through technical channels." Information security curricula at Russian universities similarly cover "leakage of information through technical channels" in depth in introductory courses.

In contrast, although TSCM tradecraft—and techniques such as RF imposition and microphonics—are known in the West, U.S. texts and courses on information security emphasize computers, software operating systems, and networks, but rarely make more than passing mention of the physics of the electronics that underlie information systems, which the Russians exploit through technical channels. In essence, the Russians look at computers and networks not just as conveyors of digital bits but also as radio transmitters and receivers, magnetic flux generators and magnetometers, optical emitters and shot sensors, and acoustic speakers and microphones.

Computers and networks were not designed to exhibit these physical characteristics, but Maxwell's equations, which describe electromagnetic fields associated with electric currents, dictate that they *do* have these characteristics. And the Russians view Maxwell's equations as offering up many opportunities both to peek and poke at computers, communications systems, and networks. The MUTS microwave attacks on the U.S. embassy (which continued at least until the early 2000s, according to a retired State Department security specialist) are an example of such peeking and poking.

U.S. texts do sometimes discuss telecommunications electronics material protected from emanating spurious transmissions (TEMPEST), a term NSA coined to describe protections against unintended electromagnetic emanations from information and communications technology,[1] but the emphasis on U.S. information security is overwhelmingly on computer science, not the physics of TEMPEST.

One reason for this difference in emphasis in cybersecurity could be that very little information about recovering information from undesired RF emanations from electronics is publicly available in the West, whereas in Russia, such information abounds. For instance, I recently found over a dozen Russian-language textbooks on the protection against "information leakage through technical channels" and PEMIN (Побочные Электро Магнитные Излучения и Наводки,[2] Russia's version of TEMPEST, literally "side electromagnetic emissions and light"), and each of these texts delved deeply into both passive (e.g., microphonics from acousto-electric transduction) and active (e.g., RF imposition) surveillance techniques. Similarly, the syllabi of most information security programs at Russian universities also describe such phenomena in great depth.

So why does the Russian government, which is well known for keeping an iron grip on "state secrets," permit such wide and open discussion of surveillance techniques that are known only to a few specialists—most with high security clearances—in the West? In fact, one of the Russian-language documents that describes surveillance techniques for electromagnetic emanations in depth, *Basic Model: The Threat of Personal Data Safety in Their Processing in the Information Systems of Personal Data,*[3] is published by the Russian government (Federal Bureau for Technology and Export Control, or FSTEK) *itself!*

Another explanation is that, in a nation rampant with organized crime, businesses—upon which the fragile Russian economy depends—put an extremely high priority on protecting themselves from industrial espionage and theft carried out by highly skilled former KGB or FSB technical operatives.

In the preface to a comprehensive textbook describing ultrasophisticated technical surveillance techniques, *Technical Methods of Protecting Information,* PEMIN expert Yuri Sidorin (at a Russian government-run polytechnic university in Saint Petersburg) wrote:

The collapse of the former Soviet Union, the formation of new states, lack of clear boundaries, a crisis in the economy, weakening of all kinds of responsibility and imperfect legislation resulted in a sharp increase in criminal groups. The presence of criminals with considerable money allows [these criminals] to create technically well-equipped mobile groups. The use of new technology and the bribing of employees (or introducing their people into the firm) allows criminals to successfully conduct their operations. The objects of their activity are private firms, factories, bases and warehouses, oil and gas processing stations, museums, valuable artistic property of the state and citizens, etc. Activities of these criminal groups leads to a sharp decline in the company's income, and in some cases also to its collapse.[4]

Another reason the Russian government allows open discussion of these techniques, and openly publishes such information itself, could be that, in Russia, these surveillance methods are not worth protecting as "state secrets" because they are common knowledge.

Which raises the question: Since the Russians pioneered these surveillance techniques (e.g., the Thing, MUTS/TUMS), did they suddenly stop developing them when the Soviet Union collapsed in 1991, or did they continue apace so that they now possess vastly *more* sophisticated and capable surveillance methods that they *don't* talk about?

Common sense says that the Russians, who place an extremely high priority on intelligence gathering, *have* continued to invest heavily in technical surveillance technology and that they either have maintained— or even extended—their lead over the West in these areas.

Why do I believe that the Russians had in the past, and probably enjoy today, a lead in technical surveillance? Well, let's go back to two cases, MUTS/TUMS, and the bugging of the New Office Building (NOB) in Moscow. The functions of MUTS and TUMS were a mystery to both State and CIA, suggesting that Soviet tradecraft exceeded that of either U.S. organization. Then, when CIA first discovered the NOB implants in 1982, they told the State Department that although they did not fully understand what the Soviets were up to, they were confident that the United States could counter the implants without removing them and that construction could continue.[5]

By the late 1980s, however, CIA concluded that they *could not* guarantee the security of the embassy through countermeasures and so recommended that the entire NOB be torn down and rebuilt under very tight security. (State refused to do this and ultimately consented only to the rebuilding of the top floors that housed the most sensitive operations, so that, to this day, the bottom floors of the U.S. chancery in Moscow are riddled with Russian listening devices.[6])

What's disturbing to me about all this is that the Russian-American difference in emphasis in training on information security and level of technical surveillance tradecraft has created what I call a *cyber blind spot* in U.S. information systems. If you asked any U.S. cybersecurity expert what radar flooding or microphonic exploitation are, ninety-nine times out of a hundred, you'd get a blank stare. But if you asked almost any Russian information security specialist about these same topics (using the Russian terms *RF imposition* in place of *radar flooding* and *PEMIN* in place of *microphonics*), ninety-nine times out of a hundred, you'd get instant recognition.

So you tell me: If, in country A, almost everyone in information security is familiar with a class of exploits that are virtually unknown in country B, whose computers and networks will be at higher risk?

And by American computers and networks, I'm not confining my concerns to government national security systems: other large organizations—banks, financial institutions, utilities, election systems, and IT—also have a cyber blind spot and are open to penetration from foreign intelligence services (such as Russia's SVR, FSB, or GRU) who seek to disrupt the U.S. economy, steal industrial secrets, and/or sow dissension.

The subject of dissension brings me back to the who-hates-whom chart.

To me, the chart was not just part of the GUNMAN story but the whole story itself. Having lived on the chart as a senior intelligence official at NSA, then at ODNI, and experienced the turf wars, rivalries, and distrust (e.g., the CIA officer who was sure Gandy faked the GUNMAN discovery to build his reputation and budget, and Mike Arneson, who thought CIA might have been responsible for the bug), I can testify with some authority that the infighting inside the U.S. national security community makes us incredibly vulnerable to Russian provocations, and the Russians know this.

Hints about Russian strategies for sowing dissension in the U.S. national security community and government can be found in recent attacks attributed to them. In both the 2016 hack of the Democratic National Committee (DNC) and the 2018 nerve agent attack in the UK, Russia left subtle—or not-so-subtle—calling cards that allowed the attacks to be attributed to them, while at the same time providing plausible deniability. The DNC hack was traced to Russian intelligence by various means, including analysis of the host network and methods used by the attackers.

The problem is, Russian intelligence has world-class hackers that are extremely proficient at making attribution of their attacks impossible, so if the Kremlin had absolutely, positively wanted to mask their involvement in the DNC hacks, they were perfectly capable of doing so. This implies that Russian leaders *wanted* to leave a strong hint that Russia had carried out the attack, possibly as a policy deterrent ("See," the Kremlin might be saying, "this is what Russia is capable of when you piss us off, as Hillary did in 2011 when she encouraged Russian dissidents") and possibly to ignite a huge internal debate in the United States over Russia.

The attack on GRU defector Sergei Skripal and his daughter, Yulia, in 2018, using a nerve agent (Novichok) that was exclusive to Russia, similarly served as a warning to Russia's adversaries, while sparking further debate in the West about Russia (some in the United States advocated very forceful response to the attack, others argued for mild sanctions, while others were apparently unbothered by the attack or unconvinced of its origin).

The infighting problem within the U.S. government is troubling because it does not arise through maliciousness, ambition, or bureaucratic selfishness of flawed individuals and cannot be solved simply by replacing a few bad actors with well-intentioned public servants.

For example, I believe George Shultz (who is alleged to have made the "fox in the henhouse" comment about NSA at the Moscow embassy) was an excellent secretary of state, who did a great job fostering diplomatic— as opposed to military—solutions to the Soviet threat. His conflicts with hawks on the National Security Council and DOD (of which NSA was a part) were part of a healthy give-and-take of ideas, and his desire that spy-counterspy dramas with the Soviets not impede the larger arc of history were, in my view, well-placed.

Similarly, CIA officers such as Burton Gerber and Gus Hathaway had very good reasons for questioning Gandy's conclusions, because in the past, technologists at both NSA and CIA *had* exaggerated technical threats. For their part, such intelligence technologists weren't being malicious or self-serving either when they raised concerns, just calling the shots as they saw them.

In short, with Project GUNMAN, as with most challenges to national security, no one at the competing bureaucracies woke up in the morning thinking about how to sabotage U.S. national security.

Rather, virtually everyone in the GUNMAN saga was acting out a well-worn Washington script that says, "Where you stand is where you sit."

In essence, the U.S. national security community is designed— whether intentionally or not—to foster conflict, tension, and constant backstabbing, so it doesn't matter who the individual actors are in each agency: the tendency to fight ourselves more than our adversaries is baked into the system.

Up to a point, this conflict is healthy because it ensures a diversity of ideas and protects America from groupthink. But usually, this conflict goes unchecked and escalates to an unhealthy level, as happened with the GUNMAN typewriter incident. Mistrust and conflicting agendas allowed the Soviets to read U.S. communications out of the Moscow embassy for six full years after the initial discovery of the chimney antenna.

Another aspect of the protracted GUNMAN saga that has troubling implications for the future of U.S. national security is that it represented the volatile and dangerous intersection of two deeply entrenched problems with our defense and intelligence establishment that persist to this day: underappreciation of the technical sophistication of the Russian threat, and interagency mistrust. Just as Gandy's claims of Soviet technical surveillance capabilities were met with incredulity at CIA and State, when I recently raised the issue of the cyber blind spot in an unclassified discussion with former CIA officers, these officers' reaction were, "Oh yeah, just more fearmongering from a wild-eyed NSA geek [me]."

I can say with high confidence that skepticism to the idea that the Russians are better than us at some aspects of cyber (i.e., in our cyber blind spot) is *not* confined to retired CIA officers. For example, some government security specialists argue that because blind spot exploitations, such as RF imposition, are costly, risky, and manpower-intensive operations that are not nearly as practical or economically viable as malware, phishing, or remote firewall attacks, the prospect of such attacks are not very concerning.

This here-and-now skepticism of a Russian technical threat, born of overconfidence in America's technological superiority and historic interagency mistrust and disrespect, means that the entrenched problems that allowed the KGB to read embassy cable traffic for six years after the chimney antenna was discovered are still with us today and still leave us highly vulnerable to assaults from Russian intelligence.

So what's the solution to endemic infighting in the national security community? How do we answer Gandy's question to me about how to fix the who-hates-whom chart?

In a word, *leadership.*

Each president needs to understand the way the system really functions and to punish excessive competition in the national security arena while rewarding cooperation.

It's really very simple: we'll get the bureaucratic behavior we reward and won't get the bureaucratic behavior we punish.

When presidents embrace this idea, the United States will be safer. When they don't embrace it, we will be far less safe.

Acknowledgments

I could not have written this story without Charles Gandy's extensive contributions and patience with hundreds of hours of grueling interviews. Ditto for Gandy's late wife, Freda, who sat through and contributed to many of the interviews.

My wife (and sometimes coauthor), Chris, was incredibly helpful reviewing drafts and providing valuable editorial ideas.

Stephen S. Power, my editor, helped tremendously, as did my agent, Richard Curtis.

A very special thanks goes to Jon LeChevet, who, like Gandy, also proved essential to the telling of this story. Jon was remarkably candid and did not try to be an apologist for the State Department, for which he worked. Jon also exhibited remarkable courage and integrity, volunteering things that he had done related to the GUNMAN implants that were less than perfect. I have rarely met a public servant with more objectivity, honesty, and patriotism.

Mike Arneson has my deep appreciation for his extensive inputs on his part of the story, as does Sean Deeley, Walt's youngest son, who contributed invaluable insights about his father (who died in 1989, when Sean was fourteen). A poignant moment came in the writing of this book when I relayed to Sean Deeley Charles Gandy's response when I said, "I'm going to interview Deeley's youngest son tomorrow. What would you like me to tell him about Walt's work at NSA?" Without hesitation, Gandy said, "You tell him his father was a hero."

Sean's touching reaction to hearing those words made all the effort I'd put into researching the manuscript instantly worth it.

Others who played a direct or indirect role in the GUNMAN project and who helped with important details include Secretary George Shultz, Admiral Bobby Ray Inman, Secretary Bob Gates, former NSA deputy director Bob Rich, Burton Gerber, Milt Bearden, Marti Peterson, Nina Stewart (of the PFIAB), Steve Polnick, Ed Epstein, George Beebe, former KGB major Victor Sheymov, "Carl," and NP, along with former NSA officers CM and JD.

Thanks also to Tom Fingar, former deputy director of national intelligence, for insight on how State Department intelligence (INR) functioned and the Roger channel; and to a former CIA executive who asked to remain nameless.

Any errors in the telling of this story are mine, not those of any of my sources.

Gandy, alarmed and embarrassed that this story portrayed him as a "John Wayne, lone hero type," asked that I acknowledge the full R9 team who supported him. "Everything you said I did was really accomplished by a team of about fifteen."

So to those nameless fifteen, my profound thanks.

I want to express my deep gratitude to General Michael Hayden, who brought me into the intelligence world in 2002, taking me on the adventure of a lifetime. The whole experience, including the opportunity to meet geniuses like Charles Gandy, was what, at Disney, we used to call "an E-ticket ride."

I also want to express my appreciation to the late Lieutenant General Lincoln Faurer, who said, with respect to overcoming skepticism, infighting, and inertia that obstruct defenses against Russian espionage, "You ought to keep screaming until someone hears. We did not keep scream-ing and screaming."[1]

Finally, thanks to the men and women at NSA and CIA who toil in obscurity to keep us safe, along with the talented officers and diplomats in the State Department who also keep us safe by dealing with vexing problems "over there" before they grow into much bigger problems "back here."

Notes

1. Our Spies Are Dying

1 Central Intelligence Agency, *The CIA/NSA Relationship*, CIA-RDP79M00467 A002400030009-4 (Washington, D.C.: CIA, 1976).

2 Central Intelligence Agency, *Directors of Central Intelligence as Leaders of the U.S. Intelligence Community 1946–2005*, chapter 8, "Stansfield Turner: Ambition Denied" (Washington, D.C.: CIA, 2005), www.cia.gov/library/center-for-the-study-of-intelligence/csi-publications/books-and-monographs/directors-of-central-intelligence-as-leaders-of-the-u-s-intelligence-community/chapter_8.htm.

3 James Bamford, *Body of Secrets: Anatomy of the Ultra-Secret National Security Agency* (New York: Anchor Books 2002), 381.

4 Central Intelligence Agency, "TRIGON: Spies Passing in the Night," www.cia.gov/news-information/featured-story-archive/2016-featured-story-archive/trigon-spies-passing-in-the-night.html.

5 Milt Bearden and James Risen, *The Main Enemy* (New York: Presidio Press, 2004), 26.

6 Martha D. Peterson, *The Widow Spy* (Wilmington, NC: Red Canary Press, 2012), 87.

7 Esther B. Fein, "Toward the Summit; For Reagans, Stately Rooms but No View," *New York Times*, May 29, 1988.

8 "Estimate of Damage to U.S. Foreign Policy Interests," Federation of American Scientists, https://fas.org/irp/news/2001/03/moscowbugs.html.

9 "Spaso House," *Wikipedia*, https://en.wikipedia.org/wiki/Spaso_House.

10 "Spaso House History," U.S. Embassy & Consulates in Russia, https://ru.usembassy
.gov/embassy-consulates/moscow/spaso-house/spaso-history/.

11 "The Thing—Great Seal Bug," Crypto Museum, www.cryptomuseum.com/covert
/bugs/thing/index.htm.

12 U.S. Department of Commerce, *Microwave Radiation at the U.S. Embassy in Moscow and Its Biological Implications: An Assessment,* NTIA-SP-81-12, prepared for the
U.S. Department of State, March 1981.

13 Domani Spero, "Microwaving U.S. Embassy Moscow: Oral History from FSOs
James Schumaker and William A. Brown," *Diplopundit,* August 29, 2017, https://
diplopundit.net/2017/08/29/microwaving-u-s-embassy-moscow-oral-history
-from-fsos-james-schumaker-and-william-a-brown/.

14 Christopher Wren, "Fire Hits U.S. Moscow Embassy, Forcing Evacuation," *New
York Times,* August 27, 1977.

15 "The Embassy Moscow Fire of 1977," Association for Diplomatic Studies and Training, August 2014, https://adst.org/2014/08/the-embassy-moscow-fire-of-1977/.

16 Ibid.

17 Ibid.

18 Bearden and Risen, *The Main Enemy,* 26.

19 Stansfield Turner, *Secrecy and Democracy: The CIA in Transition* (Boston: Houghton
Mifflin, 1985), 19.

20 Ibid.

21 "Massacre at the CIA," *U.S. News & World Report,* November 14, 1977.

22 "Gardner Hathaway," *Wikipedia,* https://en.wikipedia.org/wiki/Gardner_Hathaway.

23 David E. Hoffman, *The Billion Dollar Spy: A True Story of Cold War Espionage and
Betrayal* (New York: Anchor Books, 2016), 72.

24 "Embassy Moscow Fire," Association for Diplomatic Studies and Training.

25 Steve Vogel, "Gardner R. Hathaway, CIA Chief of Counterintelligence, Dies at 88,"
Washington Post, November 26, 2013.

26 Barry Roden, "Tolkachev, A Worthy Successor to Penkovsky," *Studies in Intelligence*
47, no. 3 (2003), https://www.cia.gov/library/center-for-the-study-of-intelligence/csi
-publications/csi-studies/studies/vol47no3/article02.html.

27 Ibid.

28 Ibid.

29 Ibid.

30 Ibid.

31 Duane R. Clarridge, *A Spy for All Seasons: My Life in the CIA* (New York: Scribner,
2002), 167; Burton Gerber, in conversation with the author, 2018.

32 Turner, *Secrecy and Democracy,* 19.

2. The Counterspy

1 Adam Gordon, *Official (ISC)² Guide to the CISSP CBK*, 3rd ed. (Boca Raton, FL: Auerbach Publications, 2015), 971; National Security Agency, "TEMPEST: A Signal Problem" (Fort Meade, MD: NSA, 2007) 26–28.

2 G. Buzov, S. Kalinin, and A. Kondratev, *Protection Against Information Leakage Through Technical Channels* (Moscow: Hot Line-Telecom, 2005), 23.

3 "Rediffusion," *WikiVividly*, https://wikivividly.com/wiki/Rediffusion.

4 "Léon Theremin," *Wikipedia*, https://en.wikipedia.org/wiki/L%C3%A9on_Theremin.

5 "Microwaving Embassy Moscow—Another Perspective," Association for Diplomatic Studies and Training, September 2013, https://adst.org/2013/09/microwaving-embassy -moscow-another-perspective/; "Ambassador Gary L. Matthews," Association for Diplomatic Studies and Training, December 2013, https://adst.org/wp-content /uploads/2013/12/Matthews-Gary-L.toc_.pdf; National Archives, RG 59, Central Foreign Policy File, P840076–0378.

6 "Vladimir Vetrov," *Wikipedia*, https://en.wikipedia.org/wiki/Vladimir_Vetrov; "The Foreign Intelligence Role of the Committee for State Security," Federation of American Scientists, https://fas.org/irp/world/russia/kgb/su0521.htm.

3. In the Belly of the Beast

1 U.S. Department of State, Case No. F-2009-07012, Doc No. C17585192, September 6, 2013.

2 G. Buzov, S. Kalinin, and A. Kondratev, *Protection Against Information Leakage Through Technical Channels* (Moscow: Hot Line-Telecom, 2005), 23.

3 National Security Agency, "TEMPEST: A Signal Problem" (Fort Meade, MD: NSA, 2007), 26–28; Li Zhuang, Feng Zhou, and J. D. Tygar, "Keyboard Acoustic Emanations Revisited," *ACM Transactions on Information and Systems Security* (forthcoming), https://people.eecs.berkeley.edu/~tygar/papers/Keyboard_Acoustic _Emanations_Revisited/tiss.preprint.pdf.

4 "The Rough Road to Moscow for Malcolm Toon," Association for Diplomatic Studies and Training, May 2017, https://adst.org/2017/05/rough-road-moscow -malcolm-toon/.

5 Ibid.

6 Robert M. Clark, *The Technical Collection of Intelligence* (Washington, D.C.: CQ Press, 2010).

7 "Alexey 7558," *Information Security Blog*, message 2831, January 29, 2006.

8 "Eavesdropping methods," Studopedia, https://studopedia.ru/9_11505_podslushivanie -s-ispolzovaniem-metodov-vch-navyazivaniya.html.

9 "The question of evaluation PEMIN analog signals with low frequency scattering fields" Mascom, http://www.mascom.ru/library/statyi/k-voprosu-otsenki-pemin

-analogovykh-signalov-ci-nizkochastotnyy-poley-rasseyaniya.php; "Methods of responding," Studopedia, https://studopedia.su/9_480_fizicheskaya-sushchnost -pemin-kak-osnovi-obrazovaniya-kanalov-utechki-informatsii.html.

10 "Methods of responding," Studopedia.

11 "Potemkin village," *Wikipedia*, https://en.wikipedia.org/wiki/Potemkin_village.

4. The Chimney

1 U.S. Department of State, *The History of the Diplomatic Security Service of the U.S. Department of State* (Washington, D.C.: Global Publishing Solutions, 2011).

2 U.S. Department of State, Office of the Secretariat Staff, Special Adviser to the Secretary (S/MS) on Soviet Affairs Marshall Shulman—January 21, 1977–January 19, 1981, Lot 81D109, Box 3.

3 U.S. Department of State, Office of the Secretariat Staff, Special Adviser to the Secretary (S/MS) on Soviet Affairs Marshall Shulman—January 21, 1977–January 19, 1981, Lot 81D109, Box 8.

4 Carter Library, National Security Affairs, Staff Material, Office, Unfiled Files, Box 152, USSR: Technical Penetration of the US Embassy in Moscow: May–June 1978.

6. Obstacles

1 "Biography of Bobby Ray Inman," Federation of American Scientists, https://fas.org /irp/news/1993/931216i.htm; "Bobby Ray Inman," *Wikipedia*, https://en.wikipedia .org/wiki/Bobby_Ray_Inman.

2 Ibid.

3 Central Intelligence Agency, *The CIA/NSA Relationship*, CIA-RDP79M00 467A002400030009-4 (Washington, D.C.: CIA, 1976).

4 "William J. Perry," Historical Office, Office of the Secretary of Defense, http:// history.defense.gov/Multimedia/Biographies/Article-View/Article/571282 /william-j-perry/.

5 Steven Engelberg, "Reagan Was Told in '85 of Problem in Moscow Embassy," *New York Times*, April 3, 1987.

6 George Lardner, "Unbeatable Bugs: The Moscow Embassy Fiasco," *Washington Post*, June 18, 1990.

7 Thomas R. Johnson, *American Cryptology During the Cold War, 1945–1989, Book IV: Cryptologic Rebirth, 1981–1989* (Fort Meade, MD: NSA, 2013).

8 Central Intelligence Agency, *Department of State, PFIAB's Concern Over Employment of Soviet Nationals by Embassy Moscow*, RDP85M00364R000300340052-8 (Washington, D.C.: CIA 1983).

9 Ibid.

7. Who Hates Whom

1 "William P. Clark Jr.," *Wikipedia,* https://en.wikipedia.org/wiki/William_P._Clark_Jr.

2 Ibid.

3 Robert C. Toth, "Head of NSA Is Dismissed for Opposing Budget Cuts," *Los Angeles Times,* April 19, 1985.

4 Philip Taubman, "The Shultz-Weinberger Feud," *New York Times,* April 14, 1985.

5 George Shultz, *Turmoil and Triumph* (New York: Scribner, 2010).

6 Central Intelligence Agency, *Security and Countermeasures: Improving the SIG Process,* CIA-RDP89G00720R000100070003-0 (Washington, D.C.: CIA, 1986).

8. A Trip to the Oval Office

1 Central Intelligence Agency, *Security and Countermeasures: Improving the SIG Process,* CIA-RDP89G00720R000100070003-0 (Washington, D.C.: CIA, 1986).

2 Michael Dobbs, "Soviets Spied on Embassy, French Say," *Washington Post,* April 6, 1985; Suzanne Deffree, "Farewell Dossier Proves U.S. Tech and Research Stolen," EDN Network, July 19, 1981

3 John Vinocur, "47 Soviet Officials Expelled by Paris on Spying Charges," *New York Times,* April 6, 1983.

4 Dobbs, "Soviets Spied."

5 Ibid.

6 National Security Agency, "United States Cryptologic History: Attack on a SIGINT Collector the USS Liberty, " (Fort Meade, NSA, 2011)

7 Thomas R. Johnson, *American Cryptology During the Cold War, 1945–1989, Book IV: Cryptologic Rebirth, 1981–1989* (Fort Meade, MD: NSA, 2013).

8 Ibid.

9. Project GUNMAN

1 Bill Gertz, "Bureaucrats Resist Efforts to Fight Back Against Spies," *Washington Times,* May 4, 1987.

10. A Wife in the Wrong Place at the Right Time

1 F. T. May, "IBM Word Processing Developments," *IBM Journal of Research and Development* 25, no. 5 (1981): 741.

11. Behind the Green Door

1 Sharon Maneki, *Learning from the Enemy* (Fort Meade, MD: NSA, 2012).

12. Putting the Smoke Back in the Gun

1 Thomas R. Johnson, *American Cryptology During the Cold War, 1945–1989, Book IV: Cryptologic Rebirth, 1981–1989* (Fort Meade, MD: NSA, 2013).

2 U.S. Department of State, *The History of the Diplomatic Security Service of the U.S. Department of State* (Washington, D.C.: Global Publishing Solutions 2011), 299.

3 Ibid.

4 "Report: Former U.S. Ambassador Stymied Moscow Embassy Security," UPI, April 6, 1987, www.upi.com/Archives/1987/04/06/Report-Former-US-embassador -stymied-Moscow-embassy-security/5356544680000/.

5 George Shultz, "Department of State Bulletin," Internet Archive, July 1988, https:// archive.org/stream/departmentofstat88213621411988unit/departmentofstat8821 3621411988unit_djvu.txt.

6 U.S. Department of State, *The History of the Diplomatic Security Service*, 278.

7 U.S. Department of State, text of telegram 81MOSCOW008153.

8 U.S. Department of State, text of telegram 81MOSCOW015919.

9 James Graham Wilson, ed., *Foreign Relations of the United States, 1981–1988, Volume III, Soviet Union, January 1981–January 1983* (Washington, D.C.: U.S. State Department Publishing Office, 2016), 244.

10 "U.S.-Russian Nuclear Arms Control Agreements at a Glance," Arms Control Association, updated December 2018, www.armscontrol.org/factsheets/USRussia NuclearAgreements.

11 "Aleksandr Dmitrievich Ogorodnik," *Wikipedia*, https://en.wikipedia.org/wiki /Aleksandr_Dmitrievich_Ogorodnik.

12 "Soviets Arrest Four Scientists on Spying Charges," *New York Daily News*, September 28, 1982; "Convict Soviet a CIA Spy," *New York Daily News*, June 23, 1980.

13 U.S. Department of State, *Classification Guide (DSCG 05-01)* (Washington, D.C.: U.S. State Department Publishing Office, 2005).

14 "Sloppiness, Not Moles, Led to KGB's Exposure of CIA Agents During Cold War," *Sputnik*, September 28, 2018, https://sputniknews.com/military/20150928102 7670037-kgb-cia-agents-outing/.

15 Walter Pincus, "Naming Those Betrayed by Ames," *Washington Post*, June 12, 1995.

16 "Nitrophenyl pentadienal," *Wikipedia*, https://en.wikipedia.org/wiki/Nitrophenyl _pentadienal.

13. Lessons About the Russians for Today

1 Dimitry Prokhorov "Moscow's Sensitive Ears," *Independent Gazet,* 2005. http:// nvo.ng.ru/spforces/2005-06-03/7_ushi.html

Author's Note

1 National Security Agency, "TEMPEST: A Signal Problem" (Fort Meade, MD: NSA, 2007), 26–28.

2 "Lecture 15: Spurious electromagnetic radiation," Intuit, www.intuit.ru/studies /courses/2291/591/lecture/12702.

3 Federal Bureau for Technology and Export Control, *Basic Model of Threats to the Security of Personal Data in Their Processing in Personal Data* (Moscow: FSTEK, 2008).

4 Yuri Sidorin, *Technical Means of Information Protection Tutorial* (Saint Petersburg, Russia: Publishing House of the Polytechnic University, 2005).

5 Michael A. Boorstein, "History of the Construction of the American Embassy in Moscow" (Cambridge, MA: Harvard University Fellows Program, 1998) www .moscowveteran.org/sites/default/files/Moscow%20Embassy%20Construction%20 2012-08-21.pdf.

6 Ibid.

Acknowledgments

1 Stephen Engelberg, "Embassy Security: Story of Failure," *New York Times*, April 19, 1987.

Index